WHEN IN ROME

2000 Years of Roman Sightseeing

WHEN IN ROME

2000 Years of Roman Sightseeing

Matthew Sturgis

DRAWINGS BY NATALIE TURNER

FRANCES LINCOLN LIMITED
PUBLISHERS

For
Lavinia
and
La Famiglia Farrelly

Frances Lincoln Limited
4 Torriano Mews
Torriano Avenue
London NW5 2RZ
www.franceslincoln.com

FRONT ENDPAPERS Street plan of Imperial Rome
BACK ENDPAPERS G.B. Nolli's plan of Rome in 1748
FRONTISPIECE The pointing hand of Constantine: a fragment of
the colossal statue in the courtyard of the Palazzo dei Conservatori

CONTENTS

Rome bewails her widowed state, in a fifteenth-century manuscript of Fazio degli Uberti's *Dittamondo*

PREFACE

W HEN I FIRST went to Rome in 1980, in the summer before going to
university, I took with me a much-battered old Baedeker, borrowed from
my grandparents' bookshelves. I liked the fact that it didn't look like a
guidebook, at least not by the standards of 1980. Then every visitor to Italy clutched
either the long, tall, green-bound Michelin guide, or the bright blue and white Benn's
Blue Guide, or perhaps the garish outsized *Europe on $20 a Day*. These were books that
proclaimed their presence. They were too big to fit in a jacket pocket, and although
their forms were already distinctive enough, their titles were emblazoned in large
letters upon their shiny covers. By contrast the 1904 edition of *Baedeker's Central Italy*,
discreet and blockish, in its faded red boards, was wonderfully anonymous. It looked
like a missal. And it allowed me to indulge my affected youthful idea of not being taken
for a 'tourist' (which, of course, was exactly what I was).

The book might have been old but Rome, as I reasoned, was older: much older.
The Colosseum, the Sistine Chapel, the Pantheon and the Spanish Steps had all been
created well before 1904. The ticket prices quoted in the text would be out of date, and
the museum opening times might be wrong, but this, as I knew, could often be the case
even with modern guidebooks. What was important was the information about the
ancient monuments and Renaissance artworks, and this must still be correct, as true
in 1980 as it had been in 1904. And at the level of mere facts and dates this proved to
be pretty much the case. But, as I learnt, there is rather more to discovering a city than
mere facts and dates.

Walking one day between the Pantheon and the Piazza Navona I encountered the
striking Renaissance façade of S. Luigi dei Francesi, 'the national church of the French'.
My Baedeker encouraged me to investigate. The church contained, besides 'a monument
to the French soldiers who fell at the siege of Rome in 1849', a noted artistic masterpiece,
a starred item worthy of special attention and admiration: 'Right Aisle, 2nd Chapel:
*Frescoes from the life of St. Cecilia, one of the most admirable works of *Domenichino*.'

The name Domenichino registered only very faintly. I had perhaps heard of him, but
certainly I had no very clear idea of what his art might look like. Nevertheless I went in
and dutifully peered into the gloomy ill-lit recesses of the second chapel on the right. I
could dimly make out a large wall-painting of a girl in a turban expiring elegantly in a
monumental and crowded bathroom, with opposite a boisterous jumble sale scene of
the young saint giving away all her worldly possessions to the poor. They were all right,

I suppose, but rather posed and artificial; very different from the staid, potent, serene images I had been looking at over the previous month in Florence, Siena, and Arezzo – paintings by Giotto, Fra Angelico, Botticelli and Piero della Francesca.

As I stood, quite alone, leaning over the chapel's marble balustrade, I became aware of a muted hubbub elsewhere in the church. There was the murmur of excited voices, the hurry of footsteps over the marble floor, the drop of a coin into a machine and the sudden flare of illumination. All this excited activity, I discovered, was coming from a chapel at the far end of the church, to the left of the altar. A tourist throng was gathering there. But to look at what?

I consulted my Baedeker. It gave no clue at all. Besides the starred Domenichino frescoes, the only other artworks the book considered worthy of mention were a picture of St Cecilia by Guido Reni and Francesco Bassano's 'fine' *Assumption*, placed over the high altar.

Approaching the little crowd I found them – clutching their various modern guidebooks – all admiring a set of three arresting frescoes: rakingly lit scenes of human drama and violence. In the otherwise tenebrous church, a coin-operated lighting system gave a clear sight of the paintings. There were postcards for sale. And a notice proclaimed that here were Caravaggio's frescoes of the life of St Matthew. Caravaggio I had heard of. I could recall his painting of *The Supper at Emmaus* from the National Gallery in London. And the pictures of St Matthew had an immediate appeal, a sense of almost cinematic intensity and realism. Peering over the shoulders of a French couple I noticed that their Michelin *Green Guide* had awarded the pictures the ultimate accolade of three asterisks. Here was a trio of pictures to view which was not merely 'worth a detour' but 'worth a journey'.

Caravaggio's frescoes had become one of the star attractions of Rome, and yet seventy-five years before, they hadn't even rated a mention in the most impressively thorough guide to the city's art treasures.

At first this struck me as no more than an interesting but isolated quirk. On subsequent Roman holidays, however, I began to realize that it fitted into a much broader pattern.

Rome, I came to appreciate, is unique in that it has been a tourist destination for over two thousand years. Since the second century BC people have travelled to Rome deliberately to look at its monuments and its treasures. Almost all these visitors, it seems, have been amazed and impressed by what they have found. Yet their notions of what was worth seeing – what was amazing and impressive and why – have changed almost with each generation, certainly with every era. This, of course, is partly because Rome itself has changed with the ages; old monuments were continually being swept away and new ones were continually being erected. But there have also been regular

– and often abrupt – changes in the tastes, the interests and the expectations of those who visit the city. The eclipse of Domenichino by Caravaggio during the course of the twentieth century was, it transpired, only one instance among many.

Many of the monuments most admired by the Ancient Romans were shunned during the Dark Ages. Travellers in Renaissance Rome looked at very different things from their mediaeval counterparts. The artworks that drew the awed attention of visitors in the Baroque era were not the same as those that impressed gentlemen on the Grand Tour a century later. And so it has continued up to the present day: things admired by one generation are ignored or disparaged by the next. It was the excitement of this realization, and the desire to trace and recover some of these varied pasts, that inspired this book.

For all the dedicated research involved in the project, the enterprise rests first upon an enduring love of Rome and the slowly acquired knowledge that comes from visiting it often. Both love and knowledge have been much enhanced by those with whom I have spent happy times exploring the city – among them Christopher Young, Richard Cockett, Cristina Odone, Linda Bruce, Marcus Matthews, William Sieghart, Donald and Joan Hossack, Griff and Jo Rhys-Jones, Annabel Potter and – best companion of all – my wife, Rebecca Hossack. But, beyond even this, I have been particularly blessed in coming to know Lavinia Farrelly and her five children. Lavinia, an American from St Louis, came to Rome in 1960 with the poet George Barker to see the Olympics, and has never left. Now in her eighties, she continues to illuminate it with her wit, generosity and spirit. Two of her children, Elizabeth and Francis, live and work in Rome still, the others – George, a doctor, James, a painter steeped in knowledge of Italian art, and Edward, a Roman-born poet with a unique sensibility – return often. Each of them has, in their different way, helped me to a richer and fuller appreciation of the city.

When I embarked on this book I had fond visions that it would involve me in frequent and extended visits to Rome. That, however, scarcely proved to be the case. It was to the British and London Libraries that my visits were most frequent; and I am very grateful to the staff of both institutions for their assistance and courtesy.

I must acknowledge too the generous assistance of the Society of Authors.

Others who have helped by sharing information and expertise include Francis FitzGibbon, Ruth Guilding, Will Hobson, Martha Hossack, Lucy Hughes-Hallett, Peter Kavanagh, Jonathan Keats, Alexandra Resich, Tim and Jean Sturgis.

Many thanks too are due to John Nicoll at Frances Lincoln for seeing the worth of the idea; to Jo Christian for being such an enthusiastic supporter of it; to Sue Gladstone for tracking down so many of the pictures; and to Becky Clarke and Anne Wilson for arranging them so artfully.

· I ·

REPUBLICAN ROME

I N THE MIDDLE YEARS of the second century BC Rome was under threat. The danger, however, was not military. It was the one-legged sideboard that, apparently, posed the gravest danger to Rome's power – at least according to the historian Livy. There were other worrying signs: bed curtains, bronze couches, and a fad for female lute players at private banquets. To the stern fathers of the Roman Republic these corrupting manifestations of 'eastern luxury' were deeply troubling. It seemed as though the very moment of Rome's triumph might contain the seeds of her future downfall.

This was the period at which Republican Rome reached its apogee. After four centuries of continual warfare, the city's brilliantly organized, and ruthlessly efficient, citizen-armies had achieved an almost undisputed dominance over the Mediterranean world. They had conquered not just all the peoples and towns of the Italian peninsula, but also the powerful empire of Carthage stretching from North Africa into Spain, and – one by one – the sophisticated city states of Greece. The final victories were achieved in 146 BC, when the fabulously rich port of Corinth fell and the once-great city of Carthage was razed to the ground. But even in the decades immediately before then, Rome's position as a Mediterranean superpower was assured.

Military success brought prestige and security to Rome. It also brought change – or at least the beginnings of it. Roman armies, returning from their campaigns among the Greek cities of southern Italy, Sicily and mainland Greece, carried with them new ideas, new tastes, and new one-legged sideboards.

Other novel artefacts arrived as well. Marcus Marcellus was credited with introducing Greek art into Rome. The plundered statues and pictures that he brought back following the conquest of Syracuse in 211 BC gave Romans a first glimpse of an uncharted aesthetic world of taste and refinement. Previously most Roman statues, like their Etruscan models, were subtly stylized forms made from terracotta or wood, but here were exquisite, almost naturalistic, works in bronze and marble and ivory.

Over the next decades more arrived. The spoils of wealthy Tarentum were paraded through Rome in 209 BC. And when M. Fulvius Nobilior took Ambracia, the first city in mainland Greece to fall to Roman arms, he is said to have carried off 785 bronze and 230 marble statues for his triumph. Set up in Rome's streets and squares, they provided conspicuous evidence of change, and also of wealth.

This was the 'germ of luxury' that – according to many wise heads – was threatening to infect the austere farmer-soldiers of the Roman Republic. (By the mid-second century BC there were, it must be admitted, few actual farmer-soldiers at Rome, but the type remained the ideal of the state's carefully cultivated self-image; and a potent ideal it was.)

The infection of luxury, obvious though it was to contemporary Roman moralists, would have been very much less clear to any of the thousands of foreigners who arrived in the city from across the Mediterranean world during this same period. They came from other parts of Italy, from conquered Carthage and its former lands, from rich Egypt, from Greece, from the Asian provinces (in modern Turkey), all drawn by Rome's power and Rome's wealth. Some were shipped as slaves, not a few travelled in embassies to plead before the Roman senate; even more came to seek their fortunes, as merchants, doctors, teachers, craftsmen and artists. At one level, almost all of them must have been disappointed by what they found.

Rome, in the mid-second century BC, may have been a superpower, but she was not yet a super city – certainly not when compared to the great centres of the Greek-speaking world: Alexandria, Pergamum, Athens, Syracuse, Ephesus, Corinth and the rest. With their ordered civic spaces and elegantly appointed public buildings, these cities of the eastern Mediterranean belonged to another cultural sphere. Rome, by contrast, was a mess.

The ranks of glowing monuments that form the popular image of 'Ancient Rome' did not yet exist. The Colosseum had not been built. The Pantheon was unthought of. There were no great public baths. There were no permanent stone-built theatres. There were no marble buildings at all. The city was a sprawling labyrinth of brick and timber dwellings, of cheap stucco, of painted terracotta and low-grade local stone. It may have

TOP The beautifully laid out city of Pergamum (shown here in a model at the Pergamon Museum in Berlin) was very different from the unplanned cityscape of Republican Rome. ABOVE The Altar of Zeus at Pergamum, created in the first half of the second century BC, was an artistic masterpiece, beyond anything then existing at Rome.

been huge (with a population perhaps exceeding three hundred thousand), but it was chaotic. Nevertheless, even then, Rome held a certain fascination for all who visited it.

One such visitor was the celebrated literary critic and cartographer Crates of Mallos. (His fame rested upon his rich allegorical interpretations of Homer, and his creation of a very early geographical globe – some 3 metres/10 feet in diameter.) He arrived in 168 BC, as an ambassador from King Attalus II of Pergamum, one of Rome's staunchest Asian allies. His sojourn extended over several months (rather longer than he expected) so he had time both to explore and to consider the city. And it is possible to piece together – or, at least, to suggest – some of his impressions.

Crates had travelled from a very different place. Pergamum, capital of the powerful Attalid Kingdom (in what is now western Turkey), was one of the jewels of the Ancient World. Its population – around two hundred thousand – may have been slightly less than Rome's, but its sophistication was infinitely greater. It was a centre of art and learning, of planned space and luxurious display. Besides its celebrated and richly adorned Altar of Zeus (now the centrepiece of the Pergamon Museum at Berlin) it boasted numerous marble temples and long, regular colonnades; it had a huge permanent theatre, half a dozen palaces, a gymnasium, a dedicated health spa (presided over by the god of healing, Aesculapius) and a famous library of over two hundred thousand volumes. No such cultural amenities would have been visible in Rome.

Rome in 168 BC still wore a distinctly rough and martial aspect. Set in a bend of the river Tiber and spreading upwards on to its seven steep-sided hills, the city was enclosed within a massive and ancient defensive wall, some six and a half miles round.† This huge cliff of dark grey blocks of tufa, stacked without mortar to a height of some 10 metres/33 feet, would have greeted Crates as he sailed up the Tiber towards the Porta Trigemina. (Modern visitors to Rome are met by an impressive run of the same blocks as they step out of Stazione Termini; it is one of several vestiges of the old Servian Wall still visible today.)

---

† The famous seven hills were essentially the linked finger-like ridges of the plain through which the Tiber ran. Counting from the north they are the Quirinal, Viminal, Esquiline, Caelian and Aventine; with – in geological terms – the Palatine being a spur of the Esquiline, and the Capitoline a spur of the Quirinal. Outside the Servian Wall to the north was the Pincian mount, while across the river rose the ridge of the Janiculum and the smaller Vatican hill. In ancient times the hills were higher than they are today, their sides steeper, and the valleys between them deeper. Over time, their tops have been levelled off, valleys between them have filled up, and the escarpments have softened into gentle slopes.

A section of the ancient city wall of Rome, just outside the Termini railway station. The wall was said to have been constructed by Servius Tullius, the sixth King of Rome, in the sixth century BC, though its extant parts date, more probably, from two centuries later.

The early history of the city was written in just such poor-quality volcanic stone. Rome stood upon a great shelf of the stuff, and it was this pocked, friable – but easily worked – *cappellaccio* that was first used as a building material for large-scale projects. (The so-called Servian Wall, though it was often restored, was supposed to date from the time of the sixth king of Rome in the sixth century BC.) For centuries the dark grey stone sufficed: there were *cappellaccio* quarries running deep into the Capitoline, Palatine and Quirinal hills. Victories against neighbouring tribes, however, did bring access to new, different and slightly better grades of tufa. And these were gradually taken up: pale black-speckled *fidenae* (from modern Fidenza, just seven miles north of Rome), yellowish *grotta oscura* from the once-powerful Etruscan city of Veii, red-brown *anio*, and mottled grey *monteverde*. By the second century BC the Romans had also begun to use the dense, evenly textured blue-tinged *peperino* from the Alban Hills south of the city. Even so, for anyone coming from a metropolis of polished marble, such materials must have seemed both crude and ugly.

The modesty of Rome's building materials was matched by the prevailing scale of the townscape. For the most part the city was a warren of small buildings: small shops overhung with crowded tenements. At unexpected moments, though, the narrow alleys opened up into broader expanses – paved marketplaces and public squares. Close to the river, where Crates would have come ashore, was the Forum Boarium, Rome's ancient cattle market, with – near by – the Forum Holitorium, where vegetables were sold. (They respond roughly to the modern Piazza Bocca della Verità, and a stretch of the broad Via del Teatro di Marcello.)

In these public spaces Crates might have noted – probably with amusement – some rather tentative attempts at Roman town-planning. Small temples were ranged together along the sides of the squares, linked by short colonnades. They provided, in a modest fashion, a formal entrance or a unified backdrop to the urban scene. The relatively limited scale of these arrangements, however, can be gathered from an inspection of the ruins of the three Republican temples incorporated into the church of S. Nicola in Carcere, on the Via del Teatro di Marcello where the Forum Holitorium once stood. The best parts of the three adjoining buildings have been reused to make just one modestly sized twelfth-century church.

There were other reasons, too, why Crates might not have been greatly impressed. Evidence of sophistication was scant. The dominant note of Republican temple décor remained the celebration of military might. The vast majority of Rome's many religious buildings were so-called 'Victory Temples'. They had been vowed by generals – usually in the heat of battle – and erected afterwards in gratitude to the appropriate god for the triumph thus secured. And their principal decorations were the arms and armour of the vanquished enemy. Swords, spears, breastplates and helmets were nailed up in elaborate patterns on every available wall and column.

In architectural style the buildings were scarcely more refined. Though they sometimes varied in ground plan, almost all of them followed the simple Etruscan – or 'Tuscan' – model, with a low pediment supported on squat, plain, widely spaced, tapering columns, surmounted by unadorned Tuscan-Doric capitals. In 168 BC the Ionic and Corinthian orders were all but unknown in Rome. The first marble temple in the city – dedicated to Juno – was only erected in 143 BC.

As an ambassador – and an interested visitor – Crates would have hastened to the Forum Romanum, the political, commercial, judicial, ceremonial and social heart of the city. An irregular oblong piazza running roughly east–west in the valley between Rome's hills, it was where the Senate met, business was transacted, festivals were celebrated, court cases were heard, deals were done, and people congregated. It combined all the life of a modern Italian piazza with the functions of a parliament and a law court.

The playwright Plautus was an expert guide to its rich social mix:

Now, for perjurers, try the Comitium. Liars and braggarts, by the shrine of Cloacina; rich married wastrels, in stock by the Basilica; a good supply of harlots, too, if not in prime condition; also men for hire-purchase. In the Fish-market, members of dining-clubs, in the Lower Forum, respectable and well-to-do citizens out for a walk; flashier types, in the middle Forum, along the canal. By the Lacus Curtius, bold fellows with a tongue in their head, and a bad purpose in mind – great slanderers of other people and very vulnerable to it themselves. By the Old Shops, the money-changers – loans negotiated or accepted. Behind the Temple of Castor – but you'd better not trust yourself there . . .

For all this human confusion, Crates would have noticed that the Forum itself, in its layout and its architecture, offered rather more sense of both order and scale than most

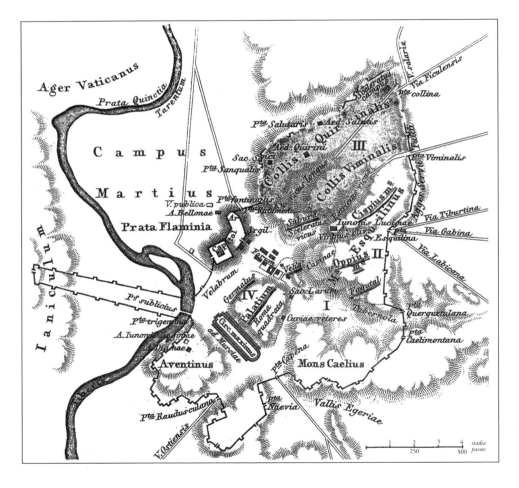

A map of Republican Rome, as drawn by the German archaeologist Theodorus Menke, 1862

urban spaces in Rome. Although it may have evolved in a piecemeal way over the centuries as a meeting place and market for the very first inhabitants of Rome's seven hills, there had clearly been some recent attempts to impose a structure upon the scene, to bring the forum closer to the civic squares of Greek cities. Certainly it was framed by larger buildings and bigger temples than any other space in Rome.

The two long sides of the paved piazza were dominated by imposing new stuctures. Along the northern flank ran a huge double-storey hall, the recently constructed Basilica Fulvia (built in 179 BC), with – facing it – across the square, the even newer Basilica Sempronia (completed only in 170 BC). These long, barn-like buildings were novelties in Rome, though they would have been familiar to Crates. Their form, like their name, was Greek: they were modelled on Hellenistic royal reception halls. Although historians think these first Roman basilicas may have been constructed as gathering places for important foreign diplomats – such as Crates – they very quickly came to serve also as law courts, and places of resort. (One of the principal attractions of the Basilica Fulvia was its ingenious water clock.)†

Although there are few traces from the Republican era in the Forum today, many elements of its essential layout do remain. The vestiges of the Basilica Aemilia (which replaced the Basilica Fulvia) and of the Basilica Julia (which replaced the Sempronia) still frame the main space, providing its form and its alignment.

---

† The Romans learnt the art of telling the time from the Greeks. The first sundial, dividing the day into hours, was brought to Rome in 264 BC after the sack of Catana, a Greek colony in Sicily. The water clock, another Greek import, arrived a century later. It operated through the controlled flow of water into (or out of) a calibrated receptacle. It was constructed using data from a sundial, but it allowed citizens to tell the time even on sunless days, and also provided scope for mechanical displays. Vitruvius describes how the rising water level in the main vessel of a water clock could be used to drive all manner of simple mechanisms: 'Statues move, goalposts are turned over, stones or eggs are thrown, trumpets blare out.' The Romans divided the day into twelve hours beginning at dawn and continuing till dusk. They maintained this twelve-part division throughout the year, so that on the shortest day – 21 December – each 'hour' was only forty-five minutes long, while at midsummer it was the equivalent of seventy-five minutes. Amazingly, this arrangement was continued in Rome even after the introduction of clockwork timepieces in the late Middle Ages allowed for time to be measured without reference to the sun's course. Right up until Napoleon's annexation of Rome in 1808, time in the city, and in the Papal States, moved at its own pace. The various mechanical clocks in Rome (which had hour but not minute hands) had to be adjusted every two weeks to allow for the lengthening or shortening of the day.

Along the front of each basilica ran a line of arcaded shops, their galleries decorated with murals 'in the popular taste'. They were the preserve of money-changers and bankers. The produce-sellers who once dominated the Forum had, during the previous century, been relocated to the area behind the Basilica Fulvia, where they were gathered in a large (and recently rebuilt) market building, the Marcellum.

If food shopping had been banished to the fringes, politics still remained at the heart of the Forum's life. In the north-eastern corner of the piazza stood the Curia Hostilia, the meeting place of the Senate, with in front of it the Comitium, an open-air stepped circle where the popular assembly met to debate and vote. Overlooking the Comitium, opposite the doors of the Curia, was the Rostra, a high speakers' platform from which the consuls and other magistrates would address the crowd. (The existing Curia and Rostra are from a much later date, but, although different in form and alignment, they stand not so very far from where the old Republican monuments once were.) The Rostra derived its name from the fearsome bronze beaks, or *rostra*, taken from the prows of defeated warships, which were fixed along the front following the famous naval victory over the Latins at Antium in 338 BC.

Facing the Rostra, further round the rim of the Comitium, was the Graecostasis (the standing place of the Greeks), another raised platform, on which foreign ambassadors – Crates among them – would stand, while following debates, or waiting for their audiences with the Senate.

Rome's original Comitium, laid out way back in the sixth century BC, had been almost square. The circular meeting place was a relatively new idea, borrowed – once again – from the Greek cities of southern Italy. There were other Greek touches too. The space was flanked by two plundered Greek statues, imposing life-sized images in gilded bronze – one of the Athenian statesman-general Alcibiades, the other of the philosopher Pythagoras.

Splendid though these works were, their interest – not only for the Romans but also for many visitors to Rome – seems to have been more political than aesthetic. Plundered artworks were a vivid symbol of Rome's foreign conquests. They were a proclamation of power. According to the Greek writer Polybius, for conquered peoples coming to Rome, the sight of 'their works of art in this new setting incite[d] jealousy and hatred.' But even among unconquered visitors from the Greek world, such as Crates, there may well have been a tinge of disquiet at Rome's implacable might, mixed with sheer admiration of the beauty on view.

Any feelings of disquiet that Crates harboured were probably increased by the general levels of philistinism that he encountered among the Roman elite. Although

Rome boasted some early connoisseurs of Greek art, Fulvius Nobilior (the conqueror of the Greek city of Ambracia) among them, there was still much ignorance. The general who sacked Corinth allowed his soldiers to use a rare painting as a dice-board. He also disgraced himself by giving the statues of two youthful warriors the names of the two oldest characters in the Iliad – 'Priam' and 'Nestor'.

Besides the choice examples of Greek art on view in the Forum there were also memorials to Rome's greatest citizens. Honorary columns dotted the space, bearing statues of generals, magistrates and heroes. Horatius Cocles (who so famously kept the bridge) was there, and also Furius Camillus, who drove the Gauls out of Rome in the fourth century BC. In the Basilica Porcia, a small basilica adjacent to the Curia Hostilia there was a huge wall-painting depicting the defeat of the Carthaginians by M. Valerius Messalla in 263 BC.

If Rome's glorious history was carefully recorded and celebrated in the Forum, so too was its more mysterious and sacred past. At the eastern end of the space – in the lee of the Palatine hill – stood a cluster of important religious buildings: the huge Temple of Castor and Pollux; the sacred marble-framed spring of Juturna; the small circular temple to Vesta, the ancient hearth of Rome, with its eternal flame tended by the Vestal Virgins (who dwelt near by in their own house); and the Regia, supposedly once the home of the kings of Rome. Most of these buildings had been recently rebuilt or heavily restored after a terrible fire swept the Forum in 210 BC, but they spoke powerfully of continuity with a long, long past.

The Regia and the Temple of Vesta belonged to the first days of Rome's legend, while the Temple of Castor and Pollux was said to have been vowed at the beginning of the fifth century BC after the two horse-riding demi-gods had miraculously appeared amidst the Roman troops during the battle of Lake Regillus, and helped to secure a decisive Roman victory over the Latin peoples; they then brought news of the battle to Rome, pausing only to water their horses at the spring of Juturna in the Forum. (The three beautiful fluted Corinthian columns which stand as one of the most conspicuous sights in the Forum belong to a first century AD rebuilding of the temple, but their scale probably reflects that of the earlier building.)

Elsewhere in the Forum stood other memorials to Rome's mythic past, reminders of the city's long history. (By the varying estimates of its own chroniclers Rome had been founded – by Romulus – some time between 758 and 728 BC, on 21 April; the Republic had been established around 250 years later, in 508 BC, after the rule of Rome's seven more or less legendary kings.) Set – rather inconveniently – between the Rostra and the Graecostasis was a square black stone slab, inscribed with an invocation in a rude, very early form of Latin. The so-called Lapis Niger (which is still visible in the Forum) was pointed out as the gravestone of Romulus.

Not far from it, in front of the Basilica Sempronia, lay the fabled Lacus Curtius, a dried-up 'pool' set in a stone surround. It was site of great importance but mysterious origin. Even in the second century BC there was no agreement as to quite what it memorialized. It was variously said to mark the spot where a Sabine warrior, Mettius Curtius, had fallen into a bog while fighting Romulus, where a Roman knight, Marcus Curtius, had sacrificed himself – and saved Rome – by leaping with his horse into a chasm that had opened up in the Forum, or where a bolt of lightning had struck in 455 BC during the consulship of Gaius Curtius.

The western end of the Forum was dominated – and closed off – by the almost sheer escarpment of the Capitoline, the smallest but the most sacred of Rome's hills. Its heights, its slopes, its base bristled with temples and monuments. It must have been clear to all visitors that here was the sacred centre of the Roman state.

Standing side-on at the foot of this cliff, facing towards the Curia, was the large and ancient Temple of Saturn, dedicated – according to tradition – on 17 December 498 BC. Its dedicatory festival, the Saturnalia, had become one of the most popular in the Roman calendar. A time of licence and foolery, when gifts were exchanged, it later provided the basis for our modern Christmas. Saturn remains a rather mysterious deity, but like most of Rome's early gods he was associated initially with the farming year. (His wooden cult statue was filled up with olive oil.) And, as agriculture was the original basis of Rome's wealth, the temple (or the vaults under it) had from early times been home to the state treasury. The twelve bronze tablets inscribed with Rome's laws were also displayed upon its walls.

Set at right angles to the Temple of Saturn, with its back against the Capitoline hill, ran the Precinct of the Harmonious Gods, a long colonnaded podium adorned with gilded statues of six matched pairs of deities – Jupiter and Juno, Neptune and Minerva, Mars and Venus, Apollo and Diana, Volcanus and Vesta, Mercury and Ceres. Crates would have recognized the arrangement, and known that it had been created in imitation of the popular Athenian cult of the Twelve Gods. He might also have thought how new it looked: it had only been dedicated in 174 BC. (The rather cramped shrine bearing the same name that exists in the present Forum is a late nineteenth-century reconstruction of a later and very much smaller version of the Precinct created during the Imperial Age.)

From these sacred buildings at the base of the hill, the eye was drawn upwards, to some 45 metres/150 feet above the Forum floor, where loomed the twin knolls of

A model of the Temple of
Jupiter Optimus Maximus

the Capitoline, their temples and other structures silhouetted against the sky. To the
right, and slightly higher, was the Arx, surmounted by the Temple of Juno Moneta
– home of the Roman mint. (It stood in the place now occupied by the church of S.
Maria in Aracoeli.) On the left-hand summit – the Capitolium – however, was a sight
even more commanding.

Looking out, slightly away from the forum and the city, almost aloof in its grandeur,
sat the great blockish form of the Temple of Jupiter Optimus Maximus – Jupiter the
Best and Greatest. Even among so many other competing temples, this was something
different. Everything about the building proclaimed its pre-eminence: its scale, its
setting, its approach, its adornments. For all who came to Rome there could be no
doubting that this was – to the Romans – the most important monument in the city,
important in itself and in its meaning.

It was considered to be nothing less than the reason for Rome's greatness – and
the guarantee that that greatness would continue. Rome, it was believed, derived her
political and military power from Jupiter Optimus Maximus. He was the official deity of
the Roman state. It was at his great temple that the city's chosen magistrates assembled
each year to be invested with the *imperium*, the mystic force of command that flowed
from the deity. Rome's chosen generals had the same power conferred upon them.
They made their sacrifices to Jupiter Optimus Maximus before departing on their
campaigns, and they gave thanks to him when he granted them victory – which he did
with quite amazing frequency. And in a world governed by military might, victory in
arms counted for much.

Certainly the most important ceremonies held at the temple were the celebrations of military triumphs, performed by victorious generals. The final destination of every cavalcade of chained prisoners and deposed rulers, of spoils piled high on carts and biers, of military banners and blaring trumpets, after it had wended its way through the Forum along the Via Sacra, was – up the steep slope of the Capitoline – to the Temple of Jupiter Optimus Maximus. The wealth of the conquered nations was piled at the feet of the Roman state's proprietary god.

The temple was (and long remained) the central shrine of the Roman people. And it certainly looked the part. It was huge – far larger than anything else not just in Rome, but in Italy – although just how much larger has become a matter of scholarly debate. Estimates now vary between a building over 30 metres/100 feet high covering an area the size of half a football pitch, and something about a third less than this. Even at the smaller dimensions the temple would have been far bigger than the Parthenon at Athens.†

The building was set on a high podium, framed within a great walled precinct, and surrounded by other, smaller, temples, shrines and altars, by commemorative columns and by statues of gods and heroes. Standing close to it was a colossal effigy of Jupiter (so large that it could, apparently, be seen from the ancient shrine of Jupiter on the Alban Mount, some fifteen miles away), as well as two giant statues of Hercules, one of them a seated bronze figure made by the great Greek sculptor Lysippus and brought as one of the spoils from Tarentum in the south of Italy. But even these gigantic images were dwarfed by the scale of the temple itself.

Squat and oblong, with a low-pitched deep-eaved roof, the building's distinctive profile dominated the skyline. As Crates looked up at the temple from the Forum, its principal feature would have been the great porch – or *pronaos* – supported on eighteen hulking Tuscan-Doric columns – six across and three deep. Across the front ran an open pediment, crowded with terracotta sculptures. On the peak of the gable was a bronze

---

† The consensus established in the late nineteenth century estimated that the temple covered a massive 53.5 × 62 metres/175 × 203 feet, and rose at the peak of its roof to 35 metres/115 feet on columns 16.6 metres /54½ feet high. Recently, however, Professor John Stamper has suggested that such a scale would have been quite impossible with the post-and-lintel construction techniques employed at the time. The span between the central columns, for instance, would have been 12 metres/39 feet, a distance unbridgeable by any timber beam. He has proposed a model reduced by about one third: 34 metres/111½ feet wide by 38.3/125½ feet metres long, with a maximum height of 22 metres/72 feet.

statue of Jupiter driving a *quadriga*, or four-horse chariot. Other statues stood, ranged on the line of the pitched roof. Columns – six in number – ran down the full length of each flank to a solid wall at the rear. And framed within them was the enclosed part of the building, a windowless block divided into three chambers – or *cellae* – each with a tall portal facing towards the front.

The whole structure glowed and dazzled in the sun. It had recently been stuccoed and whitewashed. Bronze shields had been fixed to the roof – in imitation, it was said, of the Parthenon. And the deep entablature above the columns was set with bright decorative terracotta panels, painted in red and black and white.

To the Romans it seemed a building 'so magnificent as to be worthy of the king of gods and men, the Roman Empire, and the majesty of the site itself'. To travellers from the Greek east it probably looked rather clumsy, even gross – with its squat widely spaced columns, its unadorned capitals, its low-pitched roof.† There could be no denying the temple's bulk, nor, indeed, its effectiveness. (Through the agency of Jupiter Optimus Maximus Rome had come to control much of the known world.) But, as a piece of architecture, the building would have seemed very old-fashioned. This was not entirely surprising: it was old. And that, for the Romans at least, was part of its mystique and its attraction.

According to the established legend (preserved for us by Livy) the temple had its origins in the heroic age of Rome's kings, back in the sixth century BC. It was the fifth king of Rome – the Etruscan-born Tarquinius Priscus – who was credited, at a moment of crisis during a battle against the neighbouring Sabines, with 'vowing' a temple to Jupiter on the Capitoline hill. He selected the exact site of his new temple with care, and only – as was the custom with all important state decisions – after consultation with the augurs.

Having surveyed the site, they deemed it propitious to build, not on the higher spur of the hill (the Arx), but on the southern knoll. And work was soon begun to clear the ground. This was a religious as well as a physical operation. Several ancient shrines already existed in the area and the gods to whom they were dedicated had to be persuaded to relocate. According to the augurs all the deities consented to be moved, except for two: Terminus (the god of boundaries) and Iuventas (the goddess of young men). They declared this to be an excellent omen, indicating that 'no occasion would

---

† Only a century later, the Roman architectural theorist Vitruvius, having imbibed the principles of Greek taste, would describe the Capitoline temple as 'clumsy-roofed, low [and] broad'.

ever cause the removal of Rome's boundaries, or impair the city's youthful vigour.' It was arranged that the two shrines or altars would be incorporated – as they stood – into the new temple.

Although Tarquinius Priscus completed the work of terracing and levelling the site, he died before construction could begin. Progress then stalled during the reign of his adopted son, Servius Tullius (578–535 BC). And it was only with the coming to power of his true son (or, possibly, grandson), a second Tarquinius, later to be awarded the cognomen Superbus, that building work got under way – with the creation of, first, the massive podium and then the temple itself. The building, like all Etruscan temples, was aligned facing southwards.

During the first phase of work a human head – the blood still flowing from it – was dug up by a workman. Such a bizarre discovery demanded a further consultation with the augurs. After some delay, during which all building was halted, the foremost augur – or *haruspex* – of the day (specially brought in from a neighbouring Etruscan city) pronounced it to be an omen that 'the place shall be the head of all Italy' – and, indeed, the world. (It was this incident, too, that was said to have given the Capitoline hill its name.)

Although Tarquinius Superbus relied on the local Roman population for much of the heavy labour involved in the project, he also summoned the finest masons, artists and craftsmen from across the Etruscan world to help design and embellish the building. A terracotta statue of Jupiter clutching a sheaf of thunderbolts was commissioned from the celebrated Etruscan sculptor Vulca of Veii. It was to go in the central *cella*. Two other cult statues were also ordered, because Tarquinius had decided that the temple, while dedicated primarily to Jupiter Optimus Maximus, should also be associated with the goddesses Juno and Minerva.

Besides the cult statues in the *cellae*, Vulca also created a terracotta group of Jupiter in his *quadriga* for the peak of the pediment. Although this statue was replaced by the bronze version in 296 BC, the tale was still told of how the original sculpture had miraculously expanded during the firing, and how the kiln had to be dismantled in order to remove it. The augurs at Veii had announced that this was an omen presaging the great power of whoever possessed the statue. As a result the Veiians – wanting this power for themselves – had refused to send the work to Rome. When, however, their principal augur promptly dropped dead, they relented. For the Romans the story became another instance of their cult's especial potency.

If the design and structure of the building were adapted from existing Etruscan models, the scale was something new. For the Romans of the sixth century BC the size of their new temple was an extraordinary declaration of intent. At a time when Rome was still a relatively modest settlement warring against its often more powerful neighbours, it proclaimed the city's ambition and sense of destiny. The temple was, deliberately, larger and more impressive than the ancient Temple of Jupiter Latiaris on the Alban Mount, south of Rome, which had long served as a central shrine for the various Latin peoples. Through architecture Rome was asserting its conviction that it would become the capital of the region.

Tarquinius Superbus did not remain in power long enough to dedicate the temple that he had created. He was ousted in the coup of 509 BC that established the Roman Republic. The new regime, however, was entirely in tune with his grand vision, and was eager to finish the task. It fell to the Republic's first two consuls – Valerius and Horatius Pulvillus – to draw lots for the signal honour of dedicating the temple. Horatius was successful. This greatly annoyed Valerius and his supporters, who then tried numerous ruses to sabotage their rival. In a desperate final ploy Valerius interrupted the dedication ceremony with the (false) news that Horatius' son had died. If he hoped to unsettle his rival, he was disappointed. As Livy recounts, 'Without permitting himself to be diverted from his purposes by the message, further than to order that the body should be buried, Horatius kept his hand on the door-post, finished his prayer, and dedicated the temple.'

The temple had remained unchanged in the 350 years since then, although the area around it was reinforced in 386 BC with gigantic stone-buttressed substructures – a piece of engineering that was variously described by the Roman historians as 'one of the wonders of Rome' and 'insane'.

While modern visitors tend to arrive on the Capitol from the north side, via Michelangelo's graceful staircase, in Roman times the only access to the hill's summit was from the Forum. Crates would have had to approach the Temple of Jupiter Optimus Maximus along the steep paved pathway of the Clivus Capitolinus as it zigzagged up the escarpment – past the Precinct of the Harmonious Gods, between various minor shrines and under an early example of a triumphal arch (set up in 190 BC by Scipio Africanus, the conqueror of Carthage), before passing through a gateway into the Capitoline temple precinct.

This large walled area, lined along one side with an elegant colonnaded portico (one of the first such structures built in Rome), was crowded with significant objects. Besides the colossal statues already mentioned, there were many more conventional sculptures, life-size bronzes of Hercules and Jupiter, Mars and Nemesis, as well as secular images of victorious generals and wise magistrates, and even the seven kings of Rome. Dotted about the site were various small temples and shrines – several to Jupiter in some of his other manifestations – and also a small library.

Much of what was on view commemorated Rome's long and illustrious past. A simple thatched hut was said to be Romulus' original house – or, at least a version of it. (Another – rather older – example of the same hut stood on the Palatine hill, where legend suggested Romulus had actually first made his home.) There was also an enclosure of sacred geese, kept in memory of the geese that – in 390 BC – had alerted the Romans, barricaded on the Capitol, to a night attack by the besieging Gauls.

Directly in front of the temple stood the great altar of Jupiter, upon which animal sacrifices were made at the beginning of each year, at the culmination of military triumphs and on other solemn occasions. And leading up behind it was the broad flight of the temple steps – odd in number, as was the case with all temple staircases, so that the approaching supplicant could begin and end his ascent propitiously with his right foot.

The great covered area of the temple porch was thick with yet more reminders of Rome's greatness. The widely spaced columns were hedged with statues, and fixed with military standards and proclamations. There had been a major clear-out of these accretions in 179 BC, but already the process had begun again. The altar to Iuventas, which had proved impossible to move from its original position, also stood in the *pronaos*. (The altar dedicated to Terminus had been incorporated into the *cella* of Jupiter and, since shrines to Terminus had to be open to the sky, a hole was cut in the roof directly above it.)

At the back of the *pronaos* loomed the open doorways of the three *cellae*, set with their ornate decorated bronze thresholds. Each dark windowless *cella* contained its ancient terracotta cult statue: Jupiter clutching his thunderbolts in the central – and largest – chamber, with Juno to the left, and on the right Minerva. It is possible still to catch a flavour of these archaic – and long-lost – effigies among the Etruscan collections at the Villa Giulia. A life-size terracotta group, excavated at Veii, is considered to be the work of Vulca – sculptor of the Capitoline triad. It represents Hercules stealing a stag sacred to Apollo, and the poised androgynous figure of the god, with his tilted almond eyes and long smooth limbs, perhaps carries some hint of the mystic images that once stood upon the Capitolium.

The austere restraint of these works is, however, somewhat deceptive. On feast days the statue of Jupiter in the Capitoline temple was luxuriously robed in a gold-embroidered purple toga, and its face was painted vermilion. The same elaborate outfit – as, indeed, the same vermilion make-up – was also worn by victorious generals during their triumphal processions, to emphasize their close connection with the god.

Roman temples were not places of public gathering, like modern churches. There were no set services. The necessary ceremonies and sacrifices were performed by the appropriate priests, magistrates and generals, without the need for any congregation. Individual Roman citizens did visit the temples, though, to ask for divine blessings upon particular ventures or in the face of particular crises, and also to give thanks if their requests were successful. And, as the chapels of Roman Catholic churches still are, the *cellae* of the Temple of Jupiter Optimus Maximus were decked with votive offerings – little models of limbs mended, animals cured, relatives helped. (These had to be cleared out regularly, and stored in chambers beneath the temple platform.)

Adorning the walls there were also further trophies and spoils, including plundered sculptures, paintings and jewels. Roman temples often resembled something between a museum and a bank vault. Among the earliest treasures deposited at the Temple of Jupiter Optimus Maximus had been a golden crown presented by the vanquished Latins. Among the most precious were

The *Apollo* of Veii, made by the great Etruscan sculptor Vulca, who was responsible for the terracotta image of Jupiter in the temple of Jupiter Optimus Maximus

the Sibylline Books, which held the secrets of the future. They had been bought – so it was said – by Tarquinius Superbus from the Cumaean Sibyl, and were kept in a marble chest in the basement, to be consulted only at moments of national crisis.

All these treasures have disappeared, and so has the temple itself. The building in its original form did not even survive the Republic. And although it was splendidly rebuilt several times, the depredations of later ages obliterated all trace of the structure. In recent years, however, excavations on the Capitoline, in the gardens and basement of the Caffarelli Palace, have laid bare a section of the massive podium upon which the temple once stood. These bald but impressive remains are now incorporated into the display of the Capitoline Museums. The two great parallel walls of rough-cut *cappellaccio* tufa, which mark only a small section at the corner of the podium, still give a vivid sense of the scale of the building.

A few shattered fragments of terracotta relief have also been recovered from the site. Some retain traces of pigment, red and black and white. These are perhaps remnants of the antefixes that once adorned the temple frieze: a scowling Silenus, a woman's face with arched brows, a war chariot with archaic warriors. Though small they are powerful images, but they seem redolent of an almost pre-classical world. To Crates, arrived from sophisticated Pergamum, they must have seemed quite barbarous. (To fix a sense of the cultural world from which Crates came, it should be borne in mind that the famously expressive sculpture of the *Dying Gladiator* in the Capitoline Museums – see page 220 – was probably modelled on a bronze original created at Pergamum during his lifetime.)

A painted terracotta antefix, similar to those that adorned the temple of Jupiter Optimus Maximus

If Crates was probably underwhelmed by the architectural and artistic splendours of the Capitol and the Forum, there were other sights in Rome that must have excited both his interest and his admiration.

Even as he arrived at Rome, he would have seen – rising above the teeming wharfs along the Tiber – the vast frontage of the Porticus Aemilia, a great warehouse that had been completed only six years before, to serve the new docks below the Aventine hill. It was then the largest covered building in Rome: some 487 × 90 metres/1,600 × 295 feet. Compared even to the famous Arsenal at Pergamum, which was said to hold enough grain to feed a thousand men for a year, this was something impressive. The building, moreover, had been constructed using a novel, and very Roman, building material, concrete, which allowed its relatively light barrel-vaulted ceiling to be supported on rows of piers so widely spaced that a cart could be driven between them.†

The fact that such an imposing structure should be a simple warehouse was a telling example of Republican Rome's especial genius for practicality. The same distinctive spirit was evident across the crowded metropolis: in the stone bridge that had recently been set up over the Tiber (in addition to an earlier wooden one), in the two aqueducts – the Appia and the Anio Vetus (each over a hundred years old) – that brought fresh water into the city from the surrounding countryside, in the straight stone-paved roads that led out from the principal gateways of the city. (The first of these – the Via Appia – had been laid down in 312 BC.)

Another early manifestation of Rome's practical ingenuity was its sewerage system. Pliny the Elder (always ready with a superlative) called it 'the most noteworthy achievement of all'. And as he describes it, it was impressive: the various streams running off the seven hills were channelled underground before being brought together into a single large stone-lined conduit and discharged into the Tiber. The subsidiary channels (each, apparently, big enough for a man to travel along in a small boat) 'rushing downwards like mountain torrents, sweep away everything in their path', cleaning and scouring the sides of the sewers as they went.

The system – according to legend and to Pliny – had, like the Temple of Jupiter Optimus Maximus, been the work of Rome's fifth king, Tarquinius Priscus. Certainly it must have been very early in origin for it was only with the introduction of good sewers that the marshy and often-flooded ground at the foot of the Capitoline hill could be properly drained and could begin to evolve into the Roman Forum. The small stream, called the Velabrum, which ran along the bottom of the Forum valley, provided the basis for the single stone-lined channel, gathering in all the subsidiary flows. It was

---

† The durability of Roman concrete – made from a mixture of *pozzolana* (a locally occurring volcanic sand) and lime, combined with masonry rubble – is attested by the remnants of the Porticus Aemilia's thick tufa-dotted walls still standing, just below Ponte Sublicio, in Via Rubattino and the adjoining streets. They are the earliest survivals of concrete construction in the city.

canalized and enclosed to make Rome's principal drain, the Cloaca Maxima, its path through the Forum marked by a small circular shrine – to Venus Cloacina – close to the Basilica Aemilia.

The great drain, together with the rest of the city's sewerage system, had been reviewed and probably renewed in 184 BC (as it was renewed and reviewed throughout its history). It remained a grand piece of engineering. At its mouth, where it disgorged into the Tiber, just below the Tiber Island, the Cloaca Maxima was some 3.5 metres/12 feet in diameter – large enough, as Pliny put it, 'to allow the passage of a wagon fully loaded with hay'. (Perhaps this was the same wagon that had just passed between widely spaced piers of the Porticus Aemilia.) The construction of the great vaulted tunnel combined monumental scale with a certain elegant simplicity. The massive blocks of volcanic stone (1.5 metres/5 feet long by 90 centimetres/3 feet thick) were joined without mortar or cement.

The mouth of the Cloaca Maxima, as it is today, set into the embankment of the Tiber

Of all the monuments of Republican Rome it was this ingeniously conceived and put together waste-water system that made the most profound impression on Crates of Mallos. Literally. While walking near the Palatine, he fell down an open manhole into the sewer and broke his leg. He was obliged to stay on in Rome to recuperate. He spent the time in giving an influential course of lectures, introducing his Roman audience to Greek grammar and literary theory.

The great maw of the Cloaca Maxima is still visible, set into the modern embankment of the Tiber, just below the Ponte Palatinus. It is framed within a triple circle of travertine stone, and might look more impressive but for the fact that a large fig tree and a forest of other rank saplings have grown up in front of it. You would be hard put to drive a wagonload of hay through such a thicket. A tramp, too, has taken up residence on the stone platform above the conduit. When I visited him he was carefully washing his collection of frayed and faded T-shirts in a clear little stream that trickles rather bathetically out of the once-great drain; it is the ancient Velabrum, still flowing down from the valley of the Forum.

The Cloaca Maxima remains connected to the city's drainage system, taking water from other drains, and preventing the backwash from the Tiber flowing back up into the Forum.

It was once possible also to inspect an open section of the great sewer in a space between the houses just opposite S. Giorgio in Velabro. A marble plaque on the wall across the way from the church announces that a visit can be arranged by telephoning the Department of Antiquities. Sadly, though, the arrangement no longer holds. Visits have been discontinued for 'safety reasons'. Perhaps the Department of Antiquities has belatedly turned up an old complaint form filed by Crates of Mallos.

·II·
IMPERIAL ROME

S AINT JEROME, one of the Fathers of the Church and the translator of the Bible
into Latin, had few regrets when he died in Bethlehem in 420 AD. But there were,
he admitted, three experiences that he wished he could have enjoyed: to have
beheld the face of Christ, to have heard St Paul preach, and to have seen Rome in all
its glory.

His third wish must be shared by almost all modern visitors to Rome. Standing
amidst the great fragments of the past, it is impossible not to wonder what the city
would have looked like at the height of its power, when all the great monuments were
standing, entire and glorious. If only one could travel back in time.

It can be done. Almost. Get on the Metro, and go out to EUR – the austere
modernist suburb created by Mussolini in the late 1930s, in preparation for an
Esposizione Universale Roma which never happened. The centrepiece of this rigorously
symmetrical large-scale development was a complex of grand museums – of Prehistory
and Ethnography, of Popular Art and Traditions, and of Roman Civilization. They
now stand, unvisited and unloved, the vast halls of polished marble, and dusty display
cabinets, echoing only to the sudden shrieks of visiting school parties. Yet, in the Museo
della Civiltà Romana stands one of the great sights of Rome: the *Plastico* – a huge scale-
model of the city as it was in the early fourth century AD. Constructed by the architect-
archaeologist Italo Gismondi, over four decades between 1935 and 1971, it is a labour

of love, skill and scholarship. At a scale of 1:250 it lays out the great imperial city in its pomp, on a base some 20 × 20 metres (66 × 66 feet).

It is all there: a marble wonderland of colonnaded squares and pedimented temples, of arcaded theatres and amphitheatres, of aqueducts and circuses, stretching from the banks of the Tiber up and over the seven hills. You can see – and take your bearings from – the great ring of the Colosseum. You can make out the shallow dome of the Pantheon and the position of the Forum, the long straight line of the Via Lata (which survives as the modern Corso), the grand sweep of the Circus Maximus, and the great drum of Hadrian's Mausoleum (now the Castel S. Angelo). And between these fixed points stretches an ordered patchwork of porticoes, piazzas, temples, bath complexes, gardens and reservoirs. This is no longer a city of brick and timber. Much – clearly – had changed since the time of Crates of Mallos.

An image of Ancient Rome from *Il Plastico*, the magnificent scale-model of the city preserved at the Museo della Civiltà Romana in the suburb of EUR. The Colosseum is in the bottom right-hand corner, faced by the Temple of Venus and Rome.

Rome as it appears in the *Plastico* is the record of five centuries of growth, of building and rebuilding, of increasing commercial wealth and increasing political power. The city at its height was the centre of a great empire that spread from Hadrian's Wall to the Sahara, from the Atlantic to the Euphrates. The dense, thriving, Etrusco-Latin city of the second century BC had been transformed over time into a sprawling marble megalopolis. It was larger, more crowded and more splendid than any city the world had yet seen.

It proclaimed its glory from afar. Eleven great aqueducts marched across the countryside on their tall brick-built arches, bringing water into the city. The fourteen straight well paved highways that led to Rome – through the broad expanse of the Campagna – were lined with houses, villas, shrines, mausoleums, cemeteries, temples and all the signs of thriving suburban existence, until they reached the fourteen great gateways that punctuated the city wall.

Rome's new boundary was a formidable structure of concrete-faced brick, over 8 metres (26 feet) high and some 12 miles round. It enclosed 5¼ square miles, an area more than three times greater than the old Republican wall had done. And above its rampart, vast buildings and colossal statues – raised on the city's seven hills – glistened against the skyline.

They gave a hint of what lay within. Rome was a city proud of its amenities. According to the two Regionary Catalogues which survive from the fourth century there were: 28 libraries, 8 parks, 11 fora, 10 great basilicas, 11 vast public bath-houses and 856 small private baths, 2 circuses, 2 amphitheatres, 3 theatres, 5 *naumachia* (artificial lakes), 15 great fountains, 423 temples and other assorted shrines, 2 large market halls, 290 warehouses, 1352 drinking fountains, 46 brothels (licensed and taxed by the state), and 144 public lavatories (also licensed and taxed).

Great buildings and grand monuments now stretched in an almost unbroken phalanx from the heights of the Palatine, across the Forum, past the Capitol and over the Field of Mars. They spread even across the Tiber, where, just outside the city walls, stood the barrel-like mass of Hadrian's mausoleum, close by the Vatican hill where Nero had built a lavish racetrack or 'circus'.

Thirty-six triumphal arches dotted the city, enduring reminders of military might and imperial power. Eight bridges spanned the Tiber, where – in Republican times – there had been only two. The wharves, now along both banks of the river, were busy with traffic bringing provisions up from the port at Ostia or down from the cities to the north.

The process of transformation had been long and continuous. It was Octavius – or Augustus Caesar, as he became with the institution of the Principate in 27 BC – who claimed to have 'found the city made of brick and left it made of marble'. And if his boast rather glossed over the building projects of his great predecessors – Julius Caesar, Pompey and Sulla – it was not without point. The forty-six years of Augustus' rule left an enduring imprint upon the look and layout of Rome.

He restored much and built more, always seeking to instil order and symmetry. To create additional space for the business of government, he laid out the grand Forum Augustum, to match the Forum of Julius Caesar, to the north of the old Forum. Its colonnaded square was lined with statues and dominated by the lofty bulk of the Temple of Mars Ultor – the Avenger – raised to commemorate the defeat of Caesar's assassins. He established his own modest residence upon the Palatine hill alongside a Temple of Apollo so splendid in its size and decoration that it rivalled the Temple of Jupiter Optimus Maximus on the facing bluff of the Capitoline.

He exploited the great white marble quarries at Luna (near modern Carrara, in the hills above Pisa), as well as bringing rich coloured marbles from North Africa and Greece to adorn his construction projects and confirm Rome's power and reach. New forms were adopted and old ones revived: the Corinthian column, unknown in Rome before the early first century BC, became ubiquitous.

Although he did not take up Julius Caesar's ambitious plan to prevent flooding on the Campus Martius by diverting the course of the Tiber, he did raise the ground level there and start embanking the river. And with a series of grand building schemes – two new theatres, an artificial lake, the Ara Pacis (in celebration of the universal peace brought by his rule), his family mausoleum (a vast white marble drum, surmounted with cypress trees and topped by a statue of himself), and a giant pavement-sundial (its gnomon made from an ancient Egyptian obelisk) – he confirmed the area as a zone of monuments and leisured resort.

In the centuries that followed successive emperors extended and enriched the Augustan vision, as they extended and taxed Rome's empire. Some, like Nero with his never-completed Golden House, built for their own pleasure, most – even if they sought to record their names and celebrate their victories – built to the glory of Rome's gods and the benefit of Rome's people. Vespasian, together with his sons Titus and Domitian, the three Flavian emperors, created much of enduring magnificence during the years of their triumphant rule (69–96 AD). It was Vespasian who initiated the great amphitheatre known to posterity as the Colosseum, and Titus who completed it. Domitian's enthusiasm for lavish building works developed almost into a mania. The sumptuous official residence that he created for himself on the Palatine transformed the whole hill into an exclusive imperial zone – and gave the word 'palace' to the language.

The Aurelian Walls

The Flavians' successors – Nerva, Trajan and Hadrian – added more wonders. (Hadrian was probably responsible for the great domed space of the Pantheon.) And if, after them, imperial expansion ceased and the impetus for monumental building in Rome slowed, it did not die altogether.

Septimius Severus and his 'Severan' heirs – particularly Caracalla and Alexander Severus – were energetic builders. (The Baths of Caracalla were the largest ever constructed.) And even the chaotic years of the late third century, when rival emperors pursued their independent claims across the empire, were not without construction – and reconstruction – work at Rome. Aurelian's imposing new circuit of walls dated from that period. Diocletian, the restorer of the empire's unity, though he only visited Rome once (in 305), left his mark with another vast set of baths. Maxentius restored much and began several major projects (including a private circus for chariot-racing outside the city walls). And after his defeat, his vanquisher, Constantine, completed most of these schemes and initiated several more, adding fresh accents to Rome's grandeur. His monumental Basilica Nova dominated the east end of the Forum, which had been left devastated by a fire in 281.

Fires were only too frequent throughout Rome's long history. They necessitated much rebuilding and refurbishment, and allowed for much redevelopment. The great conflagration of 64 AD (during which Nero fiddled) lasted nine days, razing three of the city's fourteen regions, and severely damaging seven others. Another fire in 80 AD burnt up much of the Campus Martius, one of the few areas that had escaped unscathed sixteen years before. When crowded residential areas were ravaged by fire, they were often redeveloped as monumental spaces; when public buildings were destroyed they were rebuilt. The Temple of Jupiter Optimus Maximus, having survived intact for over four centuries, was burnt down three times during the next 160 years (in 83 BC, 69 AD and AD 80), being rebuilt each time on the same ground plan but to a new design and at an ever-increasing height. In this way Rome grew steadily more magnificent and more congested with monuments.

Nevertheless, if it grew in splendour with the years, it diminished in power. By the mid-fourth century the highpoint of Rome's greatness had passed. The city depicted in the *Plastico*, and described in the Regionary Catalogues, was on the ebb. Its population, while still vast, had shrunk from its early third-century high of well over a million, to something perhaps closer to eight hundred thousand. The deployment of slaves as artisans and shopkeepers had sapped the vitality of the city's commercial classes. Many of Rome's citizens were content with their ancient privileges: their doles of bread and oil, and their right to attend the public games.† The old patrician families continued to control enormous personal wealth from their estates across the empire, but their political role had become largely ceremonial. (Urban government and maintenance rested with the city prefect – the emperor's deputy in the city – together with his various sub-prefects and officials.)

Administrative reforms, imperial power struggles and barbarian pressure upon the periphery of the empire had all taken a toll. Few recent emperors had lived long at Rome. Their inclinations and the demands of office had taken them away, and they had taken most of the imperial civil service with them. Even on the Italian peninsula Milan became preferred as an operational base. Meanwhile the populous and wealthy eastern provinces of the empire were increasingly the main focus of imperial energy. The new city of Constantinople, founded by the Emperor Constantine on the Bosphorus in 330, was rapidly acquiring significance as an administrative and political centre. Rome became less a place of power than an ideal – an ideal of universal government and order.

Nevertheless, the city itself was still hugely important: ideals need to be embodied. Rome held a pre-eminent position as the historic capital of the empire, the symbolic head, the *caput mundi*, the sacred city. It still had its unrivalled monuments and treasures. They were well protected, well maintained and well loved. Rome during the years of the empire had evolved gradually into a living museum. The buildings and treasures of

† In the mid-fourth century there were, according to the calendar of Philocalus, 177 designated days of games, or *ludi*: 101 days of theatrical shows, 66 of chariot racing, and 10 of gladiatorial combat.

Rome's monumental centre were a physical manifestation of her ethos. Here, in stone and metal, was a record of the city's history and the city's greatness.

Such sights must have been both a draw and an inspiration for the many citizens of the far-flung empire who came to Rome (and from 212 every free-born male within the imperial borders was accounted a Roman citizen). Which particular sights, however, had the greatest impact upon those citizen visitors? Which artworks did they most admire; which buildings most impressed them? When everything was still standing and in place, there was a great deal to choose from.

Even in the first century AD, during the reign of Augustus, when the process of Rome's beautification had only just begun, the profusion of wonders could seem overwhelming to the visitor. As the geographer Strabo recounted, 'If, on passing the Old Forum, one should see forum after forum ranged alongside it, and basilicas, and temples, and should see also the Capitol and the works of art there and those on the Palatine and in Livia's Promenade, one would easily forget the things outside. Such is Rome.' By the fourth century there were yet more forums, basilicas, temples and promenades to wonder at.

While some monuments attracted by their scale and others by their beauty, a good number owed their prominence to their historical associations. Even in Republican times Rome had a keen sense of its own history, and a gift for mythologizing it in monuments, and that had continued with the Imperial Age. The old Forum Romanum, having all but ceased to be a place of government and business, had become instead a formal showground of Rome's glorious past. New imperial temples now framed the space, while triumphal arches and honorary columns proclaimed the great deeds of the Imperial Age.

As a reminder of the city's place at the centre of the world, there stood, close by the Rostra, a golden milestone – the Milliarium Aureum – erected by Augustus to mark the point to and from which all Roman roads were measured. The ancient Republican monuments and shrines – the Lacus Curtius, the Lapis Niger, the spring of Juturna, the Regia, the Rostra, the Temple of Vesta – all remained in place, but they had been tidied up and dignified, dressed in white marble and framed with straight lines.

The two small thatched (and often restored) versions of Romulus' first home still stood – one on the Palatine the other on the Capitoline – while at the foot of the Palatine, as a further memorial to Rome's legendary founder, Augustus had also dedicated the Lupercal, an elaborately decorated cave where Romulus and Remus were supposed to have been nurtured by the she-wolf. (Its site, lost for centuries, has recently been rediscovered by archaeologists.) As a memorial to another of Rome's foundation myths, close to the Tiber, on the Campus Martius, stood a ship shed containing an ancient dug-out boat, in which – it was said – Aeneas had arrived from Troy.

If Rome was a city of history, it was also a city of art, or at least of statues. They were everywhere. They adorned the façades and rooftops of buildings, they stood in ranks in public spaces, they marked the street junctions, they crowded the temples, bath-houses, porticoes and palaces. Their maintenance and care were the responsibility of a dedicated *curator statuarum*, one of the key officials under the prefect of the city. He must have had a taxing time. By the mid-fourth century it was estimated that there were 20 great equestrian statues in Rome, 2 colossi, 80 images of gods made of gold and 77 of ivory, as well as 3,785 bronze statues. The number of marble works was left unstated, though it was said that Rome had two populations of equal size: one living, the other made of stone.

Since the time of Rome's first military incursions into the Greek world numerous masterpieces of Hellenic and Hellenistic art had been brought to the city. And over the years many Greek craftsmen had followed them. The traditions of Greek sculpture were preserved, continued and adapted in their new setting. Famous old works were copied and many new ones created. The contrasting tendencies in Ancient Greek art towards idealization and realism were both encouraged by the Romans. The former impulse contributed to many bold images of imperial propaganda, the latter to the bracing realism of much Roman portrait sculpture. By the fourth century, however, such distinctions were being obscured by a new artistic trend. Size became the one important criterion; modelling, proportion, anatomical accuracy were often ignored in the overriding quest for scale. The distinctive work of the period was the colossal statue of Constantine that was created for the Basilica Nova. (Its mammoth marble head, hand and foot can still be seen in the courtyard of the Capitoline Museums.)

The sheer variety and number of statues on view in Rome must have confounded most viewers. For many modern visitors the massed marbles of the Capitoline Museums are enough to produce a feeling of dazed satiety, but they represent only a tiny proportion of what once adorned the city. By the end of the classical period there must have been tens of thousands of statues on view. Even in the first century AD Pliny the Elder was complaining: 'At Rome, indeed the great number of works of art and their consequent effacement from our memory . . . must deter anyone from serious study.'

Nevertheless, among the many masterpieces of Greek sculpture that he lists housed in the temples, porticoes, fora, bath-houses, libraries and palaces of Rome, he did single out the marble *Laocoön*, in the Baths of Titus. This work (which we shall meet again, in the time of the Renaissance) represented the scene from the *Aeneid* when the Trojan priest Laocoön and his two sons are crushed to death by giant sea serpents after seeking to warn the Trojans against bringing the Greeks' wooden horse into the city. Ever the enthusiast, Pliny describes it as a supreme work of art, and rhapsodizes over how it had been carved by three of the most celebrated Greek sculptors of the second century BC from a single block of stone.

Pliny, however, was an aficionado. For the less-informed visitor, the most conspicuous artworks to be met with in the streets of Rome were a statue of an elephant eating grass near the Forum Boarium, a bronze group of 'nesting storks', a huge effigy of Hercules reclining on a couch, and a sculpture of Mamurius Veturius (the mythical metal-worker who fashioned eleven replicas of the *ancile*, a propitious bronze shield said to have fallen from heaven at the time of King Numa). Also particularly to be noted were the gilded equestrian statue of Constantine in the Forum, and another of Tiridates, a first-century King of Armenia, close to the Via Lata. (None of these, alas, survives.)

The much-admired *Laocoön*

The *Colossus*: the giant
bronze statue, created for
Nero, that stood before the
Flavian Amphitheatre, as
imagined by a nineteenth-
century illustrator

Dominating all, though, was the *Colossus*. This gigantic gilded bronze effigy – around 30 metres (100 feet) high – stood close to the great Flavian Amphitheatre, which, in time, would assume both its name and fame. It had originally been commissioned by Nero for the vestibule of his Golden House, and had been created as an idealized nude portrait of the emperor. After Nero's death the head was replaced (a not uncommon procedure), and the statue converted into an image of the sun god, Sol. Each of the seven great 'rays' radiating from his crown was some 7 metres (23 feet) long. And in AD 128 Hadrian, with the help of an expert engineer and twenty-four elephants, had the statue moved – in an upright position – to its new site. (The base on which it once stood can be seen, between the Colosseum and the Arch of Constantine.) From there it dominated the skyline, catching the rays of the sun in its gilded crown: literally and figuratively the greatest statue in Rome.

Size also seems to have influenced which buildings were most admired, though it was certainly not the only consideration. Contemporary testimony is frustratingly limited, but some clear outlines do emerge. There was a general awed admiration for the staggering achievement of the Roman aqueduct system. (The sight of the great brick-built arches marching across the Campagna, or rearing up unexpectedly among the streets of modern Rome, still has the power to amaze.) Even in the first century AD Pliny could write of Rome's water supply, 'We shall readily admit that there has never been anything more remarkable in the whole world.' Nevertheless, as the centuries advanced, it was less the great practical engineering triumphs of the early Romans that excited admiration than the more recent masterpieces of ostentatious display.

Pliny himself praised the Basilica Aemilia in the Forum (as rebuilt in 22 AD with 'remarkable' marble columns from Phrygia), together with the Forum of Augustus, and the huge Forum or Temple of Peace (created by Vespasian to house the spoils of Jerusalem), as 'the most beautiful [buildings] the world has ever seen'. He was writing, though, before the splendid creations of Domitian, Trajan, Hadrian, Caracalla and the rest.

The Temple of Jupiter Optimus Maximus seems always to have retained a special status for visitors. And as rebuilt by Domitian, following the fire of 80 AD, it was certainly conspicuous, its roof covered with tiles of gilded brass. Plutarch, however, complained that the beautiful columns of Pentelic marble that had been brought from Athens to adorn the temple had been 'spoiled when they were re-cut and polished [at Rome], for they were made too thin and tapering [for their great height], and the embellishment was bought at the cost of symmetry'.

Perhaps in better taste was the little Temple of Jupiter Tonans, also on the Capitoline. One of the many temples founded by Augustus, it was, apparently, decorated in such choice style, and stocked with such rarities, that some feared Jupiter Optimus Maximus himself might become jealous of it. To prevent this, Augustus hung bells from the temple's eaves, so that it could claim to be no more than the gatehouse of its great neighbour.

Another Augustine foundation that attracted enthusiastic praise was the Temple of Apollo on the Palatine. The poet Propertius, writing during the emperor's reign, gives a vivid glimpse of its splendour:

Why, you ask, do I come so late? Mighty Caesar has opened the golden colonnades of Apollo's Temple. A glorious sight it was, as it lay open to view with its columns of African marble, and set between them statues of the many daughters of old Danaus. Then, in the midst, the temple with its shining marble rose up high, which Apollo loves even more than his home in Ortygia. On its roof were two chariots of the Sun, the doors were of Libyan ivory, marvellously wrought. . . . Then, at last, there stood the god himself, between his mother and sister – Pythian Apollo, clad in a long robe, and chanting song. The marble statue seemed to me fairer than the god himself as he stood with parted lips and silent lyre. Round the altar stood the cattle of [the sculptor] Myron, four oxen that seemed to live.

Strabo, a contemporary of Propertius, was greatly impressed by the Mausoleum of Augustus on the Campus Martius, a great white marble barrel, enclosing a mound, planted with evergreen trees and surmounted by a bronze statue of the emperor.

Procopius, writing four centuries later, preferred the Mausoleum of Hadrian: 'a most notable sight, for it is made of Parian marble, and the stones fit together so closely that there are no joins visible . . . Above there are statues of men and horses, of the same marble, superb pieces of craftsmanship.'

In 7 BC the Circus Maximus, with its banks of marble seating (enough for 250,000 spectators) and ring of encircling shops, was lauded by Dionysius of Halicarnassus as 'one of the most remarkable buildings in Rome'. And it was subsequently added to and enriched by Nero, Vespasian and Trajan, becoming even more remarkable. The *Historia Augusta* noted the Baths of Caracalla as particularly 'splendid'.

The most vivid account of a visit to Ancient Rome, however, is that provided by Ammianus Marcellinus, recording the sojourn of the Emperor Constantius II in AD 357. Constantius II was the third son of the Emperor Constantine; though born in Constantinople and baptized a Christian, he was excited to be in Rome, among the monuments of the glorious – if pagan – past: 'When [Constantius] came to the Rostra, he marvelled at the renowned Forum, seat of ancient dominion: wherever he turned his gaze, the crowded display of wonderful sights was overwhelming. He addressed the Senate in the Curia, spoke to the People from the Tribunal, was received in the Palace with elaborate attentions, and there enjoyed the pleasure for which he had ardently longed.'

He attended chariot races in the Circus Maximus, showing a thoroughly Roman enthusiasm for the sport and delighting in the banter of the spectators. In thanks for his happy days at the races, he embellished the great stadium, by setting up a huge Egyptian obelisk on the *spina* – or central reservation – of the track. (He had brought the monolith with him from Alexandria, where it had long been awaiting shipment to Constantinople, as part of Constantine's original scheme to decorate his new city.)

There was time, too, for more conventional sightseeing. Constantius was impressed:

Finally, as he surveyed all the various parts of the city, disposed over the seven hills and along the plains, together with its suburbs, he thought that whatever he saw first towered above the rest. There was the Temple of Tarpeian Jove [Temple of Jupiter Optimus Maximus], excelling as divine things do human: the baths, built like whole provinces: the enormous bulk of the Amphitheatre [the Colosseum] in its framework of travertine stone, to whose highest points the human eye can scarcely reach: the Pantheon, almost a domed district of the city, vaulted over in lofty beauty: the great columns with their spiral staircases, bearing the likenesses of former emperors. There was the Temple of Venus and Rome, the Forum of Peace, the Theatre of Pompey, the Odeum, the Stadium of Domitian and among them all the other embellishments of the Eternal City.

Some of these wonders have disappeared almost completely. The glory of Domitian's Odeum (an elegant Greek-inspired concert-auditorium) now exists only as a name; even its exact site is uncertain. Nothing but a few fragments of finely carved marble remain from Domitian's gold-roofed Temple of Jupiter Optimus Maximus. Hadrian's Temple of Venus and Rome had the distinction of being the largest temple ever built in the city but only a section of its massive podium still survives, at the east end of the Forum, facing the Colosseum. (The unique back-to-back *cellae*, designed by the emperor himself, can still, however, just about be made out, providing – it has been suggested – an architectural expression of the palindrome ROMA/AMOR.)

Elsewhere, though, more than enough remains to allow us to share something of Constantius' sense of wonder. The enormous travertine bulk of the Colosseum continues to amaze the modern visitor. The serene domed space of the Pantheon endures unchanged – one of the most breathtaking survivals of antiquity. The extraordinary carved columns of Trajan and Marcus Aurelius still stand. And although the great colonnaded Forum of Peace has been obliterated (and now lies under the Via dei Fori Imperiali) one of its flanking meeting halls survives – having been converted at an early date into the Church of SS. Cosma e Damiano – to suggest its grandeur.

The massive ruins of the Baths of Caracalla, on the Via Appia, give a clear sense of how huge the *thermae* of Ancient Rome must have been. The sweeping arc of the Theatre of Pompey can still be traced in the curve of the Via di Grotta Pinta, and its echo caught in the towering remains of the Theatre of Marcellus near by; while the outline of the Stadium of Domitian – an arena for running races – is preserved in the form of the Piazza Navona. It is small wonder that Constantius II was impressed.

Then, however, Ammianus continues. The emperor came to 'a construction in my view unique under the whole canopy of heaven, admired even by the unanimous verdict of the gods, then he stood still in amazement, turning his attention upon the vast complex around him, which is far beyond any description, and not again to be rivalled by mortal men.' This was the Forum of Trajan.

The Forum of Trajan? A construction 'unique under the whole canopy of heaven', a 'vast complex . . . far beyond any description', 'not again to be rivalled by mortal men'? Constantius II came to a city crowded with architectural wonders and the thing that left him speechless with wonder was this. And there is no suggestion that his judgement was in any way contentious. The Forum of Trajan – as confirmed by 'the unanimous verdict of the gods' – was, it seems, also generally considered by mortals to be the finest thing in Rome: better even than the Colosseum and the Pantheon, more impressive than the Temple of Peace or the Baths of Caracalla. Now it is all but unknown. For

The site of the Forum of Trajan today is dominated by Trajan's Column and two lines of patched and re-erected granite columns from the Basilica Ulpia.

the tourist of today it barely registers as a name, let alone as a thing to see. What was this 'vast complex'? What did it look like? Where was it? And why did it so impress contemporary visitors to the ancient city?

There is disappointingly little to see on the ground. The general area where it once stood is now overshadowed by the elephantine 'wedding cake' of the Victor Emmanuel II Monument. Part of the forum site can just be made out in the sunken 'Archaeological Area' that lies on either side of Mussolini's Via dei Fori Imperiali. A few shattered columns have been patched, raised up and realigned; a stretch of low wall has been uncovered, a few squares of paving have been revealed. But such signs are frustratingly hard to follow. From them, however, archaeologists and historians have, over the last two centuries, managed to build up a rich – if still sometimes speculative – picture of the complex's former glory. And an image of it is preserved not only in the *Plastico* at EUR, but also in a second scale-model housed in the little visitor centre opposite the church of SS. Cosma e Damiano.

The forum was composed of several distinct elements. At its heart was a large marble-paved tree-lined piazza, the size of a rather broad football pitch, with – in the middle – a huge gilded bronze equestrian statue of the emperor. Running down the two long sides of the space were colonnaded porticoes (each giving on to a double-height semicircular exedra), while set lengthways across the far end of the square was a huge two-storey basilica with apses at each end.

Behind this great hall – its upper portion visible above the roofline – rose Trajan's massive memorial column, the emperor's ashes preserved in a chamber in the pedestal,

Il Plastico, showing the Forum of Trajan and the adjoining Imperial Fora

the emperor's gilded image standing on the summit. Facing each other on either side of the column were two small but elegantly appointed libraries, one for Greek the other for Latin literature. And then, beyond the libraries and the column, the space opened up again into a new piazza (about half the size of the main square) held in the embrace of two curving colonnades. Set on a podium against the rear wall, and filling most of the centre of this elegant arena, was a large pedimented temple dedicated to the Deified Trajan. (The arrangement seems to prefigure, on a reduced scale, Bernini's curving arcade framing the piazza in front of St Peter's.)

Trajan had built the complex following his conquest of Dacia in AD 105–6. It was one of several magnificent public-building schemes that he undertook: a new aqueduct, the new port at Ostia, a remarkable market complex on the Quirinal hill (which still survives), and the largest public baths yet seen in the city. For all these great works he employed the versatile genius of his military engineer, Apollodorus of Damascus. (Apollodurus had won fame on the first Dacian campaign by setting a bridge across the deep, fast-flowing Danube at Drobeta, to secure the army's lines of supply.) The Forum of Trajan was considered his masterpiece – and it was, perhaps, his swansong.†

The brief description of its elements certainly sounds impressive enough, but it does not quite explain why the Forum of Trajan should have been considered so pre-eminent

---

† Apollodorus had a fraught relationship with Trajan's successor, Hadrian, made more difficult by the fact that Hadrian had pretensions to being a designer himself. According to the not-always-reliable historian Dio Cassius, the problem dated back to when Trajan was consulting his architect over some building plans, and the young Hadrian interrupted 'with some irrelevance or other'. Apollodorus, much to Hadrian's chagrin, brusquely remarked, 'Oh, go and draw your pumpkins. You know nothing of these matters.'

Once established as emperor, and having completed the final phase of the Forum of Trajan, Hadrian ceased to use Apollodorus for his major building schemes. He is, though, supposed to have sent Apollodorus the plans for the huge Temple of Venus and Rome that he planned to build, to show him 'that great projects could be carried out in his absence'. In the event he was very put out when Apollodorus returned the drawings with the observation that, first, the temple should have been built on a loftier site so that it looked more impressive from the Via Sacra (and also so that its excavated basement might have served for storing stage machinery for the nearby Colosseum); and, secondly, the cult statues were too big for their *cellae*. 'If the goddesses', he said, 'ever want to get up and go out, they won't be able to do so.' To Hadrian's great annoyance both points were just, but it was too late to address them. The story that, in his pique, the emperor subsequently had Apollodorus first banished and then put to death, while almost certainly apocryphal, became part of the rich legend surrounding both the architect and his great forum.

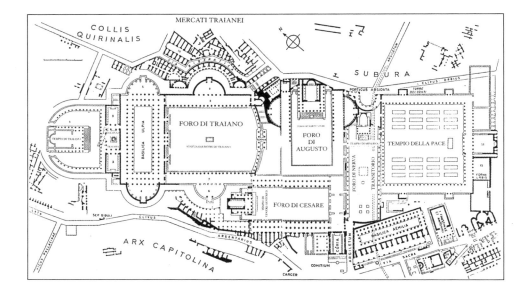

among the wonders of Rome. There were after all other spacious arcaded squares, other great basilicas, other commemorative columns, other imposing temples, even other matched pairs of Greek and Latin libraries. As a pure feat of engineering the forum was far exceeded by the dome of the Pantheon, by the aqueducts, by the ingenious concrete vaulting of Caracalla's Baths. So what was it that – in Roman eyes – raised Trajan's complex to such an exalted height? Why was it considered a construction 'unique under the canopy of heaven'?

For a start there was its position. The forum was the last of four adjoining Imperial Fora. These colonnaded squares – each enclosing a temple – had been built over the course of the first century AD to provide the ever-expanding Roman state with additional administrative and ceremonial spaces outside the old Forum Romanum (which ran roughly parallel, to the south). Trajan's forum was, it seems, intended to be approached from the east, by passing through the three connected earlier fora – the Forum of Peace, the narrow Forum of Nerva and the Forum of Augustus – providing, as it were, a climax to the series.

And there was no doubt that it was a climax. Grand though the other spaces were, the Forum of Trajan was very much grander. One only has to bear in mind that Trajan's magnificent Column, now one of the wonders of Rome, and the sole conspicuous survival from his forum, was just a single element in the great complex.

The main piazza was bigger even than the great square in front of the Temple of Peace. The principal hall – the Basilica Ulpia – was among the largest covered spaces in Rome. (To gain a clear sense of its scale it is necessary to visit the huge basilica church of S. Paolo fuori le Mura. This is one of the great spaces of Rome. Although rebuilt in the mid-nineteenth century following a fire, the church still retains its original fourth-century proportions, and these were modelled directly on those of the Basilica Ulpia. Even to a modern eye accustomed to large volumes, the lofty vastness of the long, columned nave is still humbling; the Edwardian travel writer Augustus Hare rather ungraciously likened it to a railway terminus.)

LEFT Plan of the four Imperial Fora and the Forum of Caesar
BELOW The great fourth-century church of S. Paolo fuori le Mura was modelled upon Trajan's Basilica Ulpia. Its interior still gives a sense of the grandeur and scale of an Imperial Roman public building.

In order to accommodate the forum's huge ground plan Apollodorus had to excavate a spur of the Quirinal hill which was blocking the far end of the site. An inscription on the base of Trajan's Column records that the monument marks the original height of the ground that was cut away. An estimated twenty million cubic feet of earth and rock was removed from the site and dumped outside the city walls.

But, while size was certainly important to the Romans, it had to exist together with harmony and proportion. Vitruvius, the great theorist of Roman architecture, insisted on certain 'fundamental' – if rather broadly stated – 'principles': Order, Arrangement, Symmetry, Propriety and Eurythmy (a proper agreement between the height, the breadth and the length of buildings). And in Apollodorus' design these principles were certainly observed.

He imposed a commanding symmetry upon the space, arranging each element along a strong central axis. A straight line ran from the main entrance (a triumphal arch set in the eastern boundary wall), via the emperor's equestrian statue, through the central portal of the basilica, to the great column, and then on – through the doors of the temple *cella* – to the cult statue of the deified emperor in the *cella*'s apse.

The proportions of the complex established another note of order. Every dimension was based upon a round number of Roman feet.† (The Romans – following Plato and the Greek philosphers – considered ten to be the 'perfect number'.) The forum square was 400 by 300 Roman feet; the colonnades were 300 feet long and 50 feet broad; the basilica with its apses measured 200 by 600 Roman feet, its central nave 85 by 300 Roman feet; from the base of the column to the top of the statue that surmounted it was 150 Roman feet; the shaft itself was 100 Roman feet high.

Harmony, symmetry and balance were of course key elements in almost all Roman buildings, but in the Forum of Trajan they were extended over a whole architectural complex. The symmetry would have revealed itself in stages. The harmony and balance were more allusive qualities. Yet – wandering over the patterned paving stones from the piazza, into the basilica, round the column, past the libraries, along the colonnades and up to the temple – a visitor would have felt them instinctively. And the effect was clearly profound.

It was enhanced, too, by the materials employed. Every visible surface of the forum – the square, the colonnades, the basilica façade – displayed an unabashed richness. After

† A Roman foot was equivalent to 11.7 inches or 29.6 centimetres – and is almost exactly equal to the long side of a sheet of A4.

the long centuries during which Republican Rome had built only with drab local tufa, a new age had dawned. The Romans had developed a passion for exotic marbles, and the patterned effects of coloured stone. It is a passion that continues in an unbroken strand to this day. It is discernible in the cosmatesque work of the Middle Ages, in the *pietra dura* designs of the High Renaissance, in the polychrome excesses of the Baroque era, and in the terrazzo floors of a thousand modern Roman homes. But it reaches back to the era of Imperial Rome, and found, perhaps, its fullest expression in the Forum of Trajan.

Choice marbles had been brought from across the empire to furnish the space: golden *giallo antico* from Numidia, and mauvish-white *pavonazzetto* from Phrygia in the east, white marble from the quarries of Luna above Pisa, grey granite from Egypt, black with pink *africano* from near Teos in modern Turkey, pale green *cipollino* from Karistos in Greece. The earth and the nations, it was clear, had paid their tribute to Rome.

Apollodorus orchestrated these recurring notes to create a symphony in coloured stone. The pavement in the colonnades flanking the main piazza was a bold chequerboard – alternating squares of *giallo antico* and *pavonazzetto*; while the pattern was continued but reversed in the flooring of the two hemicycles. The rear walls of the colonnades were decorated with geometric panels of coloured marble veneer set between pilasters of *giallo antico*. The thirty cabled and fluted columns that flanked each side of the square were carved from *pavonazzetto*, set off by bases and ornate Corinthian capitals of pure white marble.

The abiding sense of wealth, pattern, power and order became only more apparent when the visitor, mounting the golden-yellow steps at the head of the piazza, and passing between the great golden-yellow columns of the central portal, entered the Basilica Ulpia. The high space of the main hall, lit from above by a clerestory, hummed with controlled opulence. The large central area was framed with triple rows of grey Egyptian granite columns. The floor and walls played new and more elaborate variations in coloured marble, adding fresh elements to the mix: medallions of black and pink *africano* dotted the pavement chequerboard. The slender ionic columns of the clerestory were carved from watery green *cipollino*. And high above glowed a deeply coffered ceiling of gilded wood.

Some scant traces of the colonnade pavement survive at the site in the 'Archaeological Area', together with the two rows of patched granite columns from the basilica. But a few squares of half-shattered paving, and half a dozen shafts of battered stone can suggest little of the forum's former opulence. Two rather better preserved columns of fluted *giallo antico* were recycled during the Middle Ages and now stand in St Peter's basilica, adding a stately lustre to the chapel of St Joseph in the south transept. But perhaps a better sense of the forum's rich decorative effect can be gleaned from visiting the Pantheon, where the original Roman floor is still in place, with its patterned chequerboard of coloured marble: yellow, purple, red and grey.

The form of the forum, however, was not the only thing that made it exceptional in Roman eyes. Its content was just as important. It stood as a monument to the greatness of Trajan. It was constructed with the huge wealth that he brought to Rome through his conquest of Dacia (roughly equivalent to modern Romania). The mountains of Dacia were rich in gold and silver mines. And Trajan – tipped off by an informer – had also managed to recover the great treasure trove amassed by the defeated Dacian king, Decebalus. (At the outset of the conflict, Decebalus had diverted a brief stretch of the river Sargesia, buried the treasure in the river bed, and then restored the original current.) One conservative estimate put the trove at 180 tons of gold, and twice that weight in silver.

It was this quite extraordinary influx of booty – and mineral wealth – that financed not only the huge triumph accorded to Trajan on his return to Rome (including 123 days of public games and celebrations, during which eleven thousand wild beasts and five thousand gladiators met their deaths) but also the lavish specifications of the emperor's forum. It also dictated much of the forum's iconography.

Images of the victorious emperor and his troops were everywhere on view. The *Equus Traiani*, which showed the mounted emperor in full military dress, his hand raised in a gesture of command, was only the most conspicuous. Trajan was also represented riding in a triumphal chariot on top of the great central entrance arch, and again above the three porches gracing the façade of the Basilica Ulpia; his gilded effigy flanked each of the basilica's doorways. He stood atop his column. He sat enthroned in his temple.

The military note was insistent. Inscriptions set high on the porches of the basilica, and running along the upper sections of the colonnades, proclaimed that the forum had been paid for from Trajan's personal share of the Dacian spoils. The names of the divisions that had fought with him in the triumphant campaign of AD 105–6 were listed, and their standards – cast in bronze – adorned the parapet around the square. The very layout of the forum, with a basilica rather than the customary temple providing a backdrop to the main square, echoed the traditional arrangement of a Roman military camp.

The great column rising on its pedestal behind the basilica was carved with a continuous frieze depicting the most important incidents of the emperor's two Dacian campaigns, of 102–3 and 105–6. (Apollodorus, if he was responsible for the design, had included an image of his famous trans-Danubian bridge.) And although the reliefs towards the top of the column (even if enhanced with colour) would have been rather

A Dacian captive, reused on the Arch of Constantine; similar figures of defeated barbarians were used as caryatids along the upper storeys of the colonnades in the Forum of Trajan.

hard to 'read', the story of the conflict was well known to all.†

If Trajan and his army were a presence throughout the forum, so too were the vanquished barbarians whose wealth had paid for it. Friezes of captured arms and armour ran round the main square, while looking silently down upon the piazza were some seventy effigies of the defeated Dacians. Carved in marble – arms folded, eyes cast down, beards bedraggled – they were incorporated into the very architecture, supporting the attic storey of the long colonnades and the basilica façade upon their bowed heads. Eight such figures – their bodies carved from *pavonazzetto*, their heads and hands done in white marble – appear on the Arch of Constantine, next to the Colosseum. They were probably recycled from an Arch of Trajan that once existed on the outskirts of the city, but must be very similar to the doleful caryatids that adorned the emperor's forum, providing an image of noble but vanquished non-Romans.

Trajan's conquest of Dacia, celebrated in its own day, came to hold a special significance for later generations. It marked, as it transpired, the high watermark of Roman expansion. After Dacia no new provinces were added to the empire, and, indeed, a slow process of contraction and fragmentation began. As a monument to imperial greatness, to a supreme commander and a superlative army, the Forum of Trajan had a powerful resonance for later Romans anxious to connect with the glories of the past, and establish a feeling of continuity with their illustrious forebears.

† It has been suggested that in the original scheme the column shaft was plain, the carvings being added later as an act of piety by Trajan's successor, Hadrian.

The martial tenor of the forum's decoration was not, however, undiluted. Even in the main piazza, dominated by military ornaments, there were numerous other statues, dotting the square and lining the colonnades. These effigies of *summi viri* included poets and prefects, proconsuls and emperors. The collection was added to (and subtracted from) in a continuous process over the years. Marcus Aurelius erected a statue of his admired tutor, Marcus Fronto. The Emperor Aurelian – who, ironically, took the decision to withdraw all Roman forces from Dacia in AD 275 – was honoured with a silver-plated effigy.

Beyond the main square other aspects of Trajan's rule were emphasized. The Basilica Ulpia belonged to the official public life of Rome. (Ulpia was Trajan's family name, and the emperor had used his own money to pay for the basilica, rather than the Dacian booty that financed the rest.) It had become, primarily, a law court for the proconsuls, but could also serve other purposes, commercial, financial, political and diplomatic.

It was a fit setting for grand gestures. Trajan had chosen it as a place for greeting embassies and for issuing decrees. In AD 118 Hadrian burnt the records of unpaid taxes here, and in the late third century the Emperor Aurelian followed his example. It was in the basilica that Marcus Aurelius auctioned off the imperial jewels and state robes, to raise money for his campaign against the Marcomanni on the Danube frontier. For any citizen of Rome it was a place of impressive associations.

The twin libraries behind the basilica spoke of a world of knowledge and scholarship. The reading rooms were adorned with the statues of writers and philosophers, and, again, each was presided over by an effigy of the ubiquitous Trajan. He had his place there as an author, having produced a history of the Dacian campaigns. And then, beyond the libraries, stood Trajan's temple on its high podium, celebrating the emperor's final role – as a god. An image of the deified emperor appeared on the temple's tympanum flanked by two reclining deities (embodiments, perhaps, of the Danube and the Euphrates, the two rivers across which he campaigned with such success); and within the *cella* his image could be seen again: a seated figure in gilded bronze, the right arm raised in calm authority.†

To a Roman visitor walking through the forum, the successive spaces must have read like a record of Trajan's achievements and his legacy – from imperial triumph, to administrative order, to intellectual endeavour, to eventual apotheosis. And if the forum was an architectural embodiment of Trajan's exalted career it was also a symbol

---

† The sole but spectacular survival of the temple decoration is the set of giant stone-carved animal heads, including an ox, a ram and a deer, now preserved in the cloister behind S. Maria degli Angeli, but found on the site of the Forum of Trajan in 1586 during construction work on the nearby Palazzo Bonelli. They give a vivid sense of the scale and drama of the monument.

Two of the carved animal heads that used to adorn the Temple of Deified Trajan, now in the courtyard of S. Maria degli Angeli

of Rome's own ideal trajectory – from military success via peaceful government to eternal glory. This – above and beyond the physical splendour of the complex – perhaps explains something of the extraordinary impact of the Forum of Trajan.

Certainly Constantius II and his retinue were quite overcome – amazed both by the space and its associations. The emperor, having made his tour, stood wondering in the main piazza. Ammianus recorded the moment:

> All hope of attempting anything like it was put aside, and he simply said that Trajan's bronze horse [by which he was standing] was something that he could and would imitate. Then the Persian prince, Hormisdas . . . remarked with his native wit, 'Sire, first you must order a like stable if you can: the horse you propose to make must be as free to exercise as this which we see.'

At which Constantius 'began to rail at Fame as incompetent or spiteful because, although always exaggerating everything, in describing what there is in Rome she is so inadequate.'

·III·
ROME IN THE DARK AGES

IN 689 Caedwalla, King of the West Saxons, after a career of exemplary brutality, travelled to Rome. 'For,' as the Venerable Bede recorded, 'having learned that the road to heaven lies open to mankind only through baptism, he wished to obtain the particular privilege of receiving the cleansing of baptism at the shrine of the blessed Apostles. At the same time, he hoped to die shortly after his baptism, and pass from this world to everlasting happiness. By God's grace, both of these hopes were realized.' Caedwalla (or 'Peter' as he was christened at the font) died only days after having been received into the Church; he was buried at Rome, and given a splendid Latin epitaph.

Caedwalla may have been a conspicuous foreign visitor to Rome, but he was not an isolated one. Throughout the dark days of the Dark Ages people flocked to the city in their thousands. They were known as Romipetae or 'Rome seekers'.

The Rome they sought was not, however, the magnificent city of the Caesars. That no longer existed. The once-great metropolis was now a worn and broken husk. The living city had shrunk to a pitiful rump, lost within the vast ambit of the patched and battered Aurelian Wall. The population – in so far as can be gauged – was little more than twenty thousand.

The river Tiber had become the broken city's crooked spine. Its ancient wharves carried what very limited trade there was. Floating mills, moored in mid-stream, ground the city's meagre supply of grain. The river was the principal source of water. Of the six bridges that had once spanned the stream, only three still survived: one at the Tiber Island, another just below it, the third upstream at Hadrian's Mausoleum. And it was close to these crossing places, and along the old streets that connected them, that life was concentrated. The marshy and insalubrious Campus Martius, scarcely a residential area in ancient times, became the busiest quarter, together with Trastevere, directly across from it. The whole inhabited area on the right bank was effectively bounded to the south by the Forum Boarium (now the Piazza Bocca della Verità), to the east by the long straight line of the Via Lata (now the Corso) and to the north by the Via Recta (now the Via dei Coronari).

Old tenements and houses were still in use, though time and wear had steadily reduced their amenities. Upper storeys were abandoned as roofs fell in and plumbing systems gave out.

Beyond this huddled settlement beside the Tiber, Rome was almost a wasteland. Some four-fifths of the ancient walled city had been abandoned. Streets were blocked with the debris of floods and collapse. The heights of Rome's hills, where water was hard to come by, were all but deserted. The once gracious estates on the Caelian and the Esquiline had been given over to wilderness, grazing or the occasional market garden. Great houses had been left empty and forlorn. Colonnades had toppled. Weeds grew through ornamental pavements.

There were some small pockets of habitation and life clustered around key sites and street junctions. A few great mansions had been turned over to religious communities, and a handful of fair-sized churches dotted the empty urban landscape. But that was all.

Amidst this scene of material decay, however, there still rose many of the great monuments of the Imperial Age. Of the grand marble-dressed show area that once stretched from the Colosseum to the Mausoleum of Augustus, much still stood. Most of the famed temples, bath complexes, theatres and forums remained intact. But they were eerily empty, unloved and, for the most part, unused. Cattle were herded through the Forum of Peace. Cobwebs hung thick in the temples. Everything bore the marks of long neglect, and slow spoliation. In many places marble fascias, stone surrounds, iron clamps, lead pipes and bronze tiles had been stripped away.

The last gladiatorial contest held in the Flavian Amphitheatre had been in 434, although wild animal hunts continued there for almost another century. By the seventh century, however, the building had lost all trace of its original purpose: a small church had been erected in the auditorium, while the arena was used as a cemetery; the great vaulted arches were invaded by workshops and dwellings. Nor was it the only monument of Imperial Rome to have found new life with the passing years. Hadrian's massive mausoleum had become a fortress, a defensive bastion guarding the Pons Aelius bridgehead.

The Forum Romanum had reverted to a marketplace. And several old buildings in the vicinity were converted into churches. As early as the mid-sixth century the spacious marbled reception hall of the City Prefect, once part of the Forum of Peace, was turned into the church of SS. Cosma e Damiano. And in the century that followed the Senate House and the Senate Court in the Forum Romanum were transformed into, respectively, the churches of S. Adriano and S. Martina, while a nearby guardhouse became the church of S. Maria Antiqua.

Rome's pagan temples, however, whether in the Forum or beyond, were not pressed into the service of the new religion. Although elsewhere in the old Roman world, pagan shrines frequently became Christian churches, in Rome itself there persisted a strong superstition against the practice. They stood locked, empty and decaying. One exception, though, was made. In 609 the glorious domed Pantheon, created by the Emperor Hadrian to honour all the gods, was consecrated as S. Maria Rotonda, dedicated to the Blessed Virgin and all the martyrs. The conversion was minimal: an altar was simply installed in the main niche opposite the entrance, and an icon of the Virgin and Child set above it.

The great gilded *Colossus* still stood close by the Flavian Amphitheatre, along with several other prominent works (the elephant near the Forum Boarium, the *Horse-Tamers* on the Quirinal) but they were the great exceptions. Rome's once-celebrated population of statues had shrunk quite as drastically as its human one.

Clearly a lot had happened to city during the three centuries since the visit of Constantius II in 364. And all of it bad.

At the beginning of the fifth century Roman imperial rule in Europe had collapsed with alarming speed. The principal manifestation – if not the sole cause – of this collapse was the influx of successive waves of 'barbarian' peoples from across the Rhine and Danube frontiers, driven by movements further to the east.

In 410 Rome was sacked by Alaric the Goth. The Basilica Aemilia was burnt. (The green stains are still visible where the money-changers' scattered coins melted into the pavement.) Several palatial villas also went up in flames. The physical damage may have been quite limited but, for all citizens of the once-great empire, the psychological blow was immense.

Other blows followed. Although Attila the Hun was dissuaded from entering Rome in 452, three years later the Vandals came over from their base in North Africa to ransack the city. Two weeks of pillage saw them carry away several tons of loot, including the treasure – and the furniture – from the Imperial Palace, the spoils taken by Titus from the Temple of Solomon at Jerusalem, half the gilded roof tiles of the Temple of Jupiter Optimus Maximus, and a whole shipload of statues (which unfortunately sank on the way back across the Mediterranean.) Seventeen years later the Germanic general Ricimer sacked the city yet again, when deposing a puppet emperor whom he had previously supported.

The last recognized 'western' Roman emperor, Romulus Augustulus, was deposed in 476 by the barbarian warlord Odoacer. Henceforth the Roman Empire survived only in its eastern half, centred on Constantinople (or Byzantium as it came to be called).

The distinctly pro-Roman Ostrogothic King Theodoric did bring some order to Italy in the first decades of the sixth century, as well as restoring some prestige to Rome. He had, though, much to contend with – not least the Romans. They were already embarked on their long tradition of cannibalizing their own city: plundering monuments for masonry, melting down bronze statues, turning marble ones into lime for cement.

Theodoric's death, in 526, signalled the beginning of a debilitating struggle between the eastern emperor and the Ostrogoths for control of the Italian peninsula. The so-called Gothic Wars raged for almost twenty years, from 535 to 554, and were disastrous for Rome. The city was thrice besieged and twice taken as the balance shifted back and forth between the two sides.

It was the Gothic king Witigis, who – during one siege – broke the aqueducts in order to cut off the city's water supply. The Great Imperial Baths never functioned again. The countryside around Rome, the Campagna, already deserted, became flooded in places, developing into an unhealthy marsh, a breeding ground for malarial mosquitoes. Henceforth the unhealthiness of the Roman climate during the summer months became an enduring fact for visitors. Roman fever was a common hazard right up until the twentieth century.†

There was much physical damage to the city. The walls were breached and patched. When the Castel S. Angelo was under attack by the Goths, the Byzantine commander ordered the beautiful marble statues adorning its parapet to be broken up and hurled

---

† Until the late nineteenth century any connection between the bouts of fever suffered by visitors and the bite of the female anopheles mosquito went unnoticed. Instead the condition was blamed on the 'bad air' – or *mala aria* – that was thought to rise up from the ground each evening.

down upon the besiegers. But the real cost was human. By the time the Byzantine forces achieved a final 'victory' over the Goths, war, famine and epidemics had reduced Rome to a virtual ghost city, its population no more than a few hundred.

And this was not all. The long decades of military strife were compounded by a long trail of natural disasters. Floods were frequent as management of the Tiber and its banks was neglected. The chronicles record major inundations in 398, 411, 555, 570 and 589, carrying mud, silt and debris deep into the city. Earthquakes too took their toll: great tremors in 484 and 508 toppled columns, weakened buildings and caused landslides.

The population of Rome, after reaching its nadir in the immediate wake of the Gothic War, did creep back up as refugees returned and displaced peasants arrived to settle close by the Tiber bend. Their meagre settlement could spread eastwards over the Campus Martius because the old Aqua Virgo, which served the area, was still working. (It ran for most of its length underground and had thus escaped the attentions of Witigis and his Goths.)

The defeat of the Gothic forces left Rome nominally under the control of the Byzantine emperor. But the victorious Byzantines (like the late western emperors and, indeed, Theodoric) kept their main Italian base at Ravenna on the Adriatic coast. At Rome they merely installed a bureau of rapacious officials amidst the echoing halls of the Palatine, and a garrison on the Quirinal hill.

And for the Byzantine viceroy (or exarch) at Ravenna, Rome soon became a very minor distraction indeed. His main energies were directed to holding in check a new barbarian threat on the Italian peninsula: the Lombards – more warlike, less 'Romanized' and less tractable than the Ostrogoths. Although he succeeded for the most part in keeping them north of the river Po, they became a bellicose and disruptive presence across the country in the ensuing century.

By the beginning of the seventh century Rome had been obliged to accept its position as a place of no administrative, political or economic importance. This sad truth was, however, tempered by another, happier, reality. Rome had emerged as something else: the religious and spiritual centre of western Europe.

This had been a long and slow process. Constantine, after his conversion in the early fourth century, had begun proceedings by building three monumental churches on the fringes of the city: S. Giovanni in Laterano (for the bishop of Rome); S. Croce in Gerusalemme (to house the relic of the True Cross that the emperor's mother, Helena, had brought back from the Holy Land); and – most significantly – the basilica of St Peter's.

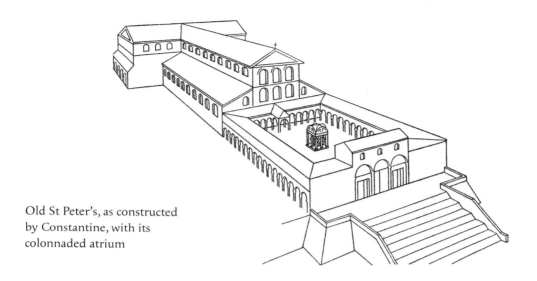

Old St Peter's, as constructed
by Constantine, with its
colonnaded atrium

St Peter, according to early tradition, had been martyred at Rome during the
persecutions of Nero, crucified upside down on the central reservation – or *spina* –
of the Circus of Nero. His body had been buried in a cemetery on the Vatican hill,
immediately next to the racetrack. As early as the second century Christians had begun
furtively to seek out St Peter's grave. Graffiti, scrawled on the modest 'trophy' that had
been built – rather like a mantlepiece – above it, records their visits and prayers. It was
a venerated site.

Constantine recognized this when he built his great basilica church. He set his
building directly over the grave of St Peter, levelling much of the Vatican cemetery and
obliterating the Circus of Nero to accommodate the church. The top of the 'trophy'
was left, rising out of the pavement in the middle of the nave, set within a new marble
enclosure.

Reverence for the graves of dead saints came to be one of the distinctive traits of
the new Christian religion. It was one that suited Rome, for the city could boast many,
many saints. Besides St Paul (who had also been executed during the reign of Nero),
thousands of Christians had been martyred in the city during successive imperial
persecutions from the time of Nero to Diocletian.

They all lay buried – layer upon layer – outside the city walls. Ancient Roman civil
law had not allowed interment within the sacred ambit of the city, so the metropolis's
numerous cemeteries – pagan, Christian and mixed – had sprung up along the roads
leading out of town. Pressure of space, the high cost of land, and a preference for

LEFT The catacombs, with narrow burial places carved into rock
RIGHT The familiar bearded figure of St Peter, sitting to the right (as the viewer sees it) of the enthroned Christ, with St Paul on the left; from a late fourth-century fresco in the church of S. Pudenziana in Rome

inhumation rather than cremation, had led in time to the creation of great subterranean necropolises – or 'catacombs' – dug out of the soft tufa of the surrounding countryside. By the end of the classical period Rome was encircled by a vast underground suburbia of the dead.

Many of these graves belonged to men and women killed during the periodic anti-Christian pogroms. And in due course these graves – of Rome's own saints and martyrs –became venerated like the resting place of St Peter.

To acknowledge these sainted martyrs, to encourage people to visit their graves, and to allow later Christians to be buried close to the sacred sites, Constantine set up five large funerary halls – or covered cemeteries – near the graves of St Sebastian, St Agnes, St Marcellinus and St Peter (not the Apostle), St Lawrence, and a now unknown martyr buried in the catacombs near the Villa Gordiani. A large basilica was also built at the end of the fourth century above the grave of St Paul on the Ostian Way.

Despite all this building work, Constantine's attempt to transform the city into a great Christian capital was not an instant success. The Romans themselves were slow to embrace his vision. Over time, however, the proud old pagan metropolis had

accommodated itself to the new religion. The grand Roman families converted and began to take up the offices of episcopal power – as they had once sought senatorial office.

During the course of the fifth and sixth centuries successive bishops of Rome – or 'popes' as they came to be called – began to evolve a vision of themselves as the true heirs of Rome's lost imperial splendour. In this Christianized version, Rome owed its pre-eminent position to the fact that it was the resting place of the two most important Apostles, St Peter and St Paul. They were – according to the papal vision – the Romulus and Remus of the new Rome. They became a ubiquitous presence in the décor of the city's churches: burly St Peter with his tight grey curls, bald St Paul with his sleek black beard, both dressed in their senatorial togas.

Since it was understood that St Peter had come to Rome to encourage and organize the early Christian community in the city, the popes lost no time in characterizing him as the first bishop of Rome, and in casting themselves as his direct successors and the inheritors of his unique commission. St Peter was the 'rock' upon which Christ planned to build his church. According to St Matthew's Gospel he had been given 'the keys of the kingdom of heaven' and the power of 'binding and loosing' souls.

And the pope, as his successor, claimed the same position, the same importance and the same power.

From the late fourth century onwards the popes used this connection with St Peter to assert their primacy in ecclesiastical and theological matters, and with considerable success. By the mid-fifth century Pope Leo I could proclaim, with no more than the usual exaggeration, that 'Rome has become the Head of the World through the Holy See of St Peter.'

The 'world' was, of course, confined largely to patches of western Europe, and the headship was severely limited. In the ecclesiastical sphere, the popes assumed the power of confirming bishops and ruling on matters of doctrine. But, in time, papal influence increased. It was the popes who took on the task of converting the new barbarian peoples who were pouring into the old Roman Empire, drawing them away either from their traditional paganism or from the Arian heresy.

On this front the great Pope Gregory I (scion of an old Roman senatorial family) led the way. It was he who, in 597, dispatched a party of Roman monks to convert the Anglo-Saxon kingdoms of Britain – so touched was he by the sight of some fair-haired young Anglian slaves in the Forum. (According to his official biography he marked the occasion with his celebrated pun, 'Non Angli, sed angeli', 'They aren't Angles but angels'). He also sent missions to the Arian Visigoths of Spain, and presents to Theodolinda, the Catholic-born Bavarian queen of the half-Arian half-pagan Lombards. And he established a happy correspondence with Brunhild, the formidable queen of the recently converted Catholic Franks.

It was Gregory, too, who extended the papacy's involvement into the practical administration of Rome. Taking up the duties neglected by the city's ineffective Byzantine administration, he used the Church's still-considerable resources to set up food distribution stations and other essential services. He initiated a church-building programme, and he made special provision for visitors arriving at Rome. There were lots of them, and their numbers were growing. By the beginning of the seventh century Rome was ready to assume a new mantle: the premier pilgrimage destination of Christendom.

The reasons for the city's prominence were several. The cult of relics had grown ever more important with the years; the bones and bodies of dead saints came to be seen not merely as objects to be honoured on account of their associations, but as things of intrinsic power in themselves. It was believed that miracles and cures could be affected through contact with relics.

Even more important than this, though, was the understanding that the saints were somehow fully present both in their tombs and in heaven; as a result the earthly relics provided a sort of direct line to the celestial sphere. To visit a martyr's bones was to come into actual contact with that martyr's presence in heaven: he, or she, would be able to hear the pilgrim's prayer and then relay it directly to God.

The idea of saints relaying prayers – 'intercession' as it came to be called – was a potent one. According to the teaching of the seventh-century Church, if you had committed a sin (and who had not?) you were unworthy to petition God directly. You had to ask the saints, who clustered around His throne, to make your requests for you.

All this was well calculated to make saints, and hence relics – and hence Rome – ever more important. For Rome had the biggest and best supply of sainted bones: it had the myriad martyrs, it had St Paul and, above all, it had St Peter.

St Peter stood at the pinnacle of the whole system of relics. He was the saint closest to Christ's heavenly throne and so the best able to intercede. He even held the keys of heaven in his own hand. To pray at his graveside was to be sure of having a good hearing in the court of heaven.

And increasingly the heavenly court was deemed to be the court best able to dispense justice or exact vengeance. The growth in the importance of relics took place against the breakdown of political power in western Europe. The continent was fragmenting into a patchwork of petty kingdoms. Secular governments had become very limited in their scope. They struggled to enforce even the most basic decrees. The saints filled a power void in the ongoing battle for order. The effects of their intercession might be hard to gauge – they could be instantaneous, or they might be deferred to the afterlife – but they were deemed to be inescapable, and that counted for a great deal.

These were powerful reasons drawing people to Rome, but there were more. The rapid rise and spread of Islam during the opening decades of the seventh century had a huge impact, altering at a stroke the long-familiar political landscape of the Near East. Some of the richest provinces of the old Roman world were swept out of reach, and with them three of the greatest classical metropolises: Alexandria, Antioch and Carthage. More importantly the Holy Land itself fell under Muslim control, and for a time became closed off to pilgrims. Up to that point the great biblical sites, especially Bethlehem and the Holy Sepulchre at Jerusalem (over both of which Constantine had also built impressive churches), had been the prime pilgrimage destinations in Christendom. Now they were out of bounds. Pious Christians, from across the Mediterranean world and beyond, who might once have set out for Palestine, now made instead for Rome.

Meanwhile, in the northern part of Europe, Pope Gregory's missionaries, and those who followed them, were creating new generations of Christians who looked solely to Rome for spiritual guidance. As the seventh century advanced the whole world of Northern Europe found itself drawn into the ambit of the papacy, and drawn towards Rome as the centre of spiritual power. The Anglo-Saxons were only the keenest among the throng of moustachioed Goths, barbate Lombards, Franks and Bavarians, ascetic Irishmen and – according to one contemporary chronicler – 'sex-hungry and ignorant Swiss', all heading towards the 'Threshold of the Apostles'. It was a period when – in Bede's phrase – 'numerous English people vied with one another in following this custom, both noble and simple, layfolk and clergy, men and women alike.' The journey may have had its travails and even dangers but they should not be exaggerated. The indefatigable Northumbrian abbot Benedict Biscop made five visits to Rome between 653 and 680.

What, though, did all these seventh-century Romipetae do when they reached the city of their hopes and dreams? What did they look at? What did they admire?

The great monuments of classical Rome were inescapable. They towered over the shrunken settlement around the low-lying Tiber bend. And they certainly impressed and interested visitors arriving from Byzantium and the still-Roman world of the eastern empire. The Byzantine Emperor Constans II, on a twelve-day visit in 667, made a thorough inspection of the city's monuments. He even carved his name at the top of Trajan's Column, and on the Janus Quadrifrons in the Forum Boarium. But his sightseeing had a distinctly practical edge. Constans was less interested in Roman monuments than Roman metal. He wanted the stuff to forge into arms. When he left Rome he took with him almost all of the remaining bronze statues (including, most probably, the gilded images of Trajan from his forum), the metal clamps from many of the city's great edifices, and – with a disregard for the building's new Christian status – the bronze roof-tiles from the Pantheon.

Other eastern visitors, however, were content merely to look, to admire and to muse upon the fallen greatness of the one-time *caput mundi*. They would certainly have noticed with interest the most recent – and last ever – addition to the monuments of the Forum: a (recycled) statue dedicated to the Byzantine Emperor Phocas, set up in 608, on an existing commemorative column close to the Rostra.

The Romipetae, however, arriving from the barbarian kingdoms of the north, had rather different attitudes. They had never known Roman imperial rule, nor experienced the metropolitan life of the empire. The great works of the past seemed strange and dangerous to them, the scale all but incomprehensible. The Anglo-Saxons considered the ruins of Roman Bath – or Aquae Sulis – to be 'the work of giants'. The monumental centre of Rome itself must have seemed to them an eerie and titanic wonderland.

Every battered monument appeared touched with mysterious significance and power. Of the great gilded *Colossus* beside the Flavian Amphitheatre Anglo-Saxon pilgrims learned the ditty, 'While stands the *Colossus*, Rome shall stand/When falls the *Colossus* Rome shall fall/And when Rome falls – the World shall fall.'

As recent converts the northern pilgrims were wary of the taint of paganism that clung to the old buildings. They shunned the ancient temples as the haunts of demons. Even the Pantheon, which was nominally a place of Christian worship, they approached with suspicion. According to the popular legend Pope Gregory had had to carry out a vigorous campaign of exorcism prior to the building's conversion, driving out a whole host of devils. It was said that the hole – or *oculus* – in the centre of the Pantheon's dome had been left by the devil as he made his escape.

If the consecrated Pantheon held little attraction for the Romipetae, the other churches inside Rome were of even less interest: what the pilgrims had come to see was bones. And these were all to be found outside the city. For seventh-century visitors Rome was effectively turned inside out.

The eager pilgrims spent their time in making a circuit of the extramural shrines. Several manuscripts survive from the period recording the procedure. It was a punishing schedule involving visits to dozens of churches and catacombs encircling the city, with long tramps on dusty roads, much tripping down steep time-worn stairs, and edging along narrow subterranean passages lit only by the occasional skylight. The number of saints encountered was – as the *De Locis Sanctis Martyrum* manuscript makes clear – literally innumerable:

And proceeding not far west from there [Via Salaria Nuova], next to the road [Via Salaria Vecchia], in a crypt eighty steps below ground, lie Saint Pamphilius and Saint Candidus and Saint Cyrinius, with many other martyrs. Continuing west from thence one reaches the [subterranean] church of Saint Hermes, where that martyr lies deep underground. There also are interred [the virgin] Basilessa and Saint Iacintus and Saint Protus and Saint Leopardus with many martyrs. From there, not far to the west, is the church of St John the martyr, whose head is placed under the altar, and whose body is in another part; also buried there are Saint Diogenis and Saint Fistus and Saint Liberatus and Saint Blastus and Saint Maurus and Saint Longina, the mother of John, and another 1,312 martyrs.

Although, in these contemporary accounts, the pilgrimage churches are listed in relation to the major roads leading out of Rome, it was not necessary for pilgrims to return to

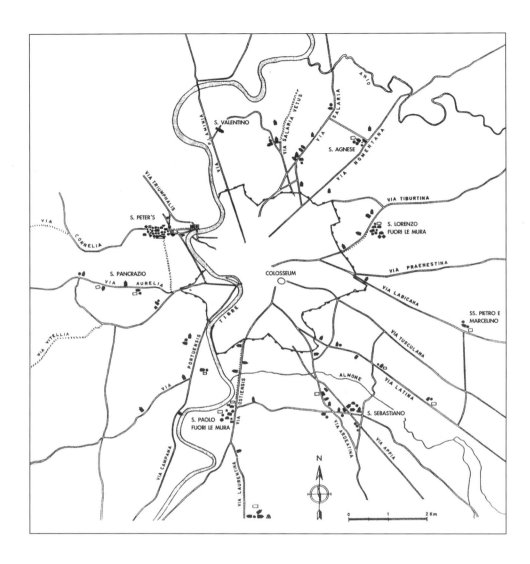

the city between visiting each cluster of shrines. A series of cross-paths linked most of the sites, providing a sort of pious orbital. Around the more important churches thriving little satellite settlements grew up. And at every shrine the scene that greeted the traveller must have been a crowded and a colourful one, flowing with its human tide of priests, monks, custodians, guides, food-sellers, tradesmen, mountebanks, beggars and, indeed, fellow pilgrims.

At each stop on the pilgrim trail the aim was to get as close as possible to the saintly relics. This posed certain problems of crowd management and security for the church authorities. It could be an awkward business getting people in and out of an ill-lit subterranean site, with those arriving trying to edge past those departing. And there was the danger, too, of unsupervised visitors trying to steal bits of bone, or even whole bodies.

Many churches were redesigned specifically to address the problem. It was a technical challenge: Roman practice at this date was very much against disturbing or translating the bones of saints. Radical measures had to be adopted. To give better access to the grave of St Lawrence, Pope Pelagius II cut away a whole section of the hillside cemetery where it lay, leaving the martyr's tomb isolated and exposed, and allowing him to build

LEFT Rome in the seventh century, showing the principal shrines surrounding the city
RIGHT The east end of S. Lorenzo fuori le Mura, with the galleries framing the tomb of the saint, which now lies beneath the raised high altar

a spacious new basilica around it. (The main elements of this late sixth-century church, with the saint's tomb set on the ground level, framed by tiered galleries, still survive at the east end of the present, thirteenth-century, basilica.)

Elsewhere the problem was different. For churches where a saint's body was already buried directly under the altar, Pope Gregory I developed the so-called 'annular crypt'. Entered down a flight of steps to one side of the altar, it ran as a curved passage – following the line of the church's apse – round the back of the altar, before emerging up another flight of steps on the other side; at the vertex of this subterranean passage a straight shaft was cut, running directly to the grave chamber of the saint under the altar. Pilgrims were thus able to file into the crypt down the flight of steps at one end, pause at the mouth of the straight corridor – from which they had a clear view of the saint's tomb – offer up their prayer, and then proceed along the curved passageway, emerging up the steps at the opposite end. It was orderly, efficient and secure.

To allow even closer contact with the relics, a small window – or *fenestrella* – could also be let into the base of the altar, giving a direct sight down into the grave-chamber below. Access to this was only available to the most favoured and distinguished pilgrims.

At every church or shrine along the way the pilgrims would offer up a prayer. Exactly what they prayed for is hard to know for sure. But we have an idea.

Some shrines were famous for healing miracles. The relics of St Martin at Tours in France, for example, helped the lame to walk, the blind to see. In the Roman churches, however, there are no miracle books preserving a record of such cures. It seems that pilgrims to Rome were not, on the whole, seeking immediate and conspicuous intervention for current ills.[†] Romipetae wanted, above all, forgiveness of their sins. They wanted the saints to intercede with God on this score. And they wanted St Peter – keeper of the celestial keys – to let them into heaven when the time came.

It was a solemn, even an awesome, business. As Pope Gregory I remarked, 'the bodies of the Apostles Peter and Paul glitter with such . . . awe that no one can go to pray there without considerable fear.'

Nevertheless, with so many pilgrims visiting the various shrines, quiet contemplation must often have been hard to achieve. Officialdom, too, was apt to be uncooperative and peremptory. The experience of Amandus, Bishop of Maastricht, who visited Rome

---

[†] There are some early references to the sick being cured at the church of SS. Cosma e Damiano in the Forum, but it seems this was a service sought by local Romans as much as by visiting pilgrims; it was, moreover, probably related to the church's proximity to the old temple of the healing pagan gods Castor and Pollux.

three times in the seventh century, was probably not untypical. 'One day, towards evening, this holy man of God was sitting in a small church after everyone had left, and the *custodi* were as usual tidying up, for he wished in his devotion to pray through the night: but one of the *custodi*, finding him there, ejected him from the church with contempt and blows.'

A rather brisker approach to prayer was adopted by Agilulf, a Frankish deacon, who travelled to Rome during the pontificate of Gregory I. Describing his visit to St Peter's he recalled, 'If anyone wishes to pray, the gates by which the spot [i.e. the altar] is enclosed are opened, and he enters above the sepulchre; then he opens a little window [the *fenestrella*] there and puts his head inside, and makes his requests according to his needs. Nor is the result delayed, if only his petition is a just one.'

Pious souvenirs were an important part of any pilgrimage. For most visitors, the ideal was to return home with an actual splinter of bone from some sainted body. But such precious gifts were rare. It was easier to gather earth from the tombs of the saints, or chippings from their sepulchres, or little strips of cloth that had been lowered on to the relics to gather up some of their power. Small glass ampules were also available for collecting oil from the lamps that burnt around the various shrines. The chaplain of the Lombard Queen Theodolinda made a complete collection of such phials, each neatly labelled and ordered. At St Peter's very important pilgrims might be presented with a small golden key that fitted into the lock on the gates of the sepulchre.

All these mementoes were considered to have more or less miraculous properties. Certainly they were efficacious against minor ailments. They could reveal their power more forcibly too. One king, who thought to melt down his golden key, was struck dead on the spot.

At some of the shrines on Rome's pilgrimage circuit – besides the bones of dead saints – specific sacred objects were also pointed out to the pilgrims. In the porch at S. Lorenzo fuori le Mura stood the millstone that had been tied around St Abundus's neck before he was thrown down the well; while on the altar at the oratory of S. Stefano on the Via Ostiense lay one of the rocks used in the stoning of St Stephen. They were among the first of those 'associative relics' that would in later centuries help to assuage the public's ever-growing thirst for contact with the sacred.

For the various churches inside the city walls, deprived as they were of martyrs' bones, such objects were the best that could be hoped for. The griddle upon which St Lawrence had been roasted was displayed at S. Lorenzo in Lucina, while the chains that held St Peter captive could be seen at S. Pietro in Vincoli. Both these relics certainly attracted visitors. There are records of favoured pilgrims receiving filings from both the chains and the

gridiron. Nevertheless the interest in these pious curiosities should not be overstated. Throughout the Dark Ages they remained very much less regarded than bones.

All sainted bones were deemed to be efficacious, but there was a definite hierarchy, running from the skeletons of unknown martyrs up to the pinnacle of St Peter. And, by and large, the status of the saint was reflected in the splendour of his, or her, shrine.

For the Rome-seekers of the seventh century there were some new architectural highlights to take in. During a concerted campaign of ecclesiastical refurbishment carried out by Pope Honorius I between 625 and 638 the pilgrimage churches of S. Agnese, S. Valentino, and S. Pancrazio were rebuilt, extended and adorned. All the resources of those straitened times were directed towards the work, and with some success. These three buildings were among the very few specifically referred to in the contemporary guides as being beautiful: *formosa, mirae pulchritudinis, mirifice ornata.*

S. Valentino is now a pile of stones beside the road a mile outside the Porta del Popolo, but the other two churches survive. S. Pancrazio stands on the Janiculum, close to the Villa Doria Pamphili and its park. Although it was made over in the seventeenth century, it retains its surprisingly large seventh-century form. The rather bare and unloved interior bears no trace of Honorius' decorative scheme, but the annular crypt giving access to the saint's relics under the altar is the earliest and best preserved in Rome.

St Pancras – an unremarkable boy-martyr of the second century – held a special place in the affections of Anglo-Saxon visitors. (Even before he became famous as a London railway terminus, he was revered in Britain. One of the earliest churches in London was dedicated in his name, and in 664 Pope Vitalian sent one of the saint's bones to Oswy, King of Northumbria, as a confirmation present.) And over the course of the seventh century he developed an additional importance. He came to be regarded as the special protector of oaths. Perjurers on approaching his tomb would, it was said, be immediately struck down. As a result pledges made in his church were considered to have a special sacredness – and effectiveness. In an age when a man's word was often his bond, this made it a very important place.

At S. Agnese beside the busy Via Nomentana much of the seventh-century beauty remains, in both the form and the decoration of the church. Like S. Lorenzo fuori le Mura, the new church was cut into the hilltop graveyard, to allow the saint's grave to be

LEFT ABOVE The simple façade of S. Pancrazio, the largest church built in Rome in the seventh century

LEFT BELOW The radiant seventh-century mosaic in the apse of S. Agnese fuori le Mura

incorporated within the building. The apse glows with a gold-ground mosaic depicting the saint perched between the popes Honorius and Symmachus (the original founder of the church), above the gloriously over-the-top inscription:

> Golden painting comes out of the enamels, and daylight both embraces and is itself confined. Dawn might think of plunging out of snow-white springs into the clouds, watering the fields with her dews: here is such a light as even the rainbow will produce between the stars or the purple peacock bright with colour. God who might bring an end to night or light has banished chaos from here out of the tombs of the martyrs. What all can see in a single upward glance are the sacred offerings dedicated by Honorius. His portrait is identified by robes and by the building. Wearing a radiant heart, he radiates in appearance also.

Of the many other churches on the grand orbital circuit, the basilica of S. Sebastiano on the Via Appia Antica was specially reverenced. It owed its status, not just to the presence of St Sebastian's body, but also to the tradition that the relics of both St Peter and St Paul had been temporarily removed to the catacombs there during a time of particularly stringent persecution in the third century. Indeed in its early years the church was known as the Basilica Apostolorum; only as the focus of religious interest shifted from past associations to present relics, did the name change to its still-current form.

Above it in the hierarchy stood the great basilicas of S. Lorenzo and S. Paolo fuori le Mura. The Apostle Paul's prominence is easily understood, but quite why St Lawrence, a minor Roman deacon who endured martyrdom in 258, should have risen to such heights is less clear. It was, though, an early and enduring phenomenon.

Both churches were connected to the city by colonnaded porticoes, which offered shade or shelter to the visiting pilgrims as they made their way out along the arterial roads. The colonnade running to S. Paolo fuori le Mura was an ingeniously assembled structure of over 750 plundered columns, each different in height, diameter and quality with, apparently, no base or capital the same. (Sadly all trace of these impressive structures has vanished. The churches are now reached along traffic-choked multi-lane highroads.)

Among all Rome's saints, however, St Peter was of course pre-eminent. In the fractured and parochial world of Dark Age Europe he remained as one of the few universal figures – and probably the most important. He was the keeper of the keys; he could actually ensure a pilgrim's safe entry into heaven. And it was generally understood that such safe entry was a very precarious business: many were called but few were chosen. To secure the support of St Peter was a hugely significant step.

The decorated façade of old St Peter's, as imagined by a nineteenth-century artist

The fact of St Peter's primacy was reflected in his church. The popes ensured that it remained the largest and most splendid in Rome. Constantine's vast barn-like basilica had been continuously embellished and improved in the three centuries since its construction. It was now encumbered with side-chapels and mausoleums, aglow with gilding and mosaics, swathed in fine draperies, and crowded with monuments of polished marble and cast bronze. Pope Honorius I carried out a major refurbishment in the early seventh century, covering one of the main doors with silver panels (weighing over 430kg/975lb), adding mosaics to the interior, installing a coffered ceiling over the nave, and adorning the roof with gilded bronze tiles taken from Hadrian's great Temple of Venus and Rome.

Nothing now remains visible of this formidable edifice. It was demolished during the sixteenth century to make way for the grand new basilica. Under the present church, in the so-called 'Vatican grottoes', some scant traces of the old church's foundations can be seen, but they have only an archaeological interest. The building as it was in the seventh century can only be recovered in the imagination.

To the left of the church stood the Vatican Obelisk (which now rises in the middle of St Peter's Square). It had once adorned the central spine of the Neronian Circus, and had remained *in situ* when the stadium was demolished to make way for Constantine's basilica, left in place to mark the spot (or very nearly) where Peter had been crucified. By the seventh century its connection with the Apostle's martyrdom had been forgotten, though a small Chapel of the Crucifixion stood at its foot. The looming needle of Egyptian granite remained, however, as a conspicuous and curious sight for all those approaching St Peter's.

Immediately in front of the church was a large courtyard, framed with colonnades. About half the size of a football pitch, it would have resembled a larger and grander version of the simple atrium that still exists before the twelfth-century church of S. Clemente. At the centre of this paved area stood an ornate fountain, its principal feature a giant bronze pine cone, under a canopy surmounted by two bronze peacocks. Both the pine cone and the peacocks still survive in the Vatican museums, the former as the focus of the Cortile della Pigna. The peacocks had come from the Mausoleum of Hadrian, but the origins of the pine cone, though certainly classical, were more obscure. One early mediaeval legend insisted that it had been the topknot of the Pantheon before the devil had blasted the hole in the roof.

The porticoes running around the courtyard were embellished with inscriptions and monuments. Caedwalla's tomb stood in the left-hand corner. Many Anglo-Saxon visitors paused before it, and some even copied out its elegant Latin verse epitaph.

The simple façade of the great basilica, rising at the far end of the atrium, was set with five doors: the Door of Judgement for funerals; the Ravennati door for men; the Silver Door (so richly embellished by Pope Honorius) opened only on special occasions; the Roman Door for women, and the Guides' Door, through which visitors and pilgrims entered.

Inside, the great five-aisled interior, with its mosaic-decorated triumphal arch, would have been similar to the vast nave that still stands at S. Paolo fuori le Mura, though with the addition of a short transept, before the apse. The walls were panelled with marble, the ceiling coffered with gilded wood. As in the modern St Peter's, the space was crowded with shrines and side-chapels. The contemporary pilgrim guides mention altars dedicated to the Holy Cross, St John the Evangelist and the Blessed Virgin Mary, among others.

There was, however, no doubting where the focus of attention lay. Set below the golden span of the apse, at the centre of the transept, stood the high altar. It was literally higher than everything else: the whole area upon which it stood was raised several feet above the level of the nave. The altar itself was framed behind a screen of beautiful white barley-sugar columns, carved with circling vines. These were said – rather fancifully – to have been brought by Constantine from the Temple of Solomon in Jerusalem. (They can still be seen in the current basilica, eight of them supporting the dome, one of them in the Treasury museum)

The arrangement was a new one. It had been put in place towards the end of the sixth century (perhaps by the future Gregory I when he was papal chamberlain) to allow the altar to be set directly over the grave of St Peter, and also to accommodate a new 'annular' crypt running around the back to the shrine, to give pilgrims readier, and better controlled, access to the saint's relics. For all those who came to Rome this was the key moment of their visit, their personal encounter with the Prince of the Apostles.

Favoured visitors could still be granted even more direct contact with the saint's bones via the *fenestrella* set in the base of the altar. Agilulf, a Frankish deacon who came to Rome in 590, wishing to carry away a 'blessed memorial' of St Peter, was allowed to lower a piece of linen down through this little window. After a period of fervent prayer he drew the strip of cloth back up, and was gratified to note that it had become 'so filled with divine virtue that it weigh[ed] much more than it did before'.

St Peter's power made palpable: as souvenirs of a Dark Age Roman holiday went, this was as good as it got.

·IV·
MEDIAEVAL ROME

'I N THE TEMPLE of Jupiter and Moneta on the Capitoline was a statue representing every kingdom of the world with a bell about its neck, and as soon as the bell sounded the priest of the temple knew that the country was rebellious . . . and informed the senators.' This legend of the 'salvatio Romae' (something between a nuclear early-warning system and the bell-board in an Edwardian servants' hall) became one of the most enduring stories of the Middle Ages, and an essential part of the mediaeval vision of Rome. It conjured up a lost world of extraordinary quasi-magical technology and fixed it among the ruins of the ancient city. For all those who came to Rome during the twelfth century the city was a place full of such marvels, or the vestiges of them. It was also – rather less thrillingly – a city full lawyers.

Rome had become the centre of a great politico-legal-religious machine, a machine constructed and controlled by the papacy. For visitors, the city was no longer a lonely beacon in a dark landscape, a collection of sainted bones on the fringes of a fragmented continent, it was the busy hub of a new order. This was a great change, and it had come about gradually over the previous five hundred years.

With the waning of Byzantine power in Italy during the troubled decades of the eighth century, Rome had gradually assumed ever more autonomy. Beset by the increasingly restive Lombards, the city had been obliged to organize its own defence. A new landholding class emerged to face the challenge, but it was bound by family ties to the Church, and tended to look to the papacy either for leadership – or for a route to power. When the Lombards actually besieged Rome – as they did on several occasions – it was the popes who managed to negotiate peace settlements.

Such successes soon encouraged the popes to see themselves – rather than the Byzantine emperors – as the true heirs of the Roman imperial tradition in the west. And their grand, if wishful, vision became crystallized in a document that was written – or, more properly, forged – at this time: the Donation of Constantine. It purported to be a fourth-century decree addressed by Constantine to Pope Sylvester I on the eve of the former's departure from Rome to establish his capital at Constantinople. In it the emperor granted to the pope and his successors – as the heirs of St Peter – supreme authority in Christendom and a higher status than his own 'secular throne', as well as political control of the city of Rome and, in theory, of the whole western empire.

This ideal, however, was confronted by a rather different reality. The pope's temporal power was extremely limited and very fragile. In 753 the Lombards took Ravenna, Byzantium's last remaining stronghold in Italy, and Rome was once more besieged. Without an ally at hand, the then pope, Stephen II, appealed for aid to the Frankish king, Pepin the Short. The move proved inspired. Pepin descended on Italy and soundly defeated the Lombards. And in the wake of his victory he presented many of the former Lombard territories in central Italy to 'St Peter and the Holy Roman Church'. The papacy thus, at a stroke (and for the next thousand years), really did become a major temporal power in Italy, as well as a spiritual force.

Frankish military might, however, was necessary to support both these roles – and indeed often to protect the pope from Rome's rivalrous and over-mighty families. In order to secure such assistance, on Christmas Day 800, at St Peter's basilica, Pope Leo III crowned Pepin's successor, Charlemagne, as 'Imperator Romanorum'. By this bold act (and much to the irritation of the Byzantine emperors) the name and the idea of the 'Roman Empire' was revived in the west. But the moment of triumph also held the seeds of future strife.

The popes considered that in the creation – or restoration – of the Christian Roman Empire, they were the senior partners. It was they who conferred the imperial power (invested as it was in them and in Rome by the Donation of Constantine). Successive emperors, however, tended to adopt a different view: while acknowledging the pope's spiritual authority, they regarded supreme temporal power across the whole empire as belonging to them alone. And, given that the Church had become part of the temporal framework of the world, holding extensive tracts of land and property, the emperors felt that they had a right to intervene in many ecclesiastical matters.

The struggle between these two opposed visions – the papal and the imperial – continued for centuries as Charlemagne's descendants were followed – from the late tenth century – by a succession of Germanic imperial dynasties – the Ottonians, Franconians and Hohenstaufen. (The great families of Rome, divided by their own rivalries, allied themselves with the two contesting powers as expediency dictated, or occasionally opposed them both.)

By the eleventh century the dispute between empire and papacy had become centred upon the particular question of whether the emperor, within his own German territories (and by extension, other monarchs in their own lands), had the right to appoint bishops and to invest them with the regalia of office. This right was claimed on the grounds that bishoprics had evolved into important political posts. They were richly endowed with lands, and consequently owed military service to the monarch: a monarch, it was argued, needed to be able to control them. The papacy, however, under the direction of the reforming monk Hildebrand (who became Pope Gregory VII in 1073), fiercely contested such notions, and asserted papal supremacy in the matter.

The investiture dispute dragged on for fifty years. It was finally resolved – with inevitable compromises – largely in favour of the papacy. By the 1140s the pope could claim to be recognized as the ultimate authority across Christendom. It was an extraordinary victory. It gave Rome a new status, and also a new attraction for visitors.

Of course the pilgrim crowds continued to descend on Rome, and descend in large numbers. But there was perhaps less urgency about this traffic. The reopening of the Holy Land to Christian pilgrims after the first Crusade in 1099, coupled with the rise of such rival attractions as the body of St James at Compostela, of St Nicholas at Bari, of Cologne (where the Three Kings were supposed to be buried) and Canterbury (after the martyrdom there of Thomas à Becket in 1170), all conspired to erode Rome's absolute pre-eminence as a pilgrimage centre. After five centuries of royal patronage, the last English king to visit the shrine of St Peter had been Canute in 1027.

In the place of penitent monarchs, the most conspicuous and important visitors arriving at Rome now tended to be argumentative clerics. From the long years of the investiture struggle the papacy had emerged, reformed and empowered, at the head of a Church almost completely free of secular control. Church lands and possessions – and, indeed, all churchmen too – were now recognized as standing wholly outside lay jurisdiction. The clergy and laity were considered to inhabit parallel realms, with – in theory – the lowest member of the clergy being superior to the highest layman. The clergy were no longer subject to secular courts, although they themselves could judge laymen in spiritual cases.

Of this remarkable new system, the papacy was the legislative and administrative head. Papal legates and officials toured Europe hearing cases and investigating abuses, while the Curia at Rome provided the court of ultimate appeal. And, in a litigious age, when disputes were many and the hard evidence of written documents scarce, almost all cases ended up there. As a result educated churchmen from across Europe found themselves drawn to Rome, to make their petitions and appeals at the papal court. They arrived in droves with their pleas for episcopal preferment, church dignities and land holdings. Such questions were never quickly dealt with. Cases dragged on. They cost large amounts of money. (The two most important saints in twelfth-century Rome, so it was said, were no longer Peter and Paul; according to contemporary satirists they had been supplanted by Saints Albinus and Rufinus – or, to speak less metaphorically, pale silver and red gold.)

But the slow turning of the papacy's legal machinery left supplicants with time on their hands, time to explore the city. They looked at the place with new eyes and they saw new things. These clerics – schooled in the great Cluniac monasteries of Europe or at the new University of Paris – arrived in the city full of expectation and curiosity. They were pious churchmen for the most part, but they belonged to a generation fired by a novel enthusiasm for the learning and art of the classical past. (There had been recurrent flickerings of such interest in earlier centuries, during the Carolingian Age or at the court of Otto III, for example, but the revival of classical learning in the twelfth century was something more concerted and more widespread.)

Classical Latin texts were being rediscovered, and appreciated anew, both for their language and their content. Cicero, Ovid, Horace and Pliny were names once more to play with. Understanding may often have been limited and partial, but interest was keen. Roman law had become a subject of concerted study. In art and architecture classical motifs were being again taken up, however awkwardly. For those fired by such interests, the very name of Rome inspired a sense of awe – rather more, perhaps, than the city itself.

Twelfth-century Rome, despite its claims to worldwide hegemony, was still rather a modest town. The population had perhaps crawled up to around thirty thousand. There had been some slight expansion of the city's inhabited area since the bleakest days of the Dark Ages. The plateau of the Aventine, which, because of its elevated position, was considered a healthful and pleasant place to live, had become colonized by a few fortified mansions. Restoration work on the aqueduct system carried out at the end of the eighth century by Pope Hadrian I had improved the water supply to both the Vatican hill and the area around the Lateran.

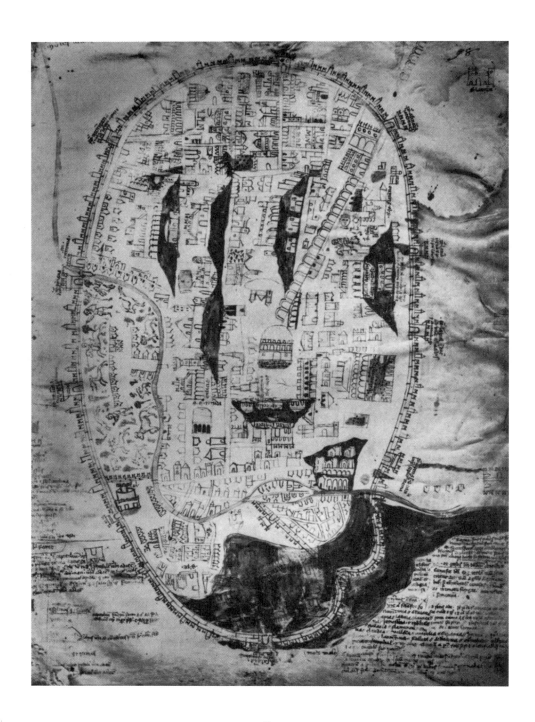

After Saracen raiders had sailed up the Tiber in 846 and looted St Peter's, Pope Leo IV had built a defensive wall around the church and its immediate quarter, creating the so-called 'Leonine City' as a linked but distinct district of Rome. (In the face of renewed raids in the 880s, Pope John VIII had also fortified the area around S. Paolo, to form the settlement of Ioannipolis.)

The long-neglected Capitoline had recently been drawn back into the life of the town with the erection of the Palazzo del Senatore on the ruins of the Tabularium – following the re-establishment of a Roman senate in 1143 by a group of municipally minded lawyers, merchants, tradesmen and minor clergy. A thriving market had also grown up on the hill's western slope (where Michelangelo's stairway now rises).

But, despite such accretions, living Rome remained – for the most part – crowded into the same limited patch, ranged along the banks of the Tiber bend. It had merely become yet more densely settled. The streets were narrow, choked with rubbish and humanity. Wooden balconies, porticoes and stairways scaffolded the modest brick-built house fronts, and impeded the flow of traffic. At many places it was impossible for two horsemen to pass.

Viewed from the hilltops, Rome's skyline was now dominated by dozens – even hundreds – of fortified towers, set up by the great local families as bases for their power struggles and disputes. Trastevere, which had evolved as the commercial core of the city, bristled with them; they rose thickly on the Tiber Island (home of the powerful Pierleoni clan), and along the eastern fringe of the inhabited city.

Among this forest of mediaeval skyscrapers there still loomed the outsized remains of many old Roman monuments. There were not, though, quite as many as in the days of Gregory the Great. During the intervening centuries much of the great imperial city had disappeared from view. The substructures of the Capitoline had been undermined, landslides had all but buried the Temple of Vespasian in the Forum. Earth tremors had continued to topple buildings and colonnades, and floods to cover them in silt and refuse. In many places the street level was rising at the rate of almost a metre every century. A major quake in 801 levelled numerous ancient structures, including much of the Forum of Trajan. It had been followed by another hugely destructive tremor in 847.

The lime-burners, too, were ceaseless in their depredations: lime mortar was always needed as the city struggled to repair and renew itself. Major projects such as the

The earliest surviving map of Rome, drawn by Fra Paolino di Venezia in 1323, but based on a thirteenth-century original, and relating to an early version of the *Mirabilia Urbis Romae*

The interior of S. Clemente, with its impressive ranks of antique columns

restoration of the city walls or the construction of the Leonine City consumed huge quantities of the stuff. During this period all the seating in the Circus Maximus, some '250,000 running feet of stone and marble benches', disappeared into the kilns. Rome's population of marble statues was purged. (A nineteenth-century excavation in the Forum unearthed an unfired mediaeval lime kiln, packed with the broken limbs of over a dozen statues.)

The ruined Forum became a centre for such activity, but there were others. The area around what is now Largo Argentina had become the lime-burners' quarter; and they also gathered near the Mausoleum of Augustus: anywhere where marble was readily to hand. Stone-cutters and architectural salvage merchants also took a steady toll. The three great Roman churches rebuilt in the twelfth century – S. Clemente, S. Maria in Trastevere and the Quattro Coronati – all rose on antique columns removed from earlier buildings. Nor was the demand for spolia confined within the city: building materials were exported from Rome to the abbey churches of Monte Cassino, St Denis and Winchester.

Nevertheless, much of Rome's monumental heritage yet remained – battered, broken, half-buried but still compelling. The Pantheon (or S. Maria Rotonda) was still there, of course, along with the theatres of Marcellus and Pompey and the imperial mausoleums; also a dozen triumphal arches, the massive ruins of the seven imperial baths, stretches of broken aqueduct, the palace complex on the Palatine, the Columns of Trajan and Marcus Aurelius, the temples of the Forum and beyond. And over everything towered the vast Flavian Amphitheatre, or Colosseum as it was now called[†]: as other monuments had collapsed and crumbled, its vast bulk became ever more conspicuous. (The various schematic depictions of Rome that survive from the Middle Ages all make it a – if not the – central feature of the city.)

Some of these ancient buildings stood forlorn and empty, but many had been pressed into new service. The vaults of the theatres and of the Colosseum were invaded by shops, storerooms, workshops and dwellings. The Porticus of Octavia sheltered two

---

[†] The great gilded statue known as the *Colossus* had disappeared by the late eighth century. (It is not mentioned in a topographical manuscript of that period called the Einsiedeln Itinerary.) Its memory persisted, however, and its name had transferred to the ampitheatre by around 1000.

convents, a church and a fish market. The porticus attached to the Theatre of Balbus housed a collection of small industries, including a bronze foundry and a glassworks. The little Temple of Portunus and the quaint circular temple that both stand, still intact, close by the Tiber near Ponte Palatino, owe their remarkable survival to the fact that they were converted into churches during the Dark Ages.

A few of the largest monuments had been transformed into strongholds for Rome's rivalrous family factions. Hadrian's Mausoleum, controlling the bridgehead between the Leonine City and the rest of Rome, had been an important bastion since before the time of the Gothic Wars, and had changed hands several times, before becoming the fortress of the popes. The Frangipani fortified the Colosseum at the end of the eleventh century, making it the centrepiece of a defensive network stretching all the way across the ruined Forum. (The Arch of Titus became a gateway to the inner part of their compound; a lookout turret was perched precariously atop the Arch of Septimius Severus.) The Colonna family dominated the west slope of the Quirinal from among the massive ruins of the Temple of Serapis; they also held the Mausoleum of Augustus. The Savelli were ensconced in the upper reaches of the Theatre of Marcellus and the Orsini in the Theatre of Pompey.

Beyond the main area of settlement, however, most of the land within the ancient city walls remained uninhabited. The curious demarcation between the small crowded *abitato* and the wider encompassing *disabitato*, which would endure right up until the late nineteenth century, had become the defining feature of Rome's topography. But what had been, a few centuries earlier, a picture of urban desolation in these outlying districts had crumbled into something almost semi-rural. Away from the bustle of the Tiber bend there stretched – towards the city walls – a rolling landscape of grazing land, market gardens and vineyards, dotted with the massy remains of aqueducts and *thermae*, with isolated towers and hamlets, and – here and there – a modest farm building.

Also scattered across this oddly vacant scene was the occasional monastic settlement or hulking church. Churches rose too amidst the crowded buildings of the *abitato*. Here and there the bristling towers of the grand families were complemented and rivalled by an elegant brick-built *campanile*. Rome had gradually been transformed into a city of churches. By the beginning of the twelfth century there were some three hundred within the walls, ranging from tiny chapels devoid of ornament to large collegiate institutions such as S. Maria Maggiore and S. Maria in Aracoeli, with their magnificent decorations, the attached monasteries, their cloisters and outbuildings.

And, for all the novel interest in the classical past, it should be remembered that Rome's first importance, for most visitors, remained as a religious centre. To the great mass of common pilgrims this was the sole point of interest. But, to all who came, it was a great fact. The classically educated churchmen, in Rome to petition the Curia and excited to be among the scenes of classical antiquity, still made the round of the city's sacred sites.

The established devotional itinerary of these religious tourists was, however, very different from what it had been in the seventh century. Of course, St Peter's remained the accepted apex; the tour still included the other major extramural basilicas – S. Lorenzo and S. Paolo. The beautiful old church of S. Agnese continued to be a starred item; the Icelandic bishop Nicholas of Munkathvera, who left an account of his visit to Rome in 1150, thought it 'the most outstanding church in the whole city'. But, after the Lombard depredations of the eighth century, many of the ancient catacombs and old cemetery churches had been destroyed. They were now unvisited, if not forgotten.

During those bleak years of destruction, however, the bones of the blessed had – whenever possible – been salvaged and brought inside the city. They had arrived by the wagonload. And many churches had been built or enlarged to accommodate them. Almost every church in Rome now held the remains of martyrs in its crypt or beneath its altar.

Buried bones, though, were no longer quite the draw they had been. There was a change in the way people prayed, and in the way they used relics as aids to prayer. Twelfth-century church visitors increasingly wanted relics that they could see, perhaps even touch. Objects associated with saints developed a new importance: they were visible, approachable, tangible.

Rome laid claim to many such 'associative relics', and the churches that housed the most spectacular assumed a new importance. The chains of St Peter preserved at S. Pietro in Vincoli came to be particularly revered, and much visited. Also popular were two miraculous knee-prints set in a paving stone at S. Maria Nova (now S. Francesca Romana), the church that had been built amidst the ruins of the Temple of Venus and Rome. They were said to have been made by St Peter as he prayed to God to confound Nero's court magician, Simon Magus, who was displaying his magic powers by flying over the Forum. (The Apostle's prayer – according to the *Acts of St Peter* – was spectacularly effective: Simon Magus plummeted out of the sky on to the Via Sacra, breaking his leg 'in three places'.) Outside the Porta Latina visitors flocked to see the vat in which St John the Evangelist had been boiled alive.

At St Peter's itself a major new attraction was the Apostle's Throne, a stout ivory-adorned chair said to be the very one upon which St Peter had sat during his sojourn at Rome. Although recent tests have shown it to be a Carolingian work (probably brought

The three great bays of the Basilica Nova, were, throughout the Middle Ages and beyond, thought to have been part of the Temple of Peace.

to Rome by Charles the Bald for his coronation in 875), to twelfth-century visitors it seemed to offer a thrilling link with St Peter himself, and something more readily accessible than the saint's bones beneath the altar.

Of even greater importance at St Peter's, however, was the Veronica, the flannel with which Jesus was supposed to have wiped his brow on his way to Calvary, and upon which he had miraculously left the image of his face.

Although Rome had long been justly proud of its close connection with Apostles Peter and Paul, a feeling had grown up that some direct link with the life and story of Jesus would add to the sacred lustre of the city. (This was particularly the case after the Holy Land was once more opened up, and pilgrims could visit Bethlehem, the Holy Sepulchre and the other sites of Christ's Passion.) There was, alas, no suggestion that Jesus had ever visited Rome, and – of course – since he was supposed to have ascended bodily into heaven there were no skeletal relics to be acquired. Other connections had to be made.

The remnants of the True Cross, brought to Rome by Constantine's mother in the fourth century and preserved at S. Croce in Gerusalemme, were of course a start. But the Veronica (which seems to have arrived at St Peter's some time towards the end of the eleventh century) was an impressive addition.

Two popular and enduring legends also grew up around this time connecting actual sites in Rome directly to the Nativity. It was claimed that the ancient foundation of

S. Maria in Trastevere stood upon the spot where a miraculous spring of olive oil had erupted from the ground on the night of Christ's birth. (This story, though first recorded by St Jerome in the late fourth century, enjoyed a new currency in the twelfth century.) The site of the spring was pointed out to visitors in the confessional of the newly enlarged church. (A column close to the main altar still marks the spot.)

The story of the miraculous olive oil well was matched by the legend that, on that same fateful night, in the very heart of the Forum, either a building or a statue had collapsed. According to some sources it was a golden idol that had been set up by Romulus with the remark, 'It shall not fall until a virgin bears a child.' But popular belief gradually came to focus instead on the great broken arches of the Basilica Nova (begun by Maxentius and finished by Constantine). With their vast hexagonally coffered vaults they were (and still are) the largest and most conspicuous ruins in the Forum, and it must have seemed appropriate that they should be ascribed a prominent part in the grand drama of the Nativity.†

The sights of Christian Rome, however, were now considered to be only one part of the city's great appeal. For many twelfth-century visitors Rome's classical past held an equal and parallel attraction. And, indeed, just as there was a desire to connect places in Rome with the life of Christ, there was also a related, but rather different, concern to connect certain important pagan Romans with Christianity.

Numerous mediaeval authors played this new game. The ingenious links that they forged ranged from the notion that Virgil had prophesised the birth of Christ in his Fourth Eclogue, to Dante's rather later idea that the whole Roman Empire had been providentially created by God in order to provide a unified and universal political setting for the Nativity, thus allowing the universal redemption of mankind.

Visitors to Rome learnt that the Emperor Augustus, reluctant to allow the senate to address him as a god, was vouchsafed a vision of 'a virgin exceedingly fair standing on an altar holding a boy-child in her arms'; this – he was informed by a heavenly voice – was 'the virgin who shall conceive the Saviour of the World' standing upon 'the altar of the

---

† The true identity of the Basilica Nova had become lost with the passing years. By the twelfth century the ruins were universally assumed to have been part of the great Temple of Peace, and it was as such that they were pointed out to visitors for the next six hundred years, and described as having collapsed on the night of the Nativity. The fact that the Temple of Peace was known to have been built by the emperors Vespasian and Titus several decades after the birth of Christ, does not seem to have registered with the topographers of the Middle Ages or, indeed, of later times.

son of God'. Suitably impressed, he 'straightway fell to the ground and worshipped the Christ that should come.' According to the legend, Augustus received this miraculous vision in an imperial chamber on the Capitoline hill, on the site of what would become S. Maria in Capitolio. And by the end of the twelfth century, the church was being called – as it still is – S. Maria in Aracoeli (or St Mary of the Heavenly Altar).

Augustus was not the only Roman emperor to be claimed as a proto-Christian. A mediaeval *Life of Pontius Pilate* asserted that the Veronica (far from arriving in Rome in the eleventh century) had been brought to the city a millennium beforehand – by the pious virgin from whom Christ had originally borrowed the cloth – and that it had miraculously cured the Emperor Tiberius of some unspecified malady. As a mark of gratitude Tiberius had – it was said – proposed adding Jesus to the pantheon of Roman gods, only to be thwarted by traditionalists in the senate.

Another early legend claimed that Pope Gregory the Great, while walking one day through the Forum of Trajan, had paused before a relief carving that showed the emperor dismounting from his horse to grant justice to a poor widow. The pope wept to think that such a rare man – at once capable of building so magnificent a forum and of displaying such compassionate humility – should be condemned to eternal perdition as an unbeliever. Later, while at prayer, he heard a celestial voice saying that his plea for the emperor's salvation had been heeded.

Unsurprisingly, Marcus Aurelius, the wise philosopher-emperor, was also credited with Christian sympathies. His victory over the Quadi, in 174, was ascribed (by the third-century Christian writer Tertullian) to the prayers of the many Christians in the XII Legion. With the Roman army exhausted by thirst, they had summoned down a providential thunderstorm, terrifying the enemy and providing vital drinking water for the troops. In recognition of this service, it was later claimed – with no justification – that Marcus Aurelius had decreed toleration for all Christians in the empire. The downpour was vividly depicted on the emperor's memorial column close to the Via Lata and, despite the fact that there it was shown being effected by Jupiter, the scene – which can still be made out – came to be regarded by mediaeval visitors to Rome as a Christian miracle.

Such fanciful Christianizing of the great figures of Rome's heritage served to create a bridge between the two, otherwise opposed, worlds. This was useful for those interested in classical antiquity, as some conservative churchmen remained wary of the pagan past. There must, they considered, be a danger for Christians in looking on pagan images or pagan texts, however fascinating such things might be. Indeed, one popular mediaeval legend (again not based on any historical fact) held that much of the visible destruction

The miracle of the rain, as depicted on the Column of Marcus Aurelius; the grateful Roman legionaries, on the left, catch the rainwater in their shields, while the barbarians on the right are swept away in the flood.

of Ancient Rome had been carried out on the express orders of Pope Gregory the Great to ensure that pilgrims would not be distracted from their round of the Christian sites.

Most educated twelfth-century clerics, however, do not seem to have been dogged by such qualms. And if they felt any need to salve their conscience, they could do so readily by claiming that their interest in Rome was largely as an exemplar of the vanity of human hopes. Master Gregory, a late twelfth-century English cleric who left a wonderfully vivid account of his trip to Rome, played exactly this card. His excited apostrophe upon the magnificence of the ancient city, even in its current state of dilapidation, was abruptly terminated with the pat moral lesson, 'I believe this ruin teaches us clearly that all temporal things will soon pass away, especially as Rome, the epitome of earthly glory, languishes and declines so much every day.'

Having made this glib declaration Master Gregory certainly felt able to devote the rest of his account to describing the various surviving marvels of classical Rome with unabashed relish. And his outlook was by no means rare. Indeed the *Mirabilia Urbis Romae*, or *The Marvels of Rome* – the remarkable guidebook compiled around 1143 by Benedict, a canon of St Peter's – was almost equally classical in its emphasis.

The *Mirabilia* remained the great popular guide to the city for three hundred years, much copied (it exists in numerous manuscript versions) and much copied from (it forms the basis of numerous other accounts of the city). Although, in an era before printing, it cannot quite be supposed that twelfth-century visitors arrived in Rome clutching a copy of the book ready to 'do the sights', the *Mirabilia* clearly had a huge influence on what people saw, and how they saw it.

Canon Benedict offered a discursive 'perambulation' among the city's many classical remains, with only the occasional aside on a Christian monument. The book was derived partly from ancient sources. There were allusions to Virgil, and Ovid's calendar of Roman festivals, the *Fasti*, gave a dash of classical colour to the descriptions of temples and their rites. A version of one of the two fourth-century Regionary Catalogues seems to have provided the basic framework for the description of the city's monumental heritage. It was, however, a framework that often fitted rather ill with the facts on the ground.

Many of Canon Benedict's ascriptions were fanciful, with names plucked from the ancient record being confidently mis-attached to long-ruined buildings, and sometimes even to piles of stones that may never have been buildings at all. The Arch of Septimius Severus was transformed into the 'Arch of Julius Caesar and the Senators', the Temple of Castor and Pollux in the Forum was pointed out as the 'Palace of Catiline', while a line of broken masonry in the Campus Martius became the 'Temple of Flora'. A misreading of the inscription on the Vatican Obelisk, combined with some wishful thinking, led to the claim that Julius Caesar's ashes were contained in the bronze orb on top of the monolith.

There were also some decidedly mediaeval attempts at etymology. According to Canon Benedict the ancient Lateran palace derived its name from a frog that Nero supposedly vomited up and then concealed in a vault on the site: *latere* being the Latin for 'to hide' and *rana* the Latin for 'frog'. (Another piece of mediaeval etymology suggested that the name derived from the fact that the outline of the city of Rome was like a rampant lion, and that the Lateran was positioned on the flanks – or *latera* – of this lion.) The name, in fact, comes from Plautius Lateranus, who built the original palace, before being executed – and stripped of his property – by Nero.

A late thirteenth-century drawing showing Rome in the form of a lion

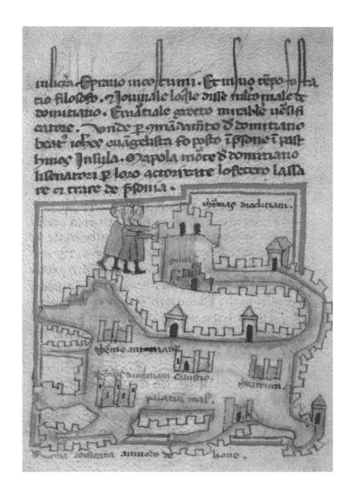

The *Mirabilia* betrays a rather limited knowledge of how the various ancient buildings might have been used. The Baths of Diocletian became the 'Palace of Diocletian', and a similar shift was also effected on behalf of the Baths of Alexander Severus, and those of Constantine. Nevertheless something of their original function was recognized. 'In the summer months,' Canon Benedict explained, 'the crypts were filled with fresh waters so the court could dwell in the upper chambers in much delight.' The Colosseum was described as having been – not a sporting arena – but a 'Temple of the Sun'.

Some of the very greatest sights of old Imperial Rome had become lost both from view and from memory. Almost nothing remained of the Temple of Jupiter Optimus

Maximus. Its battered remnant on the goat-grazed Capitoline, was now misdescribed as the 'Temple of Jupiter and Moneta' in confused conflation with the Temple of Juno Moneta that used to stand on the opposite knoll of the hill, under what had since become the church of S. Maria in Aracoeli.

The once majestic unity of Trajan's Forum had long been shattered and the various broken elements – standing amidst an orchard – were now remembered under fresh names: what remained of the Temple of Trajan was pointed out as the emperor's palace; the ruins of the Basilica Ulpia were the 'Temple of Hadrian'; the triumphal arch that once led into the great complex still stood, but as the 'Porta dei Pantani'.

Even Trajan's great column was referred to on occasion as the 'Column of Hadrian'. The inscription on its base, which might have identified it securely, had – since the ninth century – been obscured by a tiny chapel built up against the side of the monument. Nevertheless, the beautiful carved shaft was now recognized as something very special. In 1162 it became the first publicly protected classical monument in Rome, being taken under the direct care of the recently reconstituted Roman senate in order that it might 'remain whole and undiminished as long as the world lasts'.

If Trajan's Column was acknowledged as one of the most admired classical sights in twelfth-century Rome, what were the others?

Perhaps the most striking novelty in the city was the hot sulphur bath of Apollo Bianeus that continued to operate close to the Lateran. Master Gregory was certainly intrigued by it. But, like a true Englishman, though he had paid the entrance fee, he declined to take a plunge on account of the smell. (He contented himself with dipping his hand in the water to test the temperature.)

Scale seems to have been another important consideration for twelfth-century visitors. Even to men growing accustomed to the vast new cathedrals of northern Europe, the sheer size of many Roman monuments continued to command awed attention. The vastness of the Baths (or 'Palace') of Diocletian inspired Master Gregory to a characteristic burst of enthusiasm: 'It is so large in fact that I couldn't get an accurate impression of the whole structure despite spending the best part of a day there. I discovered columns so large that no one can throw a pebble as high as their capitals, and [they] say that a hundred men could scarcely cut, polish and finish one of these in the space of a year.'

The great domed space of the Pantheon provoked a similar sense of wonder. Constructed without a forest of soaring columns or flying buttresses, the building seemed an unaccountable architectural prodigy. Master Gregory tried to maintain a rational outlook when confronted by the building. He carefully paced out its diameter at

266 feet. (His feet must have been remarkably small, or his note-taking very inaccurate, as the internal width of the building is actually 145 feet.) But most visitors were less scientific in their approach. It was generally considered that the great rotunda could only have been created by some magical agency or devious trickery. The widely read compendium of saints' lives *The Golden Legend* claimed that the dome had been made by filling the whole building with earth into which coins had been mixed; after the cupola had been successfully set over this huge mound, the Roman people readily shovelled the earth out of the temple in order to get hold of the money. The *Mirabilia* ascribed the design to the goddess Cybele, who had appeared to the original builder, Agrippa, in a dream, while a popular life of St Dionysius, written around 1100, suggested that the temple had been built by Domitian with the help of witchcraft.

If Roman builders were supported by magical agency there could have been no limit to their technological capabilities. The great monuments of the ancient city became yet more wonderful in the awed imaginings of many mediaeval visitors. Master Gregory assumed that 'magic craft' had played an important part in the construction of many of Rome's 'marvels'. There certainly seemed to be something magical – or at least fantastical – about the Colosseum. The *Mirabilia* described how the building had originally been covered with a dome of gilded brass, 'where thunder and lightning and glittering fire were made, and where rain was shed through slender tubes'.

If the Colosseum, the Pantheon and the Baths of Diocletian all remain to impress modern visitors with their enduring grandeur, some of the other great sites of twelfth-century Rome have disappeared: an 'Arch of Augustus' near the Pantheon: the 'Tomb of Romulus', a marble-clad pyramid near the Vatican (matching the 'Tomb of Remus' – or Pyramid of Cestius – that still stands near the Protestant Cemetery); and the 'Septem Solia' – or Septizonium (a large, purely ornamental, façade constructed by Septimius Severus at the south-east corner of the Palatine hill).

The massive ruins of the Temple of Serapis then dominated the bluff of the Quirinal hill, sheltering the fortified enclave of the Colonna family. The temple's name, however, was long forgotten. The *Mirabilia* called it the 'Emperor's Table'; Master Gregory referred to it as the 'Palace of the Cornuti' and considered the vision of the 'large towering structure' silhouetted against the sky an arresting one. Among the ruins he noted 'many statues, all with horns. One among them, considerably larger than the others, is called "Jupiter of the Sands".' (The ruins, if not the statues, survived until the sixteenth century, when they were demolished to provide stone for various papal building projects.)

The various classical sculptures that – in spite of all vicissitudes – still remained *in situ* across the city were sources of considerable wonder and interest: the elephant by

S. Maria in Cosmedin, a suckling sow close to the Colosseum, a bronze bull on the battlements of Castel S. Angelo. All of these have long since disappeared, but *Marforio*, a river god then lounging in the Forum, close to the church of S. Martina, can now be found reclining in the courtyard of the Palazzo Nuovo on the Capitoline.

Perhaps the most conspicuous ancient statues in mediaeval Rome, however, were the two monumental *Horse-Tamers* – with their horses – standing among other, smaller, works on the Quirinal, before the ruins of the Baths of Constantine. The statues are still on the Quirinal, in pretty much the same place. They are now described as Castor and Pollux, but in the twelfth century they were considered to represent a pair of Greek naturists – and philosophers – called 'Praxiteles' and 'Phidias'. (These names, belonging to the two most famous sculptors of Ancient Greece, had been carved on the bases of the statues in the fifth century, as optimistic – but quite erroneous – attributions of authorship. But after seven hundred years the captions 'Opus Fidiae' and 'Opus Praxitelis' no longer had any resonance.)

According to the *Mirabilia* the two 'philosophers' had explained their fondness for nudity to the Emperor Tiberius with the line, 'We hold the world of no account and therefore we go naked and possess nothing.' And when the emperor wished to reward them for some great service, they replied that, having no need of money, they would prefer a handsome marble memorial. Their attendant horses 'which trample on the earth' were apparently added to suggest a disdain for all earthly power. The general drift of this legend is also preserved in Master Gregory's account of the statues as representing 'the first mathematicians, to whom horses were assigned because of the quickness of their intellects'.

Compared to the efforts of their own age, the craftsmanship, scale and verisimilitude of many classical sculptures seemed quite amazing to twelfth-century viewers. This was both exciting and troubling. Master Gregory was particularly excited and more than a little troubled by a statue of Venus that he encountered, also on the Quirinal. Despite the fact that it was some distance from his inn, he found himself drawn back three times – as if 'by some magic spell that I'm unaware of' – to contemplate its graceful form. It was 'made from Parian marble with such wonderful and intricate skill' that it appeared to him more like a living creature than a statue: 'indeed she seems to blush in

LEFT ABOVE *Marforio*; his name perhaps derives from the fact that he once lay in the Forum near a large basin inscribed with the legend, 'Mare in foro'.
LEFT BELOW The *Horse-Tamers* on the Quirinal hill, from Lafreri's *Speculum* of 1546

The *Capitoline Venus*

her nakedness, a reddish tinge colouring her face.' (The statue is, possibly, the beautiful one now in the Capitoline Museums and known as the *Capitoline Venus*, which certainly is made of Parian marble, and does have both a pinkish tinge and a touch of magic.)

A few mediaeval visitors took their enthusiasm for classical statuary even further than Master Gregory. When Henry of Blois, the Bishop of Winchester and brother of King Stephen, was attending the papal court around 1150, he spent much of his free time scouring the city, his beard unkempt, buying up sculptures to take back home with him. He, though, was regarded as something of an eccentric.

Some of the ancient statues that stood about the city had taken on a new life as Christian images. One of the pair of reclining river gods that lay close to the *Horse-Tamers* was popularly known as 'Solomon'. (It was in fact an image of the river Tigris; the statue is now in front of the Palazzo del Senatore on the Capitoline hill.) The *Mirabilia* also contains an enthusiastic account of 'a woman encompassed by serpents, who sits with a shell before her', suggesting that she 'signifies the Church, encompassed with many rolls of scriptures, but whoever desires to go to her may not unless first washed in the shell – that is, baptized.' Modern scholars suspect that this now-vanished work must, in fact, have been a statue of Hygieia, daughter of Aesculapius, god of healing, with his symbol, the serpent, coiled about her feet.

The conversion of classical statues to Christian use does not, however, seem to have been a particularly common phenomenon. It was not necessary to secure their survival, and it was not undertaken in any programmatic way. Moreover the two mildly Christianized interpretations cited above were considered – by their authors at least – as very far removed from the credulous tales of the common pilgrims, which managed to relate almost every detail of Ancient Rome back to the holy story or to the business of salvation.

Master Gregory complained, when standing before the so-called 'Tomb of Romulus', 'The pilgrims erroneously claim that this is the grain heap of the apostle Peter, which was transformed into a stone hill of the same size when Nero confiscated it. It is an utterly worthless tale, typical of those told by pilgrims.' Another of their daft notions concerned the nearby obelisk (upon which Julius Caesar's remains were thought to be perched): 'The pilgrims call this "St Peter's Needle", and they make great efforts to crawl underneath it, where the stone rests on four bronze lions, claiming falsely that those who manage to do so are cleansed from their sins having made a true penance.'

Master Gregory's comments carry a pungent sense of the very different attitudes of the two types of twelfth-century Roman visitor. Yet, interestingly, both groups agreed on one point. They shared a common view as to what was the most important sight in Rome. For classically educated clerics like Master Gregory and Henry of Blois, as much as for humble pilgrims of the most credulous sort, the undoubted highpoint of any visit was a trip to the great papal complex at the Lateran.

This was something new. Throughout the Dark Ages the focus of touristic attention had been fixed firmly upon the tomb of St Peter and the great basilica that sheltered it. Now it had shifted all the way across the city, to the home and headquarters of the pope in the south-eastern corner of the *disabitato*, close to the city walls.

A model of the Lateran basilica and palace as they would have been in the twelfth century, from the Museo Nazionale dell' Alto Medioevo, EUR, Rome

This shift of focus involved rather a trek for most people, as they struck out from their inns and hostels in the Tiber bend, across the broken ground of the Forum, around the fortified Colosseum, along the Via Maior (now the Via S. Giovanni), past the beautiful new church of S. Clemente and up the vine-clad slope of the Caelian hill. Reaching the top they found a scene very different from the one today.

The area around the modern Lateran is curiously bald and characterless: the grand eighteenth-century façade of the basilica, topped with its row of outsized saints, has a certain theatrical flair, but it looms over the unloved scrub of the Piazza Porta S. Giovanni. The adjoining palace is an essay in Renaissance anonymity. Cars race past in every direction, making the whole site seem like a traffic island. There is nothing of human scale, and little of human interest. It is not a place to linger.

In the twelfth century, however, the scene overflowed with life. It presented a formidable architectural agglomeration built up over the previous seven centuries: the huge barn-like Lateran basilica, the papal palace, the octagonal baptistery, oratories, cloisters, grand banqueting halls, council chambers, administrative offices, and other associated buildings. Gathered near by were four monasteries as well as the workshop-dwellings of numerous tradesmen. The Emperor Constantine would have been thrilled to see that his vision of the Lateran basilica standing at the heart of a new Christian Rome had finally come to fruition.

The place had an energy that drew people to it. It was the centre of the papal administration. It was there that cases were heard and judgements made. The Lateran had also become of site of rich religious associations. It boasted Rome's finest collection of relics. The basilica now contained the heads of both St Peter and St Paul. They had been transferred there for safety at the time of the Saracen raids in the ninth century and never returned. But even more attractive to twelfth-century visitors was the extraordinary gathering of 'associative relics' that the papacy had managed to build up over the years. The largest and most conspicuous item was the Scala Pilati (or Scala Sancta, as it is now called), supposedly the marble staircase – from the palace of Pontius Pilate – which Jesus had climbed during his Passion. It was attached to the papal palace, in a special building of its own.

Also attached to the palace, in the pope's private chapel, was the Sancta Sanctorum, or Holy of Holies. This was a veritable properties box for the whole biblical story. Among the wonderful relics it contained were the Ark of the Covenant, the rod of Aaron, a portion of manna, the tablets of the Ten Commandments, John the Baptist's hair shirt, some milk of the Virgin Mary (and one of her nightdresses), the last remnants of the loaves and fishes, a section of the crown of thorns, the 'coat without seam' and even some of Christ's blood.

These were things to amaze, delight and comfort the humble pilgrim. They even impressed classically educated clerics. Gerald of Wales (in Rome to stake his claim to the bishopric of St David's) spent a happy day contemplating the Lateran's remarkable haul of relics. He did not, though, get to see the 'Uronica', a miraculous portrait of Christ supposedly painted by St Luke with angelic assistance. It was thought too powerful for general exposure. Indeed one pope was said to have been struck blind after looking too closely upon it.†

Such sacred wonders were, however, only part of the Lateran's great appeal. For many visitors the principal interest of the place lay neither in the basilica nor in the papal palace but in the piazza outside them. This vast irregular square – the Campo Laterano – aside from its clusters of market booths and stalls, contained a remarkable collection of classical statues and memorials. It had been assembled there – piece by piece – over the previous couple of centuries by successive papal administrations. There were seven items on view, raised on columns and plinths above the milling throng. All of them were made from bronze. And after seven hundred years of melting, smelting and despoliation, this in itself was something extraordinary.

† The Scala Sancta was moved at the end of the sixteenth century, when the Lateran Palace was rebuilt. It now leads up to the Sancta Sanctorum, both being enclosed within a small free-standing building across the road from the basilica. Although the Uronica is still visible through the barred window of the pope's private chapel, the various other relics once housed there have not been seen publicly since the pontificate of Leo X (1513–21).

Dominating the scene, in front of the papal palace, set on a plinth supported by two lions, was the statue of Marcus Aurelius on his horse that now stands (in replica) on the Campidoglio. The only equestrian monument to have survived unscathed from antiquity, it was at that time generally believed to represent the Emperor Constantine. Near by, on columns, were placed a colossal bronze head and a hand holding a sphere, as well as an exquisite Hellenistic statue of a boy plucking a thorn from his foot. In the loggia of the Palace stood the famous Capitoline statue of the she-wolf, the *Lupa*, together with a bronze ram-cum-fountain, and – before them – a tablet recording the *Lex Vespasiani* (which included a decree by which the Senate and People of Rome transferred the imperial *potestas* first invested in Augustus to the later Emperor Vespasian).†

Taken all together these works made an arresting display – one that fixed itself vividly in the minds of all who came to Rome, simple pilgrims and clerical classicists alike. The scale of the works, their artistry, their finish, their rarity, and their value, all commanded attention. But was there more? The mediaeval mind was, after all, fond of allegory and meaning: almost everything was considered to have significance. Had the various statues been deliberately assembled to convey some message?

The question is impossible to answer conclusively. But it has been plausibly suggested that the papal officials who maintained the great showpiece may have conceived the display as a sort of visual pedigree of Rome's immortal power. Roman hegemony had been established by Romulus (who had been suckled by the she-wolf), it had been passed on by the Senate and People of Rome to the emperors (see the *Lex Vespasiani*), and it had then been transferred by Constantine (through his 'Donation') from the emperors to the pope. By gathering together enduring bronze images of the wolf, the imperial laws, the Emperor Constantine and the imperial orb, the papacy had created an ingenious piece of visual propaganda, demonstrating how control over a worldwide pagan empire run from the Capitoline had evolved seamlessly into a Europe-wide Christian administration run from the Lateran. Perhaps.

Certainly everyone who saw the Lateran sculptures must have been impressed at the power of the papacy – impressed that the popes had been able to assemble and preserve such a collection of rare things. It is doubtful, though, that many visitors took away any very complex message about the origins of papal power from their tour of the monuments. Ingenious visual propaganda has its limitations: much of it can be lost on uninformed onlookers. And, in an age before labels, visitor centres and published

---

† All the works, with the exception, of the ram, which is lost, are now in the Capitoline Museums.

guidebooks, it was impossible to fix any interpretation. Indeed there was considerable disagreement about whom the various monuments represented.

Although the great majority of pilgrims recognized the equestrian statue as 'Constantine', the first Christian emperor, by no means all did. Many Germanic visitors liked to think that it represented Theodoric the Ostrogoth – or Dietrich of Bern as he was known in German song and legend. By the twelfth century Theoderic/Dietrich had become an archetypal hero of popular romance across the Teutonic world. Proclaiming the most conspicuous statue in Rome to be Dietrich must have given the many groups of Germanic pilgrims an excuse for a good sing-song.

For those visitors anxious to find a biblical interpretation for everything, the Lateran statues presented rather a challenge. The colossal head and hand were deemed to belong, not to a Roman emperor, but to 'Samson', while the thorn-picker might be 'Absalom' (who 'from the sole of his foot to the crown of his head had no blemish in him'); and the wolf was best ignored as a dangerous 'idol'.

Failure to decipher the papal message was not, however, confined to the unlettered pilgrim throng. The Roman author of the *Mirabilia* may well have understood the ideas behind the display in the Campo Laterano but, as a canon of St Peter's (the Lateran's great rival church) and a man of Republican sympathies, he rather resented them. He pointedly refused to give a comprehensive description of the statues. Instead he makes a great play of stating that the equestrian monument was *not* of Constantine, as was generally supposed, but of a certain squire in the time of the 'consuls and senators' who had saved Rome from a besieging army by capturing the enemy king (who, apparently, in the twelfth century was represented being trampled under the horse's raised hoof).

Master Gregory had no such anti-papal bias. Nevertheless, though remarkably well informed on many issues, he seems simply to have missed any intended papal propaganda. He recognized that the monuments were important, and he devoted a great deal of space to describing them, but his response was more personal than political.

When confronted by the statue of the *Lupa* he was principally concerned with the improbability of Romulus and Remus having actually been suckled by a she-wolf – 'A tall tale indeed!' Much more likely, he thought, was that they had been rescued and nursed by a woman who was nicknamed 'Wolf' on account of her extraordinary beauty, which 'caused men to be seized with lust for her'.

He was delighted by the 'ridiculous statue' of the boy, 'which they call Priapus': 'He looks as though he's in severe pain, with his head bent down as if to remove from his foot a thorn that he had stepped on. If you lean forward and look up to see what he's doing, you discover genitals of extraordinary size.' (This last statement is something of

ABOVE LEFT The 'ridiculous' *Spinario*
ABOVE RIGHT The equestrian statue of Marcus Aurelius, with the bird-like tuft of hair between the horse's ears

a mystery, as the genitals of the *Spinario* are not, as can be confirmed at the Capitoline Museums, particularly large. Perhaps this is a further indication of the diminutive proportions of Master Gregory. Or maybe, looking up from below at the statue on its column, he had misconstrued the boy's bulging scrotum as the glans of his penis.)

Gregory stared long and hard at the bronze tablet inscribed with the *Lex Vespasiani* but found it impossible to decipher. He was told, though, not that it recorded any transfer of power from the people of Rome to the emperors, but that it 'prohibited sin'.

After consultation with 'the elders, Cardinals and men of greatest learning' he came away with two possible interpretations of the equestrian statue 'said by the Roman people to be Constantine'. According to one version it honoured a soldier named Marcus who (as in the *Mirabilia*) saved Rome from an evil king who had invested the city. The other tale was a dim recalling of the Lacus Curtius myth in which a knight – now called Quintus Quirinius – charged his horse into a gaping chasm that had opened up in the middle of the Forum, and was spewing forth a deadly plague. His sacrifice saved the city and secured the gratitude of the Roman people. Both stories involved the decisive intervention of a small bird, which Master Gregory describes as being represented, sitting between the ears of the horse. (It is, in fact, a tuft of the horse's mane.)

The great bronze head and hand, perched on their marble columns, quite stunned Gregory with their 'horrific size'. In common with the *Mirabilia* he understood that they were pieces of the famous *Colossus*, from which the Colosseum had derived its name. The statue of the Sun God had, he recounted, been destroyed as a pagan idol by Pope Gregory I (the *Mirabilia* says Silvester I). Unable to topple it, the pope had built a bonfire between its feet, 'reducing the gigantic figure to its former formless state' – except, of course, for the surviving two pieces. (Current scholarship considers that the fragments – now displayed on a smart new plinth in the Capitoline Museums – come, in fact, from a statue of Constantine.)

Although Gregory was told that the orb clutched by the massive bronze hand signified Rome's dominion over the world, it was not the symbolism of the whole work that impressed him, so much as its beauty, and – above all – its mystery. He was awestruck by 'how the fluid craftsmanship can simulate soft hairs in solid bronze, and if you look at [the head] intently, transfixed by its splendour, it gives the appearance of being about to move and speak.' It was a marvel.

That was the real effect of the Campo Laterano and its display of treasures, and the real reason that so many people were drawn to the place. Here, amidst the crush and bustle of the mediaeval city, were things that had the power to amaze.

·V·
RENAISSANCE ROME

O N 14 JANUARY 1506, while digging in his vineyard on the Esquiline hill, not far from the church of S. Pietro in Vincoli, Felice da Freddi broke through into a concealed chamber. He could make out an ornate room containing a large sculpture. It looked impressive. Word of the find spread fast. The pope, Julius II, a passionate collector of antiquities, instructed his architect, Giuliano da Sangallo, to visit the site at once. Sangallo brought his young son along with him, and also his friend and fellow Florentine Michelangelo, who was in Rome working on a monumental tomb for the pope. They were very excited. That excitement turned to something more as they peered into the hole and made out the form of a man, flanked by two boys, caught in the coils of two giant serpents. Sangallo (at least according to his son, recalling the event some sixty years later) at once remarked, 'This is the *Laocoön* that Pliny mentions.' (See pages 39–40.)

Laocoön – as described in the *Aeneid* – was the Trojan priest of Apollo, who, having tried to warn his compatriots against accepting the wooden horse left by the Greeks, was killed, along with his two sons, by a pair of sea serpents sent by Athene. A sculpture of this dramatic moment had been described by Pliny the Elder, in a celebrated passage of his *Natural History*, as being the greatest work of art known at Rome in his day: 'The *Laocoön* which is in the house of the Emperor Titus, a work to be put before all others both of painting and of sculpture. Out of one block of stone the three greatest artists of Rhodes – Hagesander, Polydorus and Athenodorus – carved according to an agreed design Laocoön himself and his sons and the astonishing coils of the serpents.'

And here, it seemed, was the very masterpiece. The hole was opened up and the statue was brought out. Amazingly, the great work was almost intact. The figure of Laocoön was missing part of an arm, as was one of the sons; the other boy was short of his lower leg. (The chamber had been walled up, perhaps – it was conjectured – to protect the statue, after the initial act of vandalism, from any further damage at some troubled moment in Rome's history.) The quality of the workmanship seemed to confirm Sangallo's initial judgment. As one informed observer remarked: it must be 'the renowned statue since [the figures] are of the most amazing excellence and display the greatest beauty and dignity'. Michelangelo was similarly impressed, describing the statue as 'a singular miracle of art'.

He and Sangallo immediately set about drawing the sculpture. Crowds began to gather. Among the first to arrive was a member of Cardinal Raffaelle Riario's household; the cardinal – one of Pope Julius's nephews – had assembled an impressive collection of classical statues, which he displayed in the courtyard of his new *palazzo*. He found other interested parties already on the scene. 'By night and day,' he reported, 'all Rome thronged to see the new discovery. Such was the interest that, for safekeeping, the sculpture was removed to the bedroom of the vineyard owner.'

In the days that followed no serious doubt was cast on the authenticity of the find. The fact that Felice da Freddi's vineyard was set among the ruins of what were supposed to have been the Baths of Titus lent weight to the ascription. (If Pliny had described the statue as residing in the 'House', rather than the Baths, of the emperor that was accounted a very minor point of detail.) On close inspection Michelangelo noted that the work was not – as claimed by Pliny – made from a single block of stone, but from several pieces ingeniously fitted together. But Pliny, it was suggested, might have been deceived, or might have been seeking to deceive his readers – and exalt the sculptors. Everyone remained convinced that they had stumbled upon the very grail of Roman antiquarianism.

A bidding war began among eager collectors. The suggestion that the sculpture should be made over to the people of Rome was ignored. Various cardinals put forward cash offers. Raffaelle Riario bid 2,000 ducats, but he was trumped by the pope. Julius II, a man of almost daemonic energy and will, nearly always got his way: he secured the masterpiece in return for granting Signore da Freddi an annuity of 600 ducats for life.

The deal concluded, the sculpture was carried to the Vatican in a triumphal procession, cheered by crowds. By early June it had been installed as the central piece in the pope's new sculpture court at the Belvedere.

This small square courtyard with bevelled corners was the still centre of the pope's sumptuous new residence, adjoining St Peter's. It stood as the final element of the Cortile del Belvedere, a long progression of stepped terrace courts devised by Bramante to link the Vatican palace with the little Belvedere garden villa erected by Pope Innocent VIII, on the northern spur of the Vatican hill. It was a Renaissance recreation of a classical sculpture garden. The paved area was softened with orange trees, cypresses and laurels; a fountain played at its centre. The atmosphere of the sacred grove was enhanced by a Latin inscription near the entrance – borrowed from the *Aeneid* – proclaiming 'Procul Este Profani' (The Uninitiated Keep Out). Ranged around the walls of the court were five elaborately decorated niches, fit settings for the choicest specimens of classical statuary in Pope Julius's collection.

The whole creation had been a splendid act of faith. At the time of the sculpture court's inception, three years before in 1503, Julius II only possessed one work worthy of the space, the serene *Apollo Belvedere* as it came to be called (see page 208), which he had acquired while he was still a cardinal. The *Laocoön* arrived right on cue, to fill one of the vacant niches. For all educated visitors to Rome the newly discovered masterpiece at once became the cynosure. It assumed a position at the head of all the wonders of Rome.

The statue still stands in its niche, though the courtyard setting has been somewhat altered over the centuries. (The elegant colonnades that now frame the space were not built until the 1770s.) It enjoys a degree of conventional attention, and remains an almost universally recognizable image (so recognizable that it has even been parodied in *The Simpsons*). But it is unrevered and unloved. The crowds that flock through the Vatican museums may pause before it, but they are hastening to the Sistine Chapel, not scrutinizing the papal sculpture collection. Among classical works taste now favours the purer, more restrained style of the earlier Greeks. And even as an example of first-century Hellenistic art, its status has been questioned. Recent scholarship has dared to scout the idea that it may not even be the original work described by Pliny.†

The huge enthusiasm for the work at the time of its discovery reflected, however, something new: a new attitude to the classical past very different from the awed wonder of the twelfth century. Excitement now was tempered with scholarly curiosity, aesthetic appreciation and the desire for ownership. The *Laocoön* inspired myriad tributes. From

† There are records of fragments of other – larger – statues of Laocoön and his sons having been discovered in Rome during the sixteenth century. Perhaps – some scholars argue – it is among these broken remnants, rather than in the surviving work of the Belvedere sculpture court, that the true original of Pliny's fabled masterpiece is to be found ...

the very moment of its discovery, images of the statue began to be produced. Prints were made, and small bronze versions. (In 1510 Bramante commissioned four of the leading sculptors in Rome to make wax models of the sculpture, and invited Raphael to judge them. The winning version – by the young Jacopo Sansovino – was then cast in bronze.) The statue became the subject of numerous poems, including one written in 1506 by the youthful Ferrarese humanist Jacopo Sadoleto, then secretary to Cardinal Oliviero Caraffa.

> Behold! From deep mass of earth and from great ruins'
> Heart, long time has brought returned Laocoön again;
> That Laocoön which once in princely halls
> Had place and dignified, O Titus, your own house.
> The image of a godlike art – skilled antiquity itself
> Looked not on nobler work – has now come back,
> Freed from the shades, to see the lofty walls of a renewed Rome.

Rome had, indeed, been renewed. Or, rather, it was in the throes of renewal. The process was relatively recent. Since the twelfth century, Rome, after a brief period of prosperity, had sunk into a long period of decline. In 1309 the papacy had removed itself to Avignon in south-western France, and remained there for almost seventy years. The long decades of exile had been followed by an equally long period of schism, during which rival popes and 'anti-popes' had contested for authority and control over the western Church. Throughout, Rome itself had been left uncared for and unloved, bereft of papal dignity and papal revenues.

By the mid-fifteenth century it bore, in the words of one contemporary chronicler, 'hardly any resemblance to a city'. Houses had fallen into ruins, churches had collapsed, whole quarters were abandoned; famine and poverty assailed the dwindling population, and so did the oppressive stench of decay: the narrow streets had become a common dumping ground for 'entrails, viscera, heads, feet, bones, blood, and skins . . . rotten meat and fish, refuse, excrement, and rotting cadavers'.

It was only in 1443 that a new pope, Eugenius IV, after long years of exile, was able to re-enter this broken and malodorous city as the undisputed head of an undivided Church. He was not merely appalled at the poverty and demoralization of the place. Having spent most of the previous decade in prosperous Florence, among the masterworks of Donatello, Brunelleschi, Fra Angelico, Masaccio and their confrères – he was also shocked to discover that Rome was a cultural backwater.

It was a shock shared by many of the educated Florentines in the papal entourage, men such as Leon Battista Alberti and the historian Flavio Biondo. The great flowering of humanist learning and artistic expression that we know as the Italian Renaissance had almost entirely passed Rome by. The situation could not be allowed to continue. With Eugenius IV the Renaissance finally entered Rome. The city was ready to be reborn.

Over the course of the next fifty years the city steadily grew from a mediaeval town into a Renaissance capital. The population doubled, from around twenty-five thousand in the 1450s to over fifty thousand in the early decades of the sixteenth century. The new inhabitants included over ten thousand Jews, expelled from Spain, Portugal and Provence and welcomed to Rome in the 1490s by the Borgia Pope Alexander VI.

The physical aspect of the city took longer to alter. The division between the crowded *abitato* and the sparsely settled *disabitato* remained a vivid fact; the Forum was still littered with shanty dwellings, lime kilns and workshops, its few half-buried and broken monuments choked with weeds and brambles. Nevertheless, everywhere about the town there were real signs of change.

Visitors to Rome at the beginning of the sixteenth century could not have missed the sense of burgeoning life and vitality. They themselves contributed to it. The return of the papal court had brought wealth and prestige back to the city. The revenues of the Papal States once again enriched the town. Papal business was flourishing, drawing hundreds of petitioners and litigants to the Curia each year.

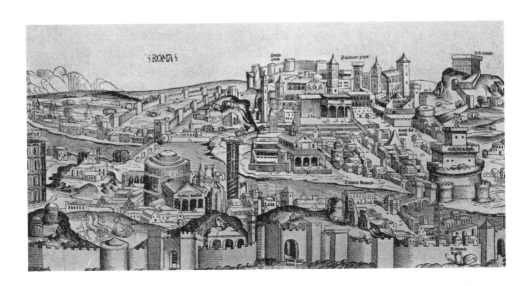

Pilgrims, too, were coming to Rome once more, and in ever greater numbers. This was a conscious revival of the glories of the past. The swansong of the mediaeval papacy at Rome had been the great Holy Year or Jubilee celebrated in 1300. It had been a huge success. According to the Florentine chronicler Giovanni Villani there were often as many as two hundred thousand visitors crammed into the city during that year. He describes how two clerks at S. Paolo fuori le Mura worked with great rakes, day and night, to gather in all the coins left by the faithful.

The pilgrims came seeking 'indulgence', as part of the detailed system of penances and punishments that the Church, extending its legalistic ideas into the spiritual realm, had evolved for the sinful. At the heart of this new system stood the novel concept of purgatory – a place where sins could be 'worked off' during the afterlife. (The concept, having been introduced, became vividly elaborated – most vividly, of course, in Dante's *Divine Comedy*, which was written in the first decades of the fourteenth century.) According to the pope's pronouncement, any pilgrim who visited the basilicas of St Peter's and S. Paolo on fifteen consecutive days during the Jubilee year would receive a 'plenary indulgence' – the remission of purgatorial punishment for all their sins. Pilgrimage was given a new sense of urgency and purpose. It is little wonder that, in 1300, the faithful came in such numbers.

The great success of that first Jubilee faded all too quickly, as the papacy was removed to Avignon soon afterwards. The return to Rome offered the popes a chance to revive the practice of holding Holy Years: they were good for the spiritual health of the world, and perhaps even better for the coffers of the papacy. (The system of granting indulgences for the remission of time in purgatory had become steadily more mechanical and commercial. It was possible to buy a pardon for most sins.)

After a false start with a very poorly attended Jubilee in 1400, subsequent Renaissance popes had refined and improved the policy of declaring Holy Years. Rather than waiting another whole century, a new Jubilee was held in 1450. It proved a huge draw – almost too much of one. The Ponte S. Angelo, leading from the city to St Peter's, became so crowded that over two hundred people died in the crush. Despite this setback, it was decided after the 1450 Jubilee to repeat the event not merely every half-century, but every twenty-five years. Cynics suggested that it was a good way for the papacy to make money for its various building schemes.

A view of Rome in *c.* 1490, from the Nuremberg Chronicle

There were, moreover, other new religious attractions to draw the pious to Rome. In 1462, the skull of St Peter's brother, St Andrew, was acquired by the pope and brought to the city amidst scenes of great pomp and ceremony. Thirty years later 'the lance of Longinus', which was said to have pierced the side of Christ while he hung on the cross, was presented to Pope Innocent VIII by Sultan Bayezid II. Installed in St Peter's, both items became important additions to the city's powerhouse of relics. The continued holiness of Rome was also attested by modern miracles. In 1480 a drunken soldier striking a picture of the Madonna in a small street-side chapel near the Piazza Navona was amazed to see it spouting blood. A beautiful new church, S. Maria della Pace, was promptly created by Sixtus IV to house the miraculous painting.

At a slightly less exalted level, the popes reintroduced and greatly augmented the carnival celebrations that preceded Lent each year. During the Middle Ages the festival had been confined to a series of popular games contested on and around Monte Testaccio, the artificial hillock close to the old Tiber docks that had been built up during classical times from the myriad shards of discarded amphorae. Under the direction of the Renaissance popes carnival was transformed into a ten-day-long riot of pageantry and fun in the heart of Rome. It became an event to witness. There were horse races along the Via Lata – which henceforth became known as the Corso (the Italian for 'run'). These were followed by a 'donkey derby', as well as a buffalo one. There were bull fights on the Capitoline, and parades of floats around the Piazza Navona. Special-category running races – from the Campo dei Fiori to St Peter's – were contested by, among others, the old, the young and the Jews. Pope Alexander VI even introduced a race for the whores of Rome.

There were plenty of them. The courtesan had emerged as a prominent – even a respected – figure on the city's new cultural scene; and, lower down the professional scale, common prostitutes were numerous. Other sectors of the service industry also rose to the challenge of Rome's returning popularity. Artisans flourished, and it was said that no city in Europe had so many – or such good – inns. During the 1450 Jubilee it was reported that there were 1,020 inns with signboards in Rome, and many more without.

Rome found herself at the centre of a changing world. In 1453 Christendom had been rocked by the fall of Constantinople to the Ottoman Turks. With all of Europe seemingly under threat from the infidel, it was the papacy that preached the need for united action and crusade. Losses at one end of the Mediterranean were, however, soon made up at the other. In 1492 King Ferdinand drove the last Moors out of Granada. That same year also witnessed Christopher Columbus' discovery of the

Americas; while on the other side of the globe the Portuguese were establishing contacts across the Indian Ocean. These were achievements that resonated in Rome, where the popes, believing that they had a spiritual responsibility for the whole of mankind, began to consider how the gospel might be propagated across the new, uncharted worlds.

The revival of Rome's fortunes was both reflected in and enhanced by the changing cityscape. When the English traveller John Capgrave had visited Rome in 1450 he noted that many of the churches were in ruins. By 1500 all that had changed, or was changing. Everywhere elegant new buildings were going up and inelegant old streets were coming down, churches were being restored, chapels were being embellished; and it was the papacy that was directing operations. Eugenius IV had made a start immediately upon his return, clearing and paving the piazza in front of the Pantheon – or S. Maria Rotonda – but it was really his successor, Nicholas V, a humanist of deep learning and broad culture, who in the 1450s mapped out a coherent vision for urban renewal. Inspired by the classically derived ideas of the Florentine architect Leon Battista Alberti, he embarked upon an ambitious plan to make Rome a fit capital for the Universal Church.

And although he was able to accomplish only a small portion of the scheme during his pontificate (1447–55), his vision was followed up over the next six decades by his successors – most notably Pius II (Piccolomini), Paul II (Barbo), Sixtus IV (della Rovere), Innocent VIII (Cibo), Alexander VI (Borgia) and Julius II (another della Rovere). Throughout this remarkable period the concerted papal effort was eagerly supported by many in the college of cardinals. Numerous princes of the Church devoted both their ecclesiastical revenues and their personal fortunes to adorning Rome.

During this campaign of regeneration the practical amenities of the city were not neglected. One of Nicholas V's first schemes was to refurbish the Aqua Virgo (or the Acqua Vergine as he rechristened it), giving the aqueduct additional outlets on the Quirinal and Pincian hills, and terminating it at a generous but unremarkable basin where the rather more spectacular Trevi Fountain now stands. The main focus was always upon the imposing and the public. Scale was considered to be of real importance. As Pope Nicholas explained on his deathbed, 'Great buildings which are perpetual monuments and eternal testimonies seemingly made by the hand of God [demonstrate that] the authority of the Roman Church is the greatest and highest.' Location too was significant. For this reason especial attention was fixed on the two key historic sites from which the city's greatness had sprung: the Capitoline (the sacred centre of Ancient Rome) and the Vatican (the sacred centre of Christian Rome).

The former, despite the presence of the church of the Aracoeli and the mediaeval Palazzo del Senatore, was still an unimpressive outcrop, known locally as the Monte Caprino – the hill of goats. Of the once-great Temple of Jupiter Optimus Maximus only traces of the massive foundation works remained, their true history unknown. They provided a drying ground. Pope Nicholas V took matters in hand, remodelling and enlarging the Palazzo del Senatore, and setting up, at right angles to it, a second building, the colonnaded Palazzo dei Conservatori, as a home for the local magistracy. The arrangement marked out the beginnings of a piazza facing west towards the *abitato*. (Although the offices of the Comune may have been improved, it should be said that this was not matched by any increase in the Comune's power. Quite the reverse: the papacy, on returning to Rome, established and maintained a firm political control over the city.)

In the ever-shifting balance of prestige between the twin seats of papal power – the Lateran and the Vatican – the scales were tilted decisively, and finally, in favour of the latter. Although Eugenius IV had made it one of his first tasks to restore the dilapidated Lateran palace and build a 'sumptuous' monastery near by, these proved minor diversions. The attraction of the Vatican site was too great to be ignored: it was the resting place of St Peter, the justification for Rome's position at the heart of Christendom; it was closer to the inhabited parts of the city, and it was easier to defend. Nicholas V signalled the shift in power when he remodelled the modest Vatican palace as the new and permanent papal residence. He brought the Florentine artist-monk Fra Angelico to Rome to decorate his private chapel in the new building.

Nicholas's successors rapidly extended his vision. The creation of the Cortile del Belvedere and its sculpture court by Julius II and Bramante was merely the culmination of a continuous process of improvement. In the decades after Nicholas's pontificate an atrium was added to the palace, and a library; the little Belvedere villa was constructed; wings were thrown out, towers set up, and façades embellished. In 1475 Pope Sixtus IV rebuilt and enlarged the old Palatine Chapel on the site (renaming it the Sistine Chapel). The finest Florentine and Umbrian painters – including Botticelli, Perugino and Ghirlandaio – were brought together to decorate its walls with scenes from the Old and New Testaments (see plates II and III). And some three decades later Sixtus's nephew Julius II commissioned Michelangelo to decorate the ceiling.

The work undertaken on the Vatican palace complex was just one element in a scheme to transform the whole Leonine city into a secure and ordered Renaissance townscape. The tenth-century walls were extended. Major repairs were carried out. The maze of narrow streets honeycombing the crowded Borgo in front of St Peter's began to be tidied up and replaced with broad, straight thoroughfares.

It was part of Nicholas V's original plan that St Peter's should be extensively restored and enlarged. After over a millennium of use, Constantine's old basilica church was in a poor state of repair. The walls, it was estimated, were leaning out of true by almost two metres. The interior had become so cluttered with tombs and monuments that there was little room for pilgrims, and scarcely more for the clergy who gathered to say Mass at the altar directly above the Apostle's tomb. To overcome these difficulties it was proposed to remodel the entire west end of the church, extending the choir, adding transepts and placing the high altar at the crossing point under a magnificent dome. A start was made, but by 1508 the scheme had been superseded by Julius II's even more radical plan to rebuild the entire church on a vastly increased plan.

Both in terms of ambition and design, all these developments looked for their inspiration to the achievements of Ancient Rome. The conception of the Christian city under the popes as heir to the imperial glory of classical Rome was, of course, a very old one, but the idea that this relationship could – and should – be reflected in the architecture and decoration of the modern Rome was something new. The great monuments were no longer regarded as 'marvels' accomplished by 'magic power', but as supreme human achievements. As early as the fourteenth century Boccaccio had suggested that some imposing classical ruin was 'a testimony of the greatness of the soul of him who built it', and this idea had gained force with the years. Roman architecture came to be seen as something not only good but also worth imitating.

Previously when architectural inspiration had been looked for in the past, the builders had turned to the examples of Constantine's early basilica churches. Now they looked further back – into the classical era.

The vision of the Renaissance popes both required and produced a new understanding of the city and its ruins. The shattered remnants of antiquity which still littered the townscape or loomed on the skyline now began to be contemplated not as a moral lesson about the fate of worldly empires, but as an inspiration and a guide to current practice. In such circumstances sound knowledge became important, and with the return of the papacy to Rome, dozens of humanist scholars – most of them attached to the papal Curia – were soon busying themselves, investigating the ruins of the old city. They looked at the broken buildings with new eyes, seeking to discover their true history: when they were built, why they looked they way they did, how they were originally used.

Leon Battista Alberti, who worked in the Curia at Rome during the early 1430s, provided the first mathematically accurate record of the surviving ruins in his *Descriptio*

Urbis Romae. Another long-serving papal secretary, Poggio Bracciolini, opened up new avenues of research through the systematic study of the inscriptions that adorned Rome's public buildings, preserving – in much-abbreviated form – a record of their origins and history. He was the first to suggest that the pyramid outside the Porta Ostiense was unlikely to be the tomb of Remus, as was popularly supposed, since a large inscription on its side – only partially concealed by weeds – declared it to be a monument to Caius Cestius. These were valuable contributions.

It was, though, yet another curial official, Flavio Biondo, who between 1444 and 1446 produced the most important and influential study of the ancient city, *Roma Instaurata – Rome Restored*. Biondo was an historian of genius. (Among other achievements he coined the term – and conceived the idea of – the 'Middle Ages', or *media aetas*, as the period dividing antiquity from his own era, an idea that stimulated a new attitude to the classical past.) Though born and educated in the north of Italy, he became an impassioned devotee of Rome, determined to recover and record as much as he could of its ancient topography.

Through his great work the old world of the *Mirabilia*, with its fanciful legends and unfounded assertions, was decisively challenged. Every traditional story and ascription was subjected to a critical re-examination, and tested against a much-enriched historical record. With the florescence of humanist scholarship during the early Renaissance many new classical sources relating to the city had been tracked down, while old ones were read more thoroughly. Greek authors, for so long indecipherable, were once again consulted, and early mediaeval texts – from Bede to the *Liber Pontificalis* – were not disdained. The two fourth-century Regionary Catalogues of Rome's monuments (in a new edition by Pomponio Leto) provided Biondo with a comprehensive structure for his book.

The author, however, did not confine himself to the library. Like Poggio and many other scholars, he roamed the city in search of clues. He embraced the new discipline of epigraphy. Even humble brick-stamps were given their due. Coins, too, he found, could be a rich source of architectural information, stamped as they often were with images of temples, triumphal arches and other structures.

Although sometimes described as the father of archaeology, Biondo lived in an age before deliberate or organized digging. Nevertheless, he did not want for material. As building activity increased everywhere in Rome, much new ground was broken and many new discoveries were made. The *Laocoön* was only the most spectacular of a host of inadvertent finds. Almost every construction project – minor or major – yielded something of interest or value.

With more information came greater understanding: huge strides were made in the interpretation of the ancient city and its monuments. The imperial baths were now recognized for what they were, and no longer designated as 'palaces'. The Colosseum was understood to have been an arena rather than the Temple of the Sun. It was acknowledged that Julius Caesar's ashes were not enclosed in the golden ball on top of the Vatican Obelisk. But despite these advances in knowledge, much, not surprisingly, remained unclear. Some old errors were perpetuated and several new ones introduced.

With the exception of the arches of Septimius Severus and Titus, none of the visible monuments in the Forum was given what is now considered its correct name. The massive ruins of the Basilica Nova continued to be labelled as the 'Temple of Peace' (and – in the popular report at least – the mediaeval legend that it had collapsed on the night of Christ's birth was maintained).

The monumental statues of the *Horse-Tamers* on the Quirinal hill, if they were no longer considered to represent a pair of nude mathematicians, were still misascribed to the Greek sculptors Phidias and Praxiteles, and – with scant regard for chronology – were now thought to commemorate the thoroughbred horses presented to Nero by Tiridates, the king of Armenia, who had come to Rome in AD 66 to receive his crown from the emperor.

The scholarly investigation of Rome's ancient monuments was always matched by a strain of practical inquiry: a desire to understand how the buildings were made. Alberti, through his reading of the Roman architectural writer Vitruvius, informed as it was by actual building experience, was really the first architect to rediscover the underlying rules of classical construction. He mapped out its modular systems (based on multiples of the Roman foot) and its ordered aesthetic, and he recorded these insights in *De re aedificatoria*, the work that he dedicated to Nicholas V in 1452.

The book proved extremely useful to the rising generation of Rome's architectural practitioners, men such as Sangallo, Bramante, Andrea Bregno and Michelangelo – anxious to emulate the achievements of the classical past. It was, though, merely a supplement to the great architectural lexicon of the city itself. The sense of vast scale, revealed by the ruins of Rome's imperial baths or the great vaults of the 'Temple of Peace' in the Forum, suggested an exciting new world of huge interior spaces, while the rediscovered Roman building technique of using brick-faced concrete showed how this world might be recreated. Classical forms and proportions, or adaptations from them, soon began to appear in the city's new buildings. After the long domination of crooked towers and crenellations, of unplanned asymmetry and narrow blank façades, this was something wholly new.

Inspired by the grand example of the Pantheon, a rather more modest dome was created for S. Maria del Popolo, the beautiful church rebuilt in 1472–8 for Sixtus IV near the Porta del Popolo. Continuing the classical theme, the church's flat façade, with its three evenly spaced doors, and its row of pilasters supporting a pediment, imitated the basic form of a Roman temple front. A similar arrangement was employed for the remodelling of S. Pietro in Montorio (1482–1500) on the Janiculum, while, next to that church, Bramante took the idea of classical emulation even further, a few years later, with his extraordinary domed Tempietto, modelled directly on the circular structure and elegant proportions of the Temple of Hercules Invictus that once stood in the Forum Boarium.

The huge *palazzo* now known as the Cancellaria, which lies just outside the Campo dei Fiori, can claim to be the first secular building in Rome since the time of the Caesars to employ the classical orders – or an approximation of them – on its façade and in its courtyard. (The columns, though not the capitals, in the courtyard were salvaged from the ruins of the Green charioteers' barracks that had once stood on the site.) Built in the 1490s by Sixtus IV's nephew Cardinal Raffaele Riario (with the 'honest fortune' he had won at cards from a fellow cardinal), the *palazzo* was one of several imposing –

and classically inspired – cardinals' palaces constructed during the period. Pope Sixtus encouraged such projects with tax breaks and liberal planning legislation. Where once the great feudal families of Rome – the Orsini, Colonna, Cenci, Savelli and Frangipani – had vied with each other in building taller and stronger towers, now the emerging papal dynasties – such as the della Rovere, Medici, Borghese and Farnese – contended through the grandness of their *palazzi*.

Among these impressive new edifices, the largest was the Palazzo S. Marco (now the Palazzo Venezia) built by Cardinal Pietro Barbo (later Pope Paul II), while the most lavish belonged to Cardinal Rodrigo Borgia (the future Pope Alexander VI): Pius II likened it to Nero's Golden House; it even had its own bull ring. Only a fraction of it now remains, as the Palazzo Sforza-Cesarini in the Via Banchi Vecchi; the rest was swept away with the construction of the Corso Vittorio Emanuele in 1870.

Through their deliberate use of classical detail, scale, proportion and symmetry, these buildings, and dozens more like them, came to transform the Roman townscape,

LEFT The classically inspired façade of S. Maria del Popolo
BELOW The Cancellaria, from an eighteenth-century print

bringing an entirely new – if suggestively antique – sense of ordered grandeur to the city's crowded streets and squares. (In an echo of Rome's ancient aqueducts, a slender footbridge, raised on high piers, ran from the upper storey of the Palazzo S. Marco to the Aracoeli on the Capitoline hill.)

The same classical influences were also making a mark on the landscape of the *disabitato*. Many cardinals, as well as other high-ranking papal officials, established suburban retreats on the city's less populated hills, garden villas where they could spend their leisure hours under vine-clad pergolas discussing classical literature. To Biondo and other humanists these so-called *vigne* conjured up the lost ambience once enjoyed in the gardens of Maecenas and Sallust.

For all the fresh interest that many in Rome felt for the city's architectural past, there was a strong admixture of very unsentimental practicality. As the pace of building activity increased, so did the pace – and scale – of destruction. This was not just a case of the lime-burners and stone-cutters, those perennial despoilers of Rome's heritage, working overtime to provide raw materials; many ancient buildings were demolished to make way for new schemes. The triumphal Arch of Gratian, Valentinian and Theodosius disappeared in the 1450s during the realignment of the Via S. Celso (now the Via dei Banchi); another arch, on the Corso, was swept away to allow the rebuilding of S. Maria in Via Lata. The remains of the Temple of Hercules Invictus near the Circus Maximus were demolished by Pope Sixtus IV. And in 1499 Alexander VI razed the Vatican pyramid – the so-called Tomb of Romulus – in order to create the Via Alexandrina leading from the Vatican palace to the Castel S. Angelo; the first straight street laid in Rome since antiquity.

Of course the stone-cutters and lime-burners played their part as well. Whole buildings were systematically plundered for their stone. The Colosseum remained, as it had long been, a giant quarry. (The rubble left by the 1349 earthquake provided many easy pickings.) Now, however, it was brought under the control of the popes. They proved as enthusiastic as anybody in their use of it. Between September 1451 and May 1452 Pope Nicholas V authorized the removal of 2,522 cartloads of stone from the site to furnish materials for his various building projects. The Ponte Sisto, built by Sixtus IV for the 1475 Jubilee – to provide an additional crossing to the Vatican, and prevent any repeat of the disaster of 1450 – was constructed largely with blocks from the same source. (Sixtus also converted much of what was left of the so-called Bridge of Horatius Cocles into cannonballs.)

Against this campaign of devastation there were some voices of dissent. Poggio and Biondo both wept over the losses to posterity, while the classical scholar Evangelista

Maddaleni di Capodiferro composed Latin epigrams excoriating papal vandalism. Pius II – a passionate humanist who, before his elevation to the papacy, had written a poem lamenting the work of the lime-burners – tried to legislate against the general plunder. But to little avail. And, indeed, he ignored his own strictures, dismantling one of the colonnades of the Portico of Octavia to gather building materials for the ongoing work at the Vatican palace.

In the second decade of the sixteenth century Raphael complained to the then pope, Leo X, that during the twelve years he had been in Rome so 'many beautiful things have been destroyed'. He urged conservation, and even received a brief – in 1515 – to halt the further destruction of old marbles. He must have struggled to enforce it. The urge to build always outweighed the urge to preserve. It remains an arresting fact that more of the ancient city was destroyed by the Renaissance popes than by all the barbarians of the Dark Ages.

This is not altogether surprising. Great though the new interest in the classical past was, in all but a very few cases (such as that of Pomponio Leto, the neo-pagan founder of the Roman Academy), it went hand in hand with a conventional Christian piety. Rome's classical grandeur was considered important by the popes and their builders because it prefigured what would become the greater grandeur of the new Christian city.

This twin perspective was also shared by most of the educated visitors who flocked to Rome during this period: they wanted both to attend the Christian shrines – for the remission of their sins – and to take in the classical ruins. Giovanni Rucellai, a cultured Florentine merchant (he commissioned Alberti to design his *palazzo*), when he visited Rome for the Jubilee in 1450, spent his mornings at the principal basilicas, and his afternoons in search of antiquities. This was probably the normal practice. What, though, did these visitors look at during their crowded days? What did they regard as the key locations on the Christian tour; and what – for them – were the most important classical monuments?

The circuit of Rome's religious sites was well established. Short, cheap, pilgrim guides to Rome's churches were plentiful throughout the period: the popular *Indulgentiae ecclesiarum Urbis* went through over sixty editions between 1475 and 1523. Several rather more ambitious fifteenth- and sixteenth-century guidebooks, however, sought to combine the two strands of interest – Christian and classical – in parallel. They list the churches in one part, ranking them by their spiritual power – the relics they contained and the indulgences that might be received by visiting them. Then they give an account of the classical sites, with their new improved ascriptions.

Although the spiritual hierarchy of Rome's churches remained largely unchanged since the early Middle Ages (with St Peter's at the top, followed by S. Giovanni in Laterano and the other major basilicas), now almost every church, however small, had its special feast day or days on which an indulgence might be granted to all who visited.

Religious potency, however, was no longer their sole point of interest for those visiting Rome's churches. The artistic concerns and enthusiasms of the period also came to play a part. This is reflected in the pages of the most influential guidebook of the period – Francesco Albertini's *Opusculum de Mirabilibus Novae et Veteris Urbis Romae* (*A Little Work on the Old and New Wonders of Rome*). Published in 1510 and reprinted five times over the next thirteen years, it gives a vivid sense of the Renaissance visitor's experience and understanding of the city.

Albertini was a child of the Florentine Renaissance: he had been taught painting (like Michelangelo) by Domenico Ghirlandaio, read the classics with Politian, and studied verse with the poet Naldo Naldi. Since 1493 he had been chaplain of the Medici church of S. Lorenzo, and he came to Rome, in 1502, as part of the household of Cardinal Santoro. His book was written at the suggestion of another cardinal, who wished to a see a guide free from the 'fables and nonsense' of the old *Mirabilia*. Putting his education to good account, he combined all the recent advances in antiquarian scholarship and artistic innovation with a comprehensive knowledge of the city's churches and a keen appreciation for the ongoing work of the Renaissance popes and their cardinals. His book embodied the new vision of the renascent Rome.

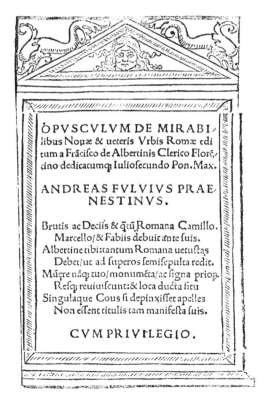

Within the conventional gazetteer of religious sites that he provided, several recently restored churches and chapels were singled out for special praise, and not

The title page of the 1510 edition of Albertini's *Opusculum*

on account of any spiritual distinction. S. Maria del Popolo and S. Pietro in Montorio were both described as 'pulcherrima' (very beautiful). And, indeed, the word is seeded throughout the whole book. 'Beauty' was a new concern, scarcely found in earlier, mediaeval, guides. For Albertini, however, it was clearly an important consideration. He applied the term with careful discrimination to a select handful of churches, palaces and other buildings, although – as both a Florentine and a humanist – he seems to have thought it most applicable to antique sculptures and Tuscan paintings.

He was very well informed about the recent productions of his various Florentine compatriots. He praised Fra Angelico's frescoes for Nicholas V's chapel at the Vatican (see plate XVII), and Filippino Lippi's cycle on the *Life of the Virgin* in the Carafa Chapel at S. Maria sopra Minerva. The decorations by Pinturicchio in S. Maria del Popolo were also singled out. All these works survive and, after centuries of neglect, are once more admired and even sought out. Another of Albertini's favourite pieces, however, has fallen rather out of view: at St Peter's he enthused over the bas-relief surrounding the altar: an 'opus mirandum' carved by Matteo Pollaiuolo with scenes of the Apostle's martyrdom. Removed during the rebuilding, it now has to be searched for in the church's 'grottoes'.

Among all the modern works listed, Albertini gave pride of place to the new Sistine Chapel. In this, of course, he established an enduring precedent. His praise of the space, however, was on account of its beautiful sequence of wall paintings (by his former teacher Ghirlandaio, Botticelli, *et al.*). Nevertheless, he did conclude his encomium with the first recorded mention of Michelangelo's painted ceiling, hailing it enthusiastically as an 'opus praeclarum'. This was up to the minute stuff: the work was still in progress, with only the central portion of the cycle completed and revealed to view.

Albertini's account of modern Rome was not confined to the city's churches. Contemporary secular architecture also received its due. He provided a thorough catalogue of the important ecclesiastical residences that were even then transforming the cityscape. Besides praising the Vatican palace and its recent additions, he accorded special prominence to the Cancellaria (or the Palazzo di S. Giorgio as it was then known), the Palazzo S. Marco, the palace of SS. Apostoli (created for Giuliano della Rovere, before he became Julius II, by Giuliano da Sangallo), and the palace of Cardinal Giovanni de'Medici (the future Pope Leo X). He also gave a loyal mention to his patron Cardinal Santoro's palace, and its 'beautiful' decorations.

His account of the glories of modern Rome was balanced with a no less thorough description of the ancient city and its remains. Just as there was a conventional hierarchy of Rome's churches, so an accepted order among Rome's classical monuments was established.

Albertini's list of the 'Seven Ancient Wonders' of the city included the Pantheon, the Colosseum, Hadrian's Mausoleum, the Aqueduct of Claudius, and the Baths of Diocletian. Within this group the Pantheon (considered as a pagan shrine rather than a Christian church) came to hold the highest place. Indeed it was during the Renaissance that the great cylindrical temple assumed a position as not merely the finest classical building in Rome, but the most perfect example of architecture *tout court* – and, indeed, the standard by which architectural excellence should be measured. This process of apotheosis was perhaps begun by Petrarch, who praised the temple church when he visited Rome in 1337. By the following century Flavio Biondo could describe S. Maria Rotonda as 'surpassing easily all the other churches in Rome', a verdict that set it above all the great basilicas built in Rome during the Christian era. And other humanist writers echoed his view – a view that endured for the best part of four hundred years.

The attractions of the Pantheon (and, indeed, of the Colosseum, Hadrian's Mausoleum, *et al.*) were – and remain – very evident to modern visitors. A rather less obvious inclusion on Albertini's list of Rome's 'Wonders' was the Forum of Nerva. This narrow 'forum', little more than a glorified thoroughfare sandwiched between

OPPOSITE A sixteenth-century drawing of the Pantheon
LEFT Two views of the half-buried 'Colonnacce' among the ruins of the Forum of Nerva

the obliterated Forum of Peace and the ruined Forum of Augustus, by the end of the fifteenth century contained little except a hulking pair of half-buried fluted Corinthian columns supporting a section of decorated entablature. This curious detail, once part of the elaborate colonnade that flanked the space, was known popularly as the 'Colonnacce' or 'those ugly columns'. The fact that the ground level had risen almost halfway up the column shafts certainly destroyed any sense of the monument's classical proportion, making the columns appear squat and top-heavy. Nevertheless it did allow spectators a close-up view of the beautifully carved entablature with its scenes of Roman domestic life (women spinning, weaving, and nursing), giving a rare sense of both the scale of classical architecture and the skill of Roman artisans.

For many classically inclined Renaissance visitors to Rome, however, the great ruins of the past were no longer the sole, or even the main, focus of interest. There was a whole new world of antiquity to be explored – and Albertini had covered it in detail.

The comprehensive listing that he provided of cardinals' palaces and *vigne* was not merely a glowing record of Rome's recent architecture. It provided him with an opportunity for mentioning which of them held collections of antique statuary. Most, it would seem. The admiration of classical sculpture was something new in Rome, but it had taken hold with real force.

There had, of course, always been a few ancient statues on very public view in and around the town: *Marforio* reclining in the Forum, the *Horse-Tamers* and the river gods set on the Quirinal. The collection of bronze statues had stood before the Lateran since the early Middle Ages. Gatherings of carved marbles and porphyries had been assembled in the porches of several churches, including St Peter's and S. Maria in Trastevere. An antique statue of a lion rending a horse had been set up outside the Palazzo del Senatore on the Capitol. And also, by this time, the *Bocca della Verità* – a classical fountain head carved with the face of a river god – had become a sight in the porch of S. Maria in Cosmedin. (Giovanni Rucellai, displaying a certain Renaissance scepticism, records how 'in ancient times it had the power to show when a woman played false to her husband.') Such works, however, had almost always been viewed as curiosities, wonders of scale and mystery, not particularly as things of beauty or historical import. That was now changing.

A new statue for the Palazzo dei Conservatori: gypsy girl or serving boy?

The aesthetic appreciation of classical statuary seems to have first taken hold in Florence during the fifteenth century. It certainly informed and inspired the great artistic flowering in that city. Lorenzo Ghiberti, the sculptor of the famous Baptistery doors, assembled in his studio a collection of classical works, including a beautiful relief of Venus and Vulcan in bed. He used them as models. Many other artists formed similar working collections. Donatello was a particularly keen student of classical sculpture; he owned a great many, and may have inspired Cosimo de'Medici to begin collecting antiquities. The Medici collection – continued and expanded by Cosimo's son Lorenzo – was only the most impressive of many. Throughout the period, dozens of wealthy Florentines, touched by the new humanist spirit, busily sought out classical sculptures – as well as gems, manuscripts, and other relics of antiquity.

Over the course of the quattrocento the novel but enduring notion was put forward that the finest examples of classical statuary represented the very height of artistic creation, the mark against which all later achievement must be measured.

The return of the papacy, after the years of exile and schism, brought these new enthusiasms and new ideas to Rome. It was fertile ground, literally. With so many building projects in hand, new (or, rather, ancient) works turned up almost weekly, as foundations were dug and old structures demolished. Some works were discovered broken up as building infill, others – like the *Laocoön* – were all but intact, and appeared to have been deliberately hidden. Among the luminaries of the papal court competition for these discoveries was fierce.

The prestige of classical statuary at Rome was, moreover, enhanced in 1471 when Sixtus IV presented the various bronze sculptures from the Campo Laterano (with the exception of the equestrian emperor†) to 'the people of Rome', installing them in – and outside – the new Palazzo dei Conservatori on the Capitoline. This gathering of works, a sort of treasure house of the city's classical inheritance, became the nucleus for the city's first museum. In due course other works were added to the *Lupa*, the *Spinario*, and the colossal head and hand. Among these was a beautiful bronze of a youth in a short tunic, now known as the *Camillus* (or serving boy) but then called the *Zingara* (or gypsy girl).

---

† The humanist scholars, although rightly convinced that the statue did not represent Constantine, continued to dispute its true identity. Various imperial models were suggested: Hadrian, Antoninus Pius, Lucius Verus; Poggio considered it to be a statue of Septimius Severus. And while Platina, in 1479, correctly recognized it as Marcus Aurelius, his ascription was not universally accepted.

Unlike many of the new cardinal-collectors, Sixtus IV seems to have been impressed more by the propagandist impact of such works than by their aesthetic power. When he came across a gilded bronze statue of Hercules, during his demolition of that demigod's temple near the Circus Maximus, he had it erected in front of the *palazzo* as a symbol of Rome's enduring power. And it was not the only symbolic intervention on view. At some moment before 1509 an anonymous sculptor added the two figures of the suckling Romulus and Remus beneath the teats of the bronze she-wolf to enhance the sculpture's point as an image of the nurturing *Mater Romanorum*. Nevertheless, the very fact of the Capitoline collection gave classical sculpture a new prominence and importance in Rome, and one that would grow with the decades. (It was to the Palazzo dei Conservatori that some hoped the *Laocoön* might be donated.)

BELOW AND OPPOSITE There were collections of antique sculpture in the courtyards of many of Rome's new *palazzi*.

The collection encouraged imitation among those fired by rather more artistic motives. By 1500 the courtyards of the Cancellaria, the Medici palace, and many of the other great residences that had sprung up across Rome, were crowded with assortments of recently discovered marble statuary – full figures, choice fragments, chipped busts, inscriptions, sarcophagi, vases and bas-reliefs. These private collections were declarations of taste and learning, as well as assertions of wealth. And they commanded the interest and admiration, not merely of rival collectors but also of less exalted observers.

Although the Palazzo dei Conservatori, as a public building, was readily accessible to interested visitors, other – privately owned – collections also seem to have been within reach. Many wealthy antiquarians were only too ready to show off their collections. The Milanese knight Giovanni da Tolentino, in his account of a visit to Rome in 1490, records how, while admiring the colossal *Horse-Tamers* on the Quirinal hill, he was approached by 'a Roman citizen' who said, 'What if you came across works in a private house probably not inferior to those you have seen in public? By Hercules, I have a few things we shall soon see.' Giovanni was then led off to

the Palazzo della Valle to inspect an impressive gathering of classical statues. (The two splendid goat-legged satyrs, balancing fruit baskets on their heads, now in the courtyard of the Palazzo Nuovo on the Capitoline, were among the stars of the della Valle collection.)

From the very beginning of the 1500s Cardinal Giuliano Cesarini was opening his collection to serious students, and others certainly followed his lead. Although Albertini's connections probably gave him privileged access to some private residences, he seems to have expected his readers to be able to follow up the recommendations he gave.

As knowledge of classical sculpture grew, so did appreciation.† Among the works pointed out by Albertini for special commendation were a satyr in the Medici collection, the *Rape of the Sabine Women* held by his patron Cardinal Santoro, a colossal crowned head in the gardens of the Palazzo S. Marco, and an image of Pompey the Great in the Sassi palace on the Via del Governo Vecchio. (It is frustratingly difficult to relate any of these works to extant pieces in Roman collections.)

Nevertheless, there can be no doubt that from its very inception the papal sculpture court at the Belvedere was regarded as the acme of all classical collections. It was supreme both in the work it contained and in the setting it provided. Albertini's guidebook, written only six years after the establishment of the sculpture court, devotes an entire chapter to describing its wonders.

By 1509 the collection had grown to include not only the beautiful *Apollo* ('which seems to speak') but also a statue of *Venus Felix* accompanied by Cupid, a powerful *Hercules and Antaeus*, and an image of the Emperor Commodus dressed as Hercules and holding the infant Hylas. Over the following two or three years these would be joined by more newly discovered masterworks: a reclining *Cleopatra* (now recognized as an image of Ariadne) and the twin recumbent river gods, *Tiber* and *Nile*. Remarkable though such works were, for Albertini – as for all Renaissance visitors – the highpoint of the Belvedere collection was indubitably the *Laocoön*.

---

† Roman pictorial art excited much less interest than Roman sculpture: less of it survived, and it was untransportable. Albertini does, however, list some examples: a mosaic of animals and birds in the church of S. Lucia in Silice salvaged from a Roman bath or temple, as well as some paintings visible amidst the ruins close to S. Pietro in Vincoli, and others just outside the town. He does not mention the decorated subterranean rooms of Nero's Golden House that had been discovered beneath the Esquiline in the 1480s, and investigated by a few intrepid artists and connoisseurs. Their decorative motifs – called 'grotesques' from the grottoes in which they were discovered – proved an inspiration for many painters, from Pinturicchio to Raphael.

For an age anxious to reconnect with the glory of the classical past, the fact that the statue had been praised by Pliny as the greatest work of its age ensured its status. But the image itself – through its drama, scale, workmanship, and indeed beauty – confirmed this primacy.

Set in its niche, it commanded the space. At this stage the missing limbs of the various figures were left unrestored.† But this in no way diminished the sculpture's power. Sadoletto, in his poem, described how, confronted with the sight of the Trojan priest wrestling vainly with the vengeful serpents, 'The mind recoils, and the mute image/ strikes the heart with a pity joined with no small terror.'

For many contemporary viewers the statue served as an *exemplum doloris*, a definitive representation of human pain. To some it suggested the woe very properly endured by the enemies of Pope Julius II. The humanist poet Evangelista di Capodiferro considered that the statue reflected the fate of Giovanni Bentivoglio, tyrant of Bologna, who, following defeat by the papal forces, was sent into exile together with his family.

Other viewers might be moved to different interpretations, but they were certainly stimulated to thought by the sculpture and its setting. The Belvedere sculpture court was, in the verdict of another humanist visitor, the ideal backdrop for philosophic contemplation; he likened it to the site beside the Ilissus near Athens where Plato had set his *Phaedrus*.

Among the many artists present in Rome, the *Laocoön* became a source not merely of contemplation, but of inspiration. On this score, as on so many others, Michelangelo led the way. He adopted, and adapted, the sculpture's defining traits for his series of naked quasi-angelic figures – the *Ignudi* – framing the various scenes of the Sistine Chapel ceiling. Depicting the nude was a new concern, and a new challenge, for the painters of the Renaissance, and one that was inevitably informed by the rediscovery of antique art.

---

† There was much debate about the position of Laocoön's missing arm. In 1506 the humanist Giovanni Cavalcanti asserted that it must have been raised, and that – following Virgil's text – it probably held a spear. Michelangelo, however, considered that it would have been bent. A copy of the statue carved by Bandinelli in the 1520s was completed with the addition of a partly bent right arm. In 1532 Michelangelo's sometime pupil Montorsoli was commissioned by Pope Clement VII to restore many of the works in the Belvedere sculpture court; he made a left arm for the Apollo, and a new, upstretched right arm for Laocoön. In 1906, however, the missing original arm was – miraculously – found, much battered, in a Roman builder's yard. It was – as Michelangelo had predicted – bent back upon itself. In 1942 this arm was fixed to the statue; it is the one seen today.

Two of Michelangelo's *Ignudi*, from the ceiling of the Sistine Chapel; their contorted poses reflected the form of the *Laocoön*.

In taking the *Laocoön*, with its highly charged *contrapposto* pose and straining musculature, as his principal model, Michelangelo forged something both spectacular and novel. In the words of one art historian, he 'created nothing less than a whole new canon of form – a canon characterized by more developed muscles, narrower hips, broader shoulders, a thicker torso, and a higher centre of gravity, which together communicated greater strength and gracefulness than ever before.'

Michelangelo's vision would influence a whole generation of artists. In the short term the very fact of his known enthusiasm for the *Laocoön* was enough to encourage others to draw upon it. Raphael, who arrived in Rome in 1508, and came to exceed even Michelangelo in his reverence for classical models, used Laocoön's head for the portrait of Homer in his fresco of *Parnassus* in the Vatican apartments.

There were, however, inevitably some less enthusiastic opinions. Not a few churchmen considered it quite inappropriate that the vicar of Christ should have a collection of profane classical statues. Gianfrancesco Pico, a puritanical follower of Savonarola, denounced the sculpture court in a poem published in 1512. He was ignored. There was rather more alarm when Adriaan Boeyens, an austere Fleming, was raised to the papacy in 1522, as Adrian VI. He dismissed the *Laocoön* and its companions as 'pagan idols', and threatened to disperse them. Fortunately he died the following year.

For Julius II, however, there had been no such conflict. He conceived his collection of classical statuary as enhancing the prestige of the papacy. And in having the very finest example of antique workmanship as the centrepiece of the display, he triumphantly achieved that purpose. The image of the Trojan priest and his sons was a reminder, too, that Rome – according to the legend of Virgil's *Aeneid* – had been born from defeated Troy. Now it was being reborn. Set in its niche in the Belvedere sculpture court, the *Laocoön* provided visitors with an arresting symbol of the continuity between Rome's glorious past and her glorious present.

·VI·

BAROQUE ROME

J OHN EVELYN came to Rome on 4 November 1644 'about 5 at night, and being greatly perplex't for a convenient lodging, wanderd up and downe on horse back, till one conducted us to one Monsieur Petit, a French man, who entertained strangers, being the very utmost house on the left hand as one ascends Monte Trinità, formerly Mons Pincius, neere the Piazza Spagnola. Here I alighted, delivered my horse to the Venurino, and having bargain'd with mine host for 20 crownes a moneth, I causd a good fire to be made in my Chamber, and so went to bed being very wet.'

When dawn broke the next day, the twenty-four-year-old Evelyn would have looked out upon a city of crowded rooftops, slender towers and looming cupolas, with the distant ridge of the tree-tufted Janiculum providing a backdrop for the scene. (The view today, from the top of the Spanish Steps, is not so very different; though in Evelyn's time, in place of the steps themselves, there was only a grassy bank running down to the piazza.)

To a young man of that time it must have appeared as a panorama of metropolitan prosperity. Rome was not merely a flourishing city but a resurgent one, resurgent in spirit and in form. Much of its new energy, however, had been fired by the dire troubles of recent times, troubles that had abruptly broken into the golden days of the High Renaissance at Rome.

The first tremor had been felt in 1517, when Martin Luther, an Augustinian friar from Wittenberg in Saxony, published his long list of grievances about the corrupt practices and false doctrines that had grown up within the Roman Church: the scandalous lives of some clergy – and some popes – the perfunctory nature of many services, the lack of vernacular texts, the accretion of superstitious beliefs, the selling of church offices, and, above all, the hugely lucrative trade in 'indulgences'– special papal favours acquired either by pilgrimage to Rome or a cash payment – that paid off the spiritual debts acquired by sin. (Although originally these indulgences could only be gained by the living for their own salvation, the concept had been extended – and the market thereby greatly increased – so that they could also be used to release the souls of the dead from purgatory.)

Luther's call for change had not been well received in Rome, but it found many echoes across northern Europe, among the German states, in Switzerland, in Scandinavia, in Bohemia, in parts of France, in Scotland, and (in due course) in the England of Henry VIII. As this Protestant Reformation spread it may have become riven by internal theological divisions, but the broad movement served to break the established power of the Roman Church.

The unfolding religious revolution was, moreover, matched by catastrophe at Rome. As the temporal ruler of the Papal States, Pope Clement VII's policy of supporting the Italian ambitions of the Kingdom of France against those of the Habsburg Holy Roman Emperor Charles V (who was also king of Spain and ruler of the Low Countries) proved disastrous. In 1525 the French king, François I, was defeated and captured at the Battle of Pavia. Two years later a huge imperial army under the command of the Duke of Bourbon, having re-entered Italy, threatened to mutiny over the non-payment of wages. To avert the crisis the troops were allowed to march on Rome. The city, unprepared and underdefended, soon fell.

The Piazza di Spagna and SS. Trinità del Monte before the construction of the Spanish Steps, from Totti's 1638 guidebook *Ritratto di Roma Moderna*

Rome was overrun by some thirty thousand ill-disciplined soldiers, and an orgy of destruction followed. Thousands were killed and raped, tens of thousands fled, and although damage to actual buildings was limited, the churches and palaces were ransacked. Only a small proportion of the imperial army had Protestant sympathies, but the desecration of sacred sites was universal. Anything portable and precious was taken. It was said that not a single chalice remained in Rome after the sack. The papal apartments at the Vatican were used for stabling horses, and Raphael's frescoes were defaced with graffiti. Rome's antiquities, however, too heavy to be carried off, escaped largely untouched.

Henceforth imperial Habsburg power became the dominant force among the Italian states, while, as a psychological blow, the Sack of Rome was a cataclysm to match the earlier predations of the Goths and Vandals. To many Romans the disaster seemed to be a sign from God. As one bishop exclaimed: 'We are not citizens of Holy Rome but of unholy Babylon; let us reform!'

It was not, however, until the end of the 1530s that a new pope, Paul III (Farnese), took up in earnest the challenge posed by the Protestant reformers, launching a vigorous programme of change – a 'Counter Reformation'. He confirmed the Jesuit order as the militant wing of this movement. A great church council was convoked in the northern Italian city of Trento to map out new policies for the reform of Roman worship, spiritual education, church design and decoration, and all aspects of Christian life. It sat for almost twenty years, from 1545 to 1563.

Rome began to revive, in energy, in wealth, in self-confidence, in appearance, in size. The inhabited part of the town spread gradually eastwards, away from the river, encroaching on the Viminal, Esquiline, Quirinal and Pincian hills. (Evelyn's lodgings were in this last quarter.) Cardinals continued to proclaim their wealth and power through their palaces and villas. Between the Sack of Rome and the end of the sixteenth century over fifty new churches were built in the city: to accommodate the directives of the Council of Trent they tended to be larger and more spacious than their predecessors, designed for preaching to large congregations, for the sharing of Holy Communion, and for the display and devotion of the host (a new feature of Counter Reformation liturgy).

After more than a century – and following numerous modifications of design – the vast new basilica of St Peter's was all but completed. Its great lead-covered dome dominated the western horizon. The Roman Church had reasserted its strength through the Counter Reformation, and this stupendous edifice was the embodiment of its triumph. It presaged a new style. The sober unadorned grandeur of late sixteenth-century Roman architecture had given way to a new exuberance and decorative invention. This shift could be seen in many of Rome's recent buildings: rigid classical discipline was

Giovanni Battista Falda's 1676 map of Rome

trumped by curving lines, by a pervading sense of light and movement. The style came to be called Baroque, the name perhaps deriving from *barocco*, the Portuguese word for a misshapen pearl. It was the spirit of the new Rome. And it was a spirit that Evelyn would have sensed on that first morning, looking out upon the jostling domes, cupolas, lanterns and other architectural flourishes.

Evelyn came as a new type of visitor; not a pilgrim, or a supplicant at the papal court, or an artist, or even a scholar: he was an educated Englishman who had simply come to have a look. Anxious to escape from England at the outbreak of the Civil War, he had received royal permission to travel, and was wandering about Europe. Taking advantage of the thaw in relations between England and the papacy, he came to Rome.† He spent almost seven months in the city, and over the course of that autumn, winter and spring he came to know it well. He explored it as a tourist – inquiring and open-minded.

He was not a lone figure. Others like him were converging from all over Europe, and three years later in 1648, when the Thirty Years War came to an end, numbers only increased. But Evelyn left, in his so-called 'Diary', a wonderfully thorough and very engaging account of his stay. This document, produced for the entertainment of the author's family, is – for all its touches of idiosyncratic wit and insight – a thoroughly representative account of the seventeenth-century north European's experience of Rome.

† For almost a century Rome had been all but barred to Protestants. A Roman Inquisition had been established in 1542 specifically to prevent the spread of Protestantism in Italy; and several unwary English Protestants who came to Rome, either by accident or drawn by an ineluctable curiosity to see the city's wonders, ended up in their dungeons. One fanatic, Richard Atkins, who, in 1581, made his way to Rome in the fond hope of converting the pope to Protestantism, was even tortured and executed.

Relations between England and the papacy were particularly bad throughout the long reign of Elizabeth I (1558–1603). The pope refused to recognize the Protestant daughter of Anne Boleyn as a rightful monarch. Of the numerous Catholic plots against the queen's life several were hatched at Rome. Moreover, in 1579, an English College was established at Rome by the Jesuits to train priests for the planned reconversion of England. Some forty priests trained at the college were captured and executed (or martyred) by the English authorities as they tried to fulfil their mission.

Rome came to be seen in England as a seat of dangerous sedition both temporal and spiritual: part of a sixteenth-century Axis of Evil. English passports of the period – 'licences for travel' – specifically forbade the holder from visiting Rome. It was only with the accession of the more religiously sympathetic Charles I in 1625, coinciding with the pontificate of the more tolerant Pope Urban VIII (Barberini), that relations began significantly to improve, and the numbers of English visitors began to increase.

Indeed, while the document's engaging colour derives from Evelyn's own observations, its thoroughness is due to the fact that Evelyn, in writing up his notes, some years after the visit, supplemented both his memory and his memoranda with much factual information drawn from the popular guidebooks of the period.† If this gives a slightly spurious omniscience to Evelyn's text (made even more spurious by Evelyn's habit of occasionally mistranslating or mistranscribing his cribs), it enhances the representative nature of the account. After all, the books he used – or others very similar – were exactly what most seventeenth-century visitors carried with them to direct their steps as they explored the city. They set out what was considered important, reflected the established canons of taste, and relayed the current cultural gossip.

Evelyn, of course, being a well connected young man (an Oxford graduate and scion of the Surrey gentry), had a few additional sources of help and information. He carried introductions to several useful figures in the city, including a couple of expatriate doctors, and – though he himself was an Anglican – several priests associated with the Venerable English College.

In his explorations Evelyn found the impression of that first morning amply confirmed. Rome, for so long the epitome of fallen grandeur, was flourishing 'beyond all expectation'. There was a hum of excitement about the city, with its elegant new streets and squares, its spacious new churches and *palazzi*, its richly painted house fronts, its ever-active building works. There were people too: over the previous hundred years the population had more than doubled, reaching 114,000: of European cities only Paris and London had more inhabitants. And there was money. The local nobles and cardinals displayed their wealth. The Italian love for luxurious wheeled vehicles was already apparent: Evelyn considered the splendid coaches that thronged the fashionable piazzas, 'generally the richest and largest that I ever saw'.

After over a millennium of relative desuetude, Rome was no longer a city tinged with a sense of decay and emptiness; it was a modern metropolis. It was still, of course, the great repository of ancient art and culture but – as John Raymond noted in his guidebook, *Il Mercurio Italico* – a new balance was being established between the past

---

† Evelyn's principal sources were J.H. von Pflaumern's *Mercurius Italicus* (1628), John Raymond's English-language *Il Mercurio Italico* (1648), Pompilio Totti's *Ritratto di Roma antica* (1627) and *Ritratto di Roma moderna* (1638) and G. Baglione's *Le nove chiese di Roma* (1639). Although Raymond's book did not appear until after his return from the Continent, Evelyn is known to have had Pflaumern's volume – first issued in 1628 – with him during his stay in Rome, and it is likely that he also owned the other titles at that time.

and present: 'the new ever emulous to exceed the old, the remnants of the old adding to the splendour of the new'.

Rome owed its new splendour not merely to individual buildings. The old muddle of mediaeval streets had in many areas been supplanted by attempts at rational order. The bold beginnings made by the early Renaissance popes in the Borgo around St Peter's had been decisively carried across the river. The two Medici pontiffs Leo X and Clement VII had been responsible for the construction of a pair of long diagonal streets on either side of the Corso. All three converged at the Piazza del Popolo to create a dramatic *trivium* or trident; it was an effect that would be replicated elsewhere across the city, becoming a distinctive feature of the new Rome. In the 1560s, another Medici, Pope Pius IV, had encouraged the expansion of the *abitato*, with the laying of the broad straight Via Pia on the Quirinal hill.

Most, however, had been achieved by the zealous reforming Pope Sixtus V (Peretti). In 1585, together with his brilliant Swiss-born architect, Domenico Fontana, he had mapped out a new urban plan, determined to make the city a fit setting for the returning crowds of pilgrims excited by the ideals of the Counter Reformation. Wide, straight thoroughfares were laid between the city's great pilgrimage centres.† The central hub from which they radiated was the newly restored church of S. Maria Maggiore. These great roads, running out beyond the Aurelian Walls, to the old extramural basilicas gave scope to Roman expansion for centuries to come. Rome, for so long a warren of alleys, became a city of imposing vistas. Looking back down the Via Pia (now the XX Settembre) towards the Palazzo Quirinale and the statues of Monte Cavallo, Evelyn declared it 'to be one of the most glorious sights for state & magnificence that any City in the Earth can show the Traveller'.

To give even greater impact to this new urban layout, several of the major junctions were marked with towering obelisks. These ancient Egyptian granite pillars had been brought to Rome during the Imperial Age to adorn the city, and had been toppled, broken and buried, for the most part, over the course of the ensuing centuries. Only the one standing before St Peter's – surmounted by its bronze orb supposedly containing the ashes of Julius Caesar – had remained unscathed from classical times.

---

† The enduring notion of Rome's 'seven pilgrim churches' – St Peter's, S. Giovanni in Laterano, S. Paolo fuori le Mura, S. Maria Maggiore, S. Lorenzo fuori le Mura, S. Sebastiano, and S. Croce – was established in 1552, when the Florentine preacher and future saint Filippo Neri urged the Romans to join him in a tour of them on the Thursday before Lent. This pious circuit became first an annual event and then a Roman religious institution.

The idea of realigning this obelisk on the axis of the new basilica had been mooted for several years as work on the church advanced, but it was only achieved in 1586 'with vast Cost, & most stupendous invention' by the formidable pairing of Sixtus V and Domenico Fontana. The story of its translation assumed the status of an heroic legend. For, despite Fontana's elaborate system of pulleys, and the efforts of nine hundred men, together with seventy-five horses, disaster almost struck. As the forty-ton monolith was being raised in its new position, the hawsers began to give way. The workmen had been commanded to absolute silence, so that they might hear Fontana's commands, but one of them – a sailor from Bordighera – seeing what was happening, cried out in panic, 'Give water to the ropes!' Just in time water was brought. The fibres stiffened, the ropes held and the obelisk was raised. (In recognition of the workman's vigilance, Bordighera still has the honour of providing the palm leaves for the Palm Sunday service at St Peter's.)

After the successful re-erection of the Vatican needle, other – fallen and damaged – obelisks were sought out and repaired. One was retrieved from the Mausoleum of Augustus and sited behind S. Maria Maggiore. The long-toppled needle erected by Constantius II in the Circus Maximus (see page 43), was excavated and placed before the Lateran, while a second from the same spot was erected in the Piazza del Popolo. Each was topped with a cross. (The ball from the top of the Vatican Obelisk was removed to the Palazzo dei Conservatori.) In this Christianized guise the obelisks became a defining element of Sixtus V's transformed cityscape.

Fountains were another ubiquitous feature of the new Rome. At great expense Sixtus V created a new aqueduct, the Acqua Felice, the first since classical times; while extensive repair work also revived some elements of the old Roman system, bringing water back into the centre of the city and even to Trastevere. The terminus of the Acqua Felice, on the Via Pia, was a magnificent sculptural affair created by Domenico Fontana, showing Moses striking the rock, flanked by Aaron and Gideon, the children of Israel and several ruminative camels. Domenico's son, Giovanni, helped to create the imposing five-bayed architectural Fontanone, near Porta S. Pancrazio, marking the end of the old Aqua Traiana, which had been restored by Pope Paul V. These large termini fed dozens of smaller fountains. Almost every street now possessed a fount of some description, while the main piazzas boasted elaborate creations. The pair of fountains in the Piazza Farnese, adapted from antique sarcophagi, were much admired, while Evelyn praised the three 'noble' fountains in the Piazza Navona, then the city's principal marketplace. (They were not the three yet more noble ones, erected soon after, that stand in the piazza now.)

Rome, in the course of the half-century before Evelyn's arrival, had also become a city of gardens. They were everywhere. Part of the old Circus Maximus was turned over to allotments, while the great ruined drum of the Mausoleum of Augustus had been converted, by the Soderini family, into an elaborate circular garden. On the slopes of the Palatine, overlooking the eastern end of the Forum, Cardinal Alessandro Farnese had created an elegant terraced park, the Orti Farnesiani, while opposite, amidst the ruins of the Basilica Nova (or the 'Temple of Peace', as it was still called), flourished the enchanting hanging gardens of Monsignor Silvestri. But it was away from the crowded core of the *abitato* where space was still plentiful that the real change had been effected. The modest *vigne* of the early Renaissance cardinals had given way to grand villas and extensive formal parterres.

The Villa Montalto (on the site of the present railway station) was set in elegantly laid out gardens, dotted with fountains, ponds, statues, inscriptions and reliefs than which, Evelyn recorded, 'nothing can be more solemn and stately'. In fact for solemnity, stateliness, scale and everything else they were rivalled by numerous others: the still-extant gardens of the Villa Borghese, created by Cardinal Scipione Borghese at the beginning of the century, were 'an Elysium of delight' with their trick fountains, grottoes, streams and groves, to say nothing of a vivarium containing 'Estriges, Peacoks, Swanns, Cranes & c.' And they stood near to the great classical sculpture parks assembled in the grounds of the Villa Giustiniani, the Villa Medici and Villa Ludovisi. It was said that the gardener at the Palazzo del Quirinale (greatly enlarged for Sixtus V by Fontana) received 2,000 scudi a year for maintaining the magnificent hedges of juniper, myrtle, laurel and box. But this was only a third of what was spent on the upkeep of the stupendous gardens of the Villa Mattei (or the Celimontana as it is now called) on the Caelian hill.

The Villa Mattei and its gardens

Nor was formal elegance confined to the horticulturalists. The city at last had a new and worthy civic centrepiece: the Piazza del Campidoglio. Beginning in 1538, Michelangelo, at the request of Pope Paul III, had redesigned the public buildings on the Capitoline, creating an ordered Renaissance piazza, a new 'forum', framed with three symmetrical palaces, and reached – from the west side – by a monumental graded ramp, the Cordonata. The sturdy balustrade bounding the square was adorned with antique marble statues. (By Evelyn's day these included monumental statues of Castor and Pollux, the celebrated 'Trophies of Marius', brought from their old site on the Esquiline hill in 1590, and two rather crudely wrought emperors – Constantine and his second son, Constantine II.) At the centre of the piazza, rising on its plinth from a slightly convex oval pavement, stood the bronze equestrian statue (by then generally accepted as an image of Marcus Aurelius) that had formerly stood before the Lateran.

The harmonious disposition of space, of modern buildings and rare antiquities, seemed a fitting form not only for the ideals of the new Rome but also for the ancient heart of the classical city – 'certainly', as Evelyn declared, 'one of the most renowned places in the World'. Although the prestige of the ancient Capitoline was well understood by classically educated seventeenth-century visitors, archaeological knowledge of the site was very limited. By Evelyn's day, it was universally – if erroneously – accepted that the Temple of Jupiter Optimus Maximus had stood on the site of the Aracoeli; the last vestiges of its actual platform, at the other end of the hill, had been levelled and obliterated with the construction of the Palazzo Caffarelli in the 1590s.

Arriving from the Protestant north, Evelyn was highly curious about the Catholic rites and rituals that he encountered at Rome. And without harming his conscience or attracting undue attention to himself, he seems to have been able to satisfy that curiosity. Indeed the spectacle and theatre of the Roman Church was emerging as one of the tourist diversions of the city. Such novelties as hearing young boys, of eight or nine, delivering orations at St Filippo Neri's Chiesa Nuova, or listening to the sublime singing of the castrati at the same church, to the accompaniment of 'Theorbas, Haspsicors, & Viols', were eagerly sought out.

Evelyn was fortunate to witness a 'Possessio', the grand procession made by the new pope, Innocent X (Pamphili), as he rode from the Vatican to take possession of the old episcopal seat at the Lateran. He was also granted an audience with the new pontiff, and kissed his toe. But even the regular ceremonies of the Christian calendar provided plenty of entertainment. On Christmas Eve, Evelyn – together with many others – stayed up all night, 'desirous to see the many extraordinary Ceremonies perform'd in their Churches'. (He specially enjoyed a nativity play acted out with giant puppets at S. Maria sopra Minerva.) And there was a similar intensity of activity during Holy Week, with curious visitors 'running from Church to Church' and the whole town steeped in 'buisy devotion, greate silence, and unimaginable Superstition'. Although many Protestant visitors had some qualms about the 'heathernish pomp' of the hooded flagellants parading through the streets on Maundy Thursday, there seems to have been genuine admiration for the splendour of much Roman Catholic church ritual.

Another aspect of the city's exoticism was its conspicuous and much put upon Jewish community. In 1555 Pope Paul IV had established a walled ghetto for them, close to the Tiber, just south of the Theatre of Marcellus. They were locked in each night. A host of punitive regulations was enacted against them: they were barred from owning property; they could live only by 'brokage & usury'; they were forced to attend a weekly sermon at an oratory near Ponte Sisto (a tradition which continued until 1847); they had to wear yellow hats. (The original ordinance had designated red hats but this was countermanded after a short-sighted cardinal had inadvertently saluted a Jew in the street, mistaking him for a fellow prince of the Church.)

Evelyn shared in the general curiosity about the life of the ghetto. He readily accepted an invitation from a Jewish acquaintance to attend a circumcision ceremony. ('The Rabby lifting the belly of the child to his face, & taking the yard all blody into his mouth he suck'd it a pretty while, having before taken a little Vinegar, all which together with the blood he spit out into a glasse of red-wine of the Colour of French wine.') He balked, however, at drinking from the glass when it was passed around the congregation.

Intriguing though such excursions might be, they remained merely a sideshow to the main event. Rome's great attraction was as a repository of treasures and curiosities: treasures of art, of architecture, treasures of religious history, treasures of antiquity and curiosities of every type. These, for the seventeenth-century visitor, were the things that made Rome unique, the things that had to be seen; and there were many of them. The prospect was almost daunting. Indeed one of the first things that Evelyn did after his arrival, being anxious 'not to waste any time', was to engage what he called a 'Sights Man' – one of those 'Persons in Rome, who get their living onely by leading strangers about to see the Citty'. These guides had emerged as a distinctive feature of Roman life. They might be hired at certain established inns, although the best known *cicerone* of the period was Giovanni Alto (or Hans Gross), a very tall member of the Vatican Swiss Guard.

The itinerary offered by such 'Sights Men' was gradually becoming formalized. It fell into three parts, covering the city's principal churches, its grand palaces, and (in prime position) the great ruins of classical antiquity.

The Pantheon, by Gian Paolo Panini, 1732

Frescoes from the walls of the Sistine Chapel
II *The Calling of Peter and Andrew,* by Domenico Ghirlandaio
III *Christ Handing the Keys to Peter,* by Perugino

IV

View of the Campo Vaccino, Rome, by Claude Lorrain, 1636

V

The *Sala Clementina* in the Vatican, with decorations by Cherubino Alberti and others

VI

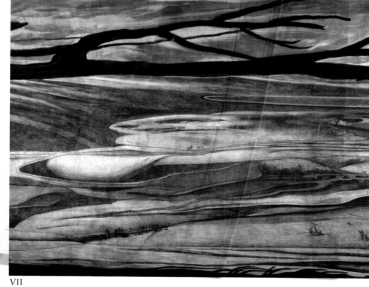

VII

Perspective frescoes by Jean-François Niceron in the cloister of SS. Trinità del Monte
VI *St Francis of Paola* VII A detail of the same fresco

VIII

VIII *The Liberation of St Peter*, by Raphael, in the *Stanza di Eliodoro*, in the Vatican
IX *The Transfiguration*, by Raphael, in the Vatican Pinacoteca

IX

x

The Deposition, by Daniele da Volterra, in SS. Trinità del Monte

XI

XII

The Last Communion of St Jerome,
by Domenichino, in the Vatican Pinacoteca

The Vision of St Romuald,
by Andrea Sacchi, in the Vatican Pinacoteca

Ancient Rome,
by Gian Paolo Panini, 1757

XIV

XIV *Shelley at the Baths of Caracalla*, by Joseph Severn, in the Keats-Shelley Memorial House
XV Supposed portrait of *Beatrice Cenci*, attributed to Guido Reni, in the Galleria Nazionale d'Arte
Antica, Palazzo Barberini

XVI

The Calling of St Matthew, by Caravaggio, in S. Luigi dei Francesi

XVII

Fresco by Fra Angelico, in the Chapel of Nicholas V in the Vatican
Pope Sixtus Handing over the Treasures of the Church to St Lawrence

XVIII

St Jerome, by Leonardo da Vinci, in the Vatican Pinacoteca

Most tours began with a thorough investigation of the Forum Romanum – or 'Campo Vaccino' as it was more familiarly called. Although the area might now be a pasture for cows, with an impressive drinking fountain erected for their convenience, it was very much more open and attractive than it had been for many centuries. Over two hundred houses and other structures had been cleared from the site in 1534, in preparation for the triumphal procession devised by Pope Paul III to welcome the Emperor Charles V back from his conquest of Tunis. And although some houses did still border the space, they were interspersed by the elegant façades and cupolas of half a dozen churches, all remodelled if not rebuilt in the forty years before Evelyn's visit (see plate IV).

S. Lorenzo in Miranda, with its dramatic broken pediment, caged within the columns of the ancient Temple of Antoninus and Faustina, dominated the Campo's northern flank, together with the church of SS. Cosma e Damiano; the graceful classical façade of S. Francesco Romana (as S. Maria Nova had been renamed in 1608) looked down from the eastern end, sentinel between the Orti Farnesiani and the hanging gardens of Monsignor Silvestri; on the southern side was the impressive (though now demolished) S. Maria Liberatrice, its ordered Renaissance front and cupola modelled on Il Gesù; while at the western end of the space jostled S. Giuseppe de Fangelami, guild church of the carpenters, with its proto-Baroque details, S. Adriano (in the old Senate House, or – as Evelyn thought – in the old Temple of Saturn), and Pietro da Cortona's SS. Martina e Luca, the painters' church, with its exuberant and innovatory curved façade.

The sixteenth century had seen the vestiges of several monuments in the Forum obliterated completely, carted off to provide lime or stone for the ongoing construction of St Peter's. (Paul III had accelerated the process by granting exclusive excavation rights to the Deputies of the Fabric of St Peter's.) But from what remained the weeds and the lean-tos had been stripped away. A handful of imposing ruins now rose up – distinct and largely unencumbered – from the undulating plane of masonry-strewn scrubland.

Some rose further than others. The three fluted Corinthian columns of the Temple of Castor and Pollux (or Jupiter Stator, as Evelyn's contemporaries had it) dominated the scene. The lower part of the Arch of Septimius Severus remained choked with 'ruines and earth', while the Temple of Vespasian and Titus (Jupiter Tonans, to Evelyn) at the foot of the Capitol, stood buried almost to its column tops. Many celebrated monuments existed only as names. Some 'heapes' of stone on the lower slopes of the Palatine were pointed out to Evelyn as 'Cicero's Palace'; and 'from there we passed by the place, rather than any signs, of the Lake into which Curtius is sayd to have precipitated himself for the love of his country.'

For all the advances in archaeology and epigraphy achieved during, and since, the Renaissance, many of the old (mis-)ascriptions persisted, as did several of the old stories from the *Mirabilia*. For seventeenth-century visitors the massive ruins of the Basilica Nova at the eastern end of the Forum continued to be pointed out as the 'Temple of Peace'. And it was still believed – or at least reported – that the building's great hexagonal vault had collapsed at the exact moment of Christ's birth.

The monumental *Horse-Tamers* on 'Monte Cavallo' – though set on smart new pedestals by Sixtus V – continued to be credited to Phidias and Praxiteles. In the inscription recording the refurbishment they were described as representing Alexander the Great with his horse Bucephalus. But this notion, which had been prompted by the idea that Constantine might have brought the statues over from Alexandria to adorn his baths, soon fell out of favour. Urban VIII removed the offending tablet in 1634, and the guidebooks subsequently asserted that the statues (in spite of their supposed early Greek authorship) represented the famous horses 'sent to Nero out of Armenia', accompanied by two naked slaves, or else (rather more plausibly) Castor and Pollux with their steeds.

The pace of destruction, which had so paradoxically quickened with the return of the Renaissance popes, was continued. Sixtus V's energetic urban regeneration schemes had swept away many classical fragments, including the great but tottering structure of the Septizonium. The unending need for building materials – and the lucrative monopoly granted to the Fabbrica (the office in charge of the construction of St Peter's) reduced such long-conspicuous ruins as the Temple of Mars Ultor in the Forum of Augustus and the Temple of Minerva in the Forum of Nerva to mere lumps. Pope Urban VIII (Barberini) removed the bronze beams from the porch of the Pantheon to provide material for Bernini's gigantic *baldacchino* at St Peter's, provoking the famous squib 'Quod non fecerunt Barbari, fecerunt Barberini' (What the barbarians did not do, the Barberini did).

With so much lost to view, the more complete survivals were especially prized. The 'Temple' – or Arch – of Janus Quadrifrons, the Arch of Constantine, the Pyramid of Cestius, the Theatre of Marcellus (despite still being home to the Savelli family), the Columns of Trajan and Marcus Aurelius (now topped respectively with statues of St Peter and St Paul) received glowing praise as 'pretty intire' antiquities.

The Colosseum, of course, continued to awe with its bulk. And, for the first time, visitors began to question the policy of its systematic spoliation. That it should have been vandalized to provide building-stone for the Cancellaria and the Palazzo Farnese was, as Raymond put it, something 'which I much merveile at'. The guidebooks supported the sense of the arena's magnificence with reams of statistics: the vast dimensions, the thousands of beasts slain, the millions spent, and the hordes of spectators who enjoyed it all. Inside, though, the amphitheatre presented a rather melancholy spectacle of decay. (Sixtus V had considered converting it into a woollen-factory to give employment to reformed prostitutes.) Built against the lowest tier of seats was the little chapel of S. Maria della Pietà nel Coliseo, established around 1519 and presided over by a not very lonely hermit; Evelyn climbed to the top of the chapel to admire the view.

Although there had been a chapel of some description in the arena since the late sixth century, the 1600s witnessed a growing sense of the Colosseum itself as a holy place. The Renaissance recognition that the building had been the site of the Roman Games (rather than a Temple of the Sun) had led on to the idea that it was here that many Christian martyrs had met their end. Although there is, in fact, no evidence to support this notion, it proved very attractive. Dust from the arena, supposedly stained with the blood of the righteous, became a sought-after relic and souvenir. When, in 1671, the sports-loving Cardinal Altieri wanted to reintroduce bullfighting in the amphitheatre, his plan provoked outrage among the pious. Three years later the Colosseum as a whole was officially declared a holy sanctuary, and its lower arches were walled in.

A different sort of religious connection gave the Arch of Titus (then flanked by ramshackle buildings) a particular interest for visitors. The reliefs carved on the archway walls showed the emperor's triumph following the Jewish War, with the spoils from the Great Temple at Jerusalem being paraded along the Via Sacra. Evelyn, as a keen student of the Bible, was excited to note the Ark of the Covenant 'upon which stands the seven-branch'd Candlestick, describ'd in Leviticus, as also the two tables of the Law, all borne upon men's shoulders'. He got Carlo Maratti, a respected painter, to make a copy of the scene 'for the light it gave to the holy history'.

At the head of the list of architectural survivals, however, stood the Pantheon 'formerly sacred to all the Gods, & still remaining [despite the depredations of Urban VIII] the most intire Antiquitie of the Citty'. For scale, beauty, ingenuity, completeness, past association and current interest (it was the resting place of 'the famous Raphael' and several other modern painters), there was nothing to match it. 'In a word,' as Evelyn put it, following the enthusiastic encomia of his guidebooks, ''tis of all the *Roman* Antiquities the most worthy of notice.'

If the great monuments of classical antiquity drew the visitor's attention first, there was also curiosity about early Christian Rome. The various churches associated with St Peter and his supposed stay in Rome – S. Pietro in Carcere, in Vincoli, and in Montorio – all exerted a definite pull.† And a marked pathos also attached to S. Maria degli Angeli, the magnificent church that Michelangelo had fashioned out of the ruined central hall of Diocletian's baths, because it was believed that the vast bath complex had been built with the sweat of 150,000 persecuted Christians, all cruelly put to death on its completion.

Evelyn carried his interest in the early Christians (along with his sense of adventure) so far as to visit the 'grottoes' – or catacombs – of Domitilla, near S. Sebastiano, which, after centuries of neglect, had been recently 'rediscovered' by the scholar Antonio Bosio. Armed with two torches and a guide, Evelyn's party set off down the 'strange and fearefull passages for divers miles'; he found the paintings adorning the walls 'very ordinary' and the skeletons in their niches 'dreadfull', but there was a pleasing frisson of terror about it all. He was subsequently told that a few years previously a French bishop and his retinue had ventured too far into the labyrinth and 'their lights going out, were never heard of more'. (The story was probably an invention, though an enduring one; versions of it are recycled even to this day.)

The catacombs, whatever their spookiness, had a real historical interest. Rather less well regarded were the so-called 'superstitious elements' of the Catholic faith, encountered in so many of the churches and chapels of Rome. Evelyn raised an eyebrow when told that women were not permitted to enter the Oratory of St John the Baptist, attached to the Lateran Baptistery, on account of 'the malice of Herodias who caus'd [John the Baptist] to loose his head'. Bones and bric-a-brac, however, were the main focus of Protestant scorn.

The authenticity – to say nothing of the efficacy – of Rome's myriad relics became a matter of amused, or outraged, scepticism among non-Catholic visitors. Evelyn's note

---

† S Pietro in Carcere, fashioned from the Tullianum, an infamous Roman dungeon at the west end of the Forum, was where the Apostle was supposed to have been imprisoned by Nero prior to his execution. S. Pietro in Vincoli, on the Esquiline, housed the chains in which St Peter had been held captive in Jerusalem, as well as those that had bound him in Rome; S. Pietro in Montorio on the Janiculum marked the supposed site of St Peter's execution; this was as a result of an early mediaeval misunderstanding of the fourth-century source that described Peter as having been crucified 'between two *metae*'; the word *meta* – which means a conical turning post such as marked the ends of the spine of the Circus of Nero (where Peter was, according to all other sources, crucified) – was taken to mean a pyramidal tomb. And there were two such in Rome: the so-called Meta Remi (or Pyramid of Cestius) that still stands by the Protestant Cemetery, and the Meta Romuli, since demolished, that stood close to St Peter's. S. Pietro in Montorio, established in the ninth century, marked a spot almost equidistant between them.

of wry detachment when discussing such matters would have found many echoes: at S. Maria Maggiore 'they pretended to shew us some of the holy Innocents bodyes slain by the cruelty of Herod'; at S. Pudenziana 'they also shew many reliques, or rags rather, of St Peter's mantle; believe it who will'; in S. Sabina a stone (in fact an old Roman weight) was pointed out which 'they report was cast by the Devil at St Dominic' while he was at prayer; at S. Croce in Gerusalemme he admired, among other things, St Thomas's doubting finger and some of Judas's pieces of silver 'if one had faith to believe it'; while during his tour of S. Giovanni in Laterano, having scrutinized a column upon which the cock was supposed to have crowed after Peter's abnegation, and the slab on which the soldiers had cast lots for Christ's garments, he was proudly shown 'the just length of the Virgin Mary's foote, as her shoomaker, it seems, affirmed'.

And the credulity of the Roman clergy was not, in Evelyn's opinion, confined to religious matters. He was startled to be told by the 'Friars' at the church of S. Crisogono, in Trastevere, that the two magnificent porphyry pillars framing the high altar were formed of 'congealed water', and had been found by chance in a stretch of old aqueduct uncovered during the construction of the church.

Historical and religious interest in a monument did not always extend to aesthetic appreciation. For the seventeenth-century visitor the physical attractions of post-classical and mediaeval Rome were minimal. The vestiges of the Middle Ages were lumped together and dismissed as 'Gothic' and 'meane'. Confronted by the attractive mediaeval house next to S. Lorenzo in Panisperna, Evelyn laments, 'the fabrique is nothing but Gotic'. And the same disparaging epithet is wheeled out to damn many other fine old buildings, from the Lateran basilica downward.

This was in marked distinction to the enthusiastic reception of modern works.

The 'incomparable' Michelangelo (who died in 1564, eighty years before Evelyn's arrival) held a special position in the consciousness of the new Rome. His status was unique. He was regarded, not unjustly, as the archetypal genius, and credited – rather less justly – with being the first to revive and match the glories of the classical era. (His reputation had been secured in no small measure by an extremely influential – and decidedly partisan – book: *Lives of the Most Excellent Painters, Sculptors and Architects* by Giorgio Vasari. First published in 1550, Vasari's account of the Renaissance revival of painting in Italy traced the story (with a strong Florentine bias) from the brave beginnings of Giotto in the thirteenth century, via the fruitful experiments of Masaccio and Mantegna and the other quattrocento masters, past the slow-ripening maturity of Leonardo, to achieve a final triumph in the works of Michelangelo and Raphael. In their work, he suggested, the pinnacle of art had been reached, a perfect balance of naturalness, colour, power and grace achieved. In Vasari's narrative Michelangelo is the hero, and almost the end, of the history of art. And this estimate echoed through almost all later accounts of Italian art. It became part of the background noise of Rome, a city that Michelangelo had marked in so many ways. In the travel literature of the period the works of 'M. Angelo' – architectural, sculptural, pictorial – were always singled out for special praise.

Among contemporary artists an almost equal pre-eminence had been achieved by Gian Lorenzo Bernini. Evelyn arrived in Rome to find Bernini an acknowledged star: 'Cavaliero Bernini A Florentine [in fact, Neapolitan] Sculptor, Architect, Painter & Poet: who a little before my Coming to the Citty, gave a Publique Opera (for so they call those Shews of that kind) where he painted the scenes, cut the Statues, invented the Engines, composed the Musique, wrote the Comedy & built the Theatre all himselfe.' Like Michelangelo before him he had been put in charge of the ongoing work at St Peter's. His gigantic bronze *baldacchino* above the main altar was already one of the marvels of Rome. The designs he provided for Pope Urban VIII's Palazzo Barberini – 'as superbe, and princely an object, as any moderne building in Europ for the quantity' – had initiated the new Baroque style.

If Bernini led the field, many other great creative talents had also contributed to the transformation of the city, to its plethora of new churches and *palazzi*. Their work, for all its novelty and invention, seems to have been readily appreciated. There was little of that incomprehension of modern architecture, or distrust of the new, with which we have since become familiar.

Evelyn, standing before Giacamo della Porta's boldly massed façade for the Jesuit church, Il Gesù (1565–78), deemed it 'as noble a piece of Architecture as any in Europe'. Fontana's new arcaded Lateran palace, completed in 1586, he thought perhaps the finest *palazzo* in Rome. He was impressed by the Baroque refurbishment of S. Maria Maggiore, and suggested that S. Maria della Vittoria (now considered a rather conventional piece of Baroque architecture, by G.B. Soria) must 'ravish the beholder with astonishment'. Even the daring innovations of Bernini's erstwhile pupil Borromini met with his approval. While the guidebooks tutted over his recently completed little church of S. Carlo as 'capriccioso e bizarro', Evelyn thought it, 'a singular fabrique for neatness as built all of a new white stone, and of an excellent oval design'.

Towering, both literally and figuratively, above all new buildings in the city, however, was the recently completed St Peter's: 'that most stupendous & incomparable Basilica, far surpassing any now extant in the World, & perhaps (Solomon's Temple excepted) any that was ever built'. It was regularly referred to as the Eighth Wonder of the World.

Although the structure was not framed within the great curving embrace of Bernini's colonnade until 1656, the basilica itself stood pretty much as it exists today. It dazzled by its sheer scale, as much as its opulence. Evelyn recorded that the façade 'is suppos'd to be the largest, and best studied piece of Architecture in the World', adding, 'to this we went up by 4 [flights of] stepps of marble: the first entrance is supported by huge Pillasters: The Volto within is certainly the richest in the Earth, overlayed with gold.'

And this was only the beginning of a long chronicle of awed superlatives. The various side-chapels and oratories were, he noted, larger than many 'ordinary churches'. Bernini's great *baldacchino* was 'a thing of that Art, vastnesse & magnificence beyond all that ever man[']s industry has produced of this kind'. There were polyglot confessionals offering to absolve sinners in every language from Hebrew to Welsh. The roof of the basilica seemed like a little town, with its various houses lived in by the church caretakers. But, within and without, everything was dominated by the 'prodigious' cupola. Following his guidebooks Evelyn declared that it was 'more in Compasse than that of the Pantheon (which was the largest amongst the old Romans, & is yet intire) or any else known in the whole World'. This is something of an exaggeration. The diameter of the dome is 138 feet, four feet less than that of the Pantheon. But it serves to show the hold that the vast new basilica had over the imagination of both Romans and visitors.

Most of the great buildings in Rome – ancient and modern, religious and secular – had an additional interest. They were repositories of Art. Churches were adorned with monumental sculptures, valuable plate, and elaborate painting cycles. Also, many of the city's aristocratic families – as well as a few impassioned individuals – had gathered in their homes extraordinary collections of sculptures, paintings, medals, coins, gems and curiosities, and they were happy to let visitors see them.

Among all these assembled treasures, antique sculpture continued to command the high ground. The notion, first adumbrated during the Renaissance, that classical art could represent an absolute standard against which all later work might be judged, had gained currency with the years. And classical sculpture as the most conspicuous artistic survival from the past had come to occupy a special position. A canon of accepted masterpieces – embodying what were considered the best artistic values – was gradually establishing itself.

Over the century and a half since the finding of *Laocoön*, many exciting new discoveries had been made in and around Rome, brought to light in the constant campaign of building. And although almost all of these works remained in the city, appreciation and knowledge of classical sculpture was become ever more widespread.

Copies – in miniature or to scale – had been made of many of the great works in the Roman collections, and they had been dispersed across Europe. The French king, François I, had led the way. Thwarted in his Italian ambitions by the defeat at Pavia, he had set about turning his royal hunting lodge at Fontainebleau into a second Rome. In 1540 as part of this ambitious project he commissioned Primaticcio to take moulds from several of the statues in the Belvedere sculpture court – including *Laocoön* and *Apollo* – and cast bronze replicas from them.

Other heads of state followed his lead, and reused his moulds. In time his example even carried to England. Charles I ordered bronze casts of a dozen Roman statues including the *Spinario* and *Commodus as Hercules*. He also acquired a copy of *Laocoön*, and several actual antiquities. His enthusiasm was matched by that of a select band of courtiers, the Duke of Buckingham, the Earl of Pembroke and – most especially – the Earl of Arundel. Arundel had visited Italy and Rome in 1613–15, together with his architect, Inigo Jones, buying several antiquities, and he presented Evelyn with a list of the things most worth seeing in the country.

Casts, copies and originals, however, were very expensive. They remained spectacular rarities, the preserve of the very, very few. Print was cheaper. And printmakers and publishers played a rather larger part in spreading abroad the fame of – and encouraging the taste for – Roman antiquities. From the early 1500s a growing stream of individual prints and compilation volumes recorded the city's notable statues. New titles and new editions strove to keep pace with the fresh discoveries.

Evelyn possessed a copy (now in the British Library) of François Perrier's 1638 selection of 'the most celebrated statues of Ancient Rome, yet extant there'. Armed with this, his letter from Lord Arundel and his various guidebooks, he might pick his way confidently through the assembled masterpieces of the city. The accepted hierarchy had changed in the century and a half since 1510: new discoveries had been made; old works had risen to new prominence; others had faded from the field.

Most of the accredited masterworks Evelyn found in the handful of great collections, put together by the powerful families that had controlled the papacy, and its wealth, over the previous century. At the Villa Medici, close to his lodging, the acknowledged stars of the display were the *Medici Venus* ('Certainly nothing in Sculpture ever approached this miracle of art'), the 'plainley stupendious' crouching *Wrestlers*, which Evelyn thought 'happily prefferable to any [sculpture] in the World', and the so-called *Niobe Group*, a gathering of fifteen terror-stricken figures, representing Niobe and her numerous offspring being attacked by the gods, arranged picturesquely on an artificial mound in the gardens.

A fanciful reconstruction of the *Niobe Group* in the gardens of the Villa Medici, from a 1638 account of Rome's statues by François Perrier

The 'famous statue' of the *Dying Gladiator* – called by Raymond the 'tyr'd gladiator' – was the jewel of the Villa Ludovisi collection, and one of the most copied statues of the period.† It had been discovered only in 1623, during the construction of the villa on a site formerly occupied by the Gardens of Sallust.

At the nearby Villa Borghese there was another, almost equally famous and very much more vigorous, *Gladiator* (of which both Charles I and the Earl of Pembroke had a copy), and a 'most incomparable' polychrome *Seneca* with enamel eyes, set in an elaborate basin supposedly representing the dying philosopher's blood-filled bathtub. Evelyn, however, seems to have preferred the 'hard-soft Hermaphrodite' lying upon its 'quilt of stone'. This unsettling erotic work had been discovered, around 1620, in the gardens of S. Maria della Vittoria, and presented to Cardinal Scipione Borghese.

† This work, now known as the *Dying Gaul,* is housed in the Capitoline Museums (see page 220).

ABOVE *The Hermaphrodite,*
now in the Louvre
LEFT The statue admired
by Evelyn as an *Adonis,* but
now considered to be a
Meleager
OPPOSITE *Pasquino* on his
street corner

(In return he had paid for the façade of the church.) The 'matarazzo' on which the figure lay was carved by Bernini. Evelyn bought a small ivory version of the piece.†

Away from the great princely collections, Evelyn reserved special praise for the '*Adonis*' – or *Meleager* – owned by Signor Picchini (a work which Lord Arundel had tried to buy).†† He also enjoyed several visits to the house of Ippolito Vitelleschi at the southern end of the Corso. Vitelleschi, the eccentric brother of the General of the Jesuits, possessed 'certainly one of the best collections of statues in Rome . . . to which he frequently talks and discourses, as if they were living, pronouncing now and then Orations, Sentences, & Verses, sometimes kissing & embracing them.' His treasures included a 'much esteemed' bust of Brutus supposedly 'scarr'd in the face by order of the Senat for his killing of Julius [Caesar]'.

In the streets and squares of Rome Evelyn admired not only the old river god *Marforio* (now incorporated into Michelangelo's Campidoglio) but also a much-battered piece depicting a soldier raising the body of a wounded comrade, mounted on a corner of the Palazzo Braschi. This was *Pasquino*, one of Rome's celebrated 'speaking statues'. Following a tradition established not long after the statue's discovery in 1501, Romans would adorn it with scurrilous or satirical broadsides – or 'pasquinades', as they came to be known. (The jibe about the barbarians and the Barberini was one such.) The interest that this gave to the sculpture was further enhanced for Evelyn by the knowledge that Bernini considered it the finest work in Rome.

Over the years the public collection at the Palazzo dei Conservatori on the Capitoline had grown considerably. Raymond fancifully reported that the palace's very name derived from the fact that it was the place where so many of Rome's statues were 'conserved'. For

† He also admired the numerous classical bas-reliefs set into the Villa's façade, including images of Marcus Curtius, Europa and the Bull, and 'Leda fuckt by a Swan . . . Most exquisite'.
†† It is now in the Pio-Clementino Museum at the Vatican.

seventeenth-century visitors acknowledged highlights of the collection included both the old-established favourites, such as 'the horse and the lion' (greatly admired, so it was said, by Michelangelo), the *Spinario* ('very popular with artists'),† and the *Zingara/Camillus* (which Evelyn supposed – perhaps because it was standing close to the bronze *Lupa* – to represent the mythical shepherd Faustulus who had rescued Romulus and Remus from the she-wolf), and various new discoveries: a beautiful marble *Adonis* (now supposed to be *Endymion*) and a 'very rare' sarcophagus front depicting the four seasons.

Evelyn for his part was particularly impressed by the four bas-reliefs showing the triumph and sacrificial offerings of Marcus Aurelius on account of 'the antiquity and rareness of worke'; he commanded Carlo Maratti to make copies of them. (The marble panels are still there, though one of them is now thought to represent Hadrian, rather than Marcus Aurelius.)

The Belvedere sculpture court at the Vatican retained its exalted position, even if there were some changes to the collection's arrangement and hierarchy. The *Hercules and Antaeus* had gone, presented to Duke Cosimo I of Tuscany and shipped to Florence. But the loss had been compensated for by additions. The final two niches had been filled. The Farnese Pope Paul III (1534–49), installed a second *Venus* in one, and a much-admired *Antinous* in the other; it was one of the pieces of which Charles I had a bronze copy. Also in the middle years of the sixteenth century, the so-called *Torso* (see page 207) had been brought into the collection – and set, as part of the fountain, in the centre of the court. This monumentally muscled fragment – probably of Hercules – had once belonged to the sculptor Andrea Bregno, but it owed its high reputation to the endorsement of Michelangelo. He was said to have copied it incessantly, and modelled many of his figures from it. (As a result of the connection the Belvedere sculpture court was sometimes referred to as 'The Study of Michelangelo'.)

Anxieties about the papacy owning such pagan works occasionally resurfaced. The ascetic Dominican Pope Pius V (1566–72) had the niches fitted with 'dores of Wainscot' to hide the corrupting images from general view. His successors left the shutters in place as protecting the statues from the weather. There was a certain drama for visitors in these doors being opened by an attendant to reveal the statue within.

---

† Evelyn's contemporary Richard Lassels called the *Spinario*, 'the prime piece in Rome', and recorded the legend that the boy was a messenger charged with bringing a vital letter to the Roman Senate. Despite picking up a thorn in his foot, he ran all the way, ignoring the pain. Only having discharged his duty did he sit down to remove the thorn – 'which the senat seeing, graced him with this very statue, which now graceth Rome too: for the world hath not a better.'

For seventeenth-century visitors the *Laocoön* remained the uncontested acme of the display. If Pliny judged it 'to be esteem'd before all pictures & statues in the World', who dared to disagree? Certainly not Evelyn. He was rapt by its dramatic force, claiming to have been quite alarmed at the verisimilitude of the serpent. Interestingly, the more serene *Apollo Belvedere* was not – during this period – singled out for especial praise. Indeed, after the *Laocoön*, the most admired statues in the papal collection were the river gods – *Tiber* and *Nile* – which flanked the *Torso*, and the 'dying Cleopatra' which adorned a fountain alcove just off the Belvedere sculpture court. Some combination of horizontality, death, tragedy and snakes seems to have been best calculated to appeal to the Baroque sensibility.

The *Nile*, with sixteen attendant children, said to represent the number of cubits that the river rose during its annual flooding; they remained unrestored until the late eighteenth century.

Cleopatra (or *Ariadne* as she is now more generally known)

But for all the glory of the *Laocoön* – to say nothing of 'those two famous images of Nylus with the children playing abut him, and Tyber' and the 'bellezza Cleopatra' – the Belvedere's absolute pre-eminence among the princely sculpture collections was no longer unchallenged. A new star had risen. For any visitor to Rome in the 1640s the greatest treasure house of antiquities in the city was now considered to be not on the Vatican hill but at the Palazzo Farnese.

Set in its own spacious piazza, just off the Campo dei Fiori, this vast palace – the largest then in private hands – had been built over the whole course of the sixteenth century. Begun by Pope Paul III while he was still a cardinal, and finished in 1589 by his charismatic grandson Gran Cardinale Alessandro Farnese, it had drawn on the talents of a whole succession of architects, including Antonio da Sangallo the Younger, Michelangelo and Giacamo della Porta. (Although, as Raymond remarked, 'for the commendation of the Architecture, it is enough to say Michael Angel had a chief part therein.') The walls and ceilings of the interior were decorated by some of the finest painters of the age. And – most importantly, for the visitors of the period – it housed an extraordinary gathering of antique sculpture. Paul III, having filled the last two niches of the Belvedere sculpture court, had begun collecting on his own account, and his grandson had continued the

LEFT The Palazzo Farnese
RIGHT The *Farnese Toro* or *Bull*, in
an illustration from a contemporary
guidebook

work with equal vigour. Their collection could be visited by arrangement with the major-domo.

Whole rooms were lined with statues. There was a chamber of philosophers, another of emperors. In one room, surrounded by other nudes, stood the *Callipygian Venus*, 'that so renowned piece of a Venus pulling up her smock, and looking backwards on her buttocks', while in another apartment rested a marble head – now sadly lost – 'found long since, and supposed the true portrait of our B[lessed] Saviour's face'. The main courtyard of the palace was dominated by the unmistakable looming bulk of the *Farnese Hercules*, the gigantic second-century AD marble statue of a weary muscle-bound Hercules leaning on his club, discovered in 1546 during excavation work at the Baths of Caracalla. Across from it stood an even larger *Flora* of the same date. Although these 'incomparable' statues were justly celebrated 'as two of the most rare pieces of Sculpture in the World', they had to cede pole position to another work in the Farnese collection.

Standing in the second courtyard, in a sort of shed, was a huge sculptural group:

A bull with a dog and five persons every one bigger than the Naturall[,] cut to wonder out of one stone, the work of Apollonius and Tauriscus of Rhodes, from whence it was conducted & plac't in Antoninus [Caracalla] his bathes, where it was dug up a hundred years since [in 1545], as Intire as if made but yesterday; and now stands in this palace astonishing all that behold it.

The work was taken to be one mentioned in fulsome terms by Pliny as representing Dirce, the haughty second wife of Licus, King of Thebes, who was tied to the tail of a wild bull by her disgruntled stepsons. The combination of the sculpture's size (it was described as a 'mountain' of marble), its dramatic subject matter, and the endorsement of Pliny, carried the work into the front rank. For many it surpassed even the *Laocoön*. Adopting the tones of conventional hyperbole, Evelyn lauded it as 'that most stupendous, and never sufficiently to be admired, *Toro* . . . to be valued beyond all the marbles of the World, both for its antiquity and workmanship'. (It was a judgement that scarcely outlasted the century. It soon became a commonplace that the work was 'considerable only because of its large size and the quantity of figures all carved from one stone', rather than for any intrinsic beauty.)

Although the appreciation of antique statuary might dominate the traveller's cultural horizon, the interest was not exclusive. Certainly mediaeval sculpture – like mediaeval architecture – tended to be ignored. (The 'old brasse' statue of St Peter in the new

The tomb of Pope Paul III, supported by the images of *Justice* (represented by the pope's sister) and *Prudence* (represented by the pope's mother)

basilica was only interesting to Evelyn because 'devout persons' rubbed their heads under its feet, and it was fancifully said to have been cast from the image of Jupiter once housed in the Capitoline temple.) But 'modern' sculpture was sought out and admired. At its best it was believed to revive the achievements of the classical past.

The 'incomparable' Michelangelo was regarded as a worthy successor to the ancients. And Rome was scattered with his masterworks: the 'never sufficiently to be admired' *Moses* at S. Pietro in Vincoli, *Christ at the Column* in S. Maria sopra Minerva, and the 'most glorious' *Pietà* at St Peter's. His pupils, too, had maintained the legacy. In St Peter's Evelyn was much struck by Pope Paul III's monumental sculptural tomb, the masterpiece of Michelangelo's disciple Guglielmo della Porta. It included – as he noted – 'two naked incumbent figures of an old, & a young woman, upon which last, there now lys a covering, or apern of brasse, to cover those parts, which it seemes occasioned a pigmalian Spanyard to be found in a lascivious posture, so rarely to the life was this warme figure don'. It was said that the model for the statue had been the pope's beautiful sister, Giulia Bella, mistress of his predecessor, the Borgia Alexander VI. The legend – or fact – of the work's erotic charm continued down the ages. The early nineteenth-century Roman dialect poet Giuseppe Belli wrote two scurrilous sonnets about, respectively, an English lord and a Roman altar boy being caught *in flagrante* with the 'stone doll'.†

In most collections the distinction between antique and modern work was left unfixed. Contemporary sculptors were often required to supply missing limbs or heads for antique fragments. Guglielmo della Porta made a pair of legs for the *Farnese Hercules* when the huge trunk of the statue was first excavated. And although the original legs were subsequently unearthed, Michelangelo persuaded Paul III to retain his pupil's contribution in order to demonstrate how the work of the moderns could match that of the ancients. (The original legs were only reunited with the rest of the statue in 1787.)

This desire to measure modern achievement against the standard of antiquity also encouraged the habit of exhibiting contemporary works alongside classical ones. In this, as in so much else, Michelangelo led the way: even in the early 1500s his *Bacchus* had stood in the collection of the wealthy banker Jacopo Galli surrounded by antique pieces. Such juxtaposing now became a common device. Many of the works in the

† The figure of the young woman is not in fact nude. Beneath her brass apron she was clad in a loose chemise. The work, set in a niche at the back of the apse, to the left of the high altar, is now almost impossible to get near (whatever your intentions), as most of the upper end of the basilica is barricaded against the tourist throng. Very good eyesight – or binoculars – are necessary to appreciate its charms.

Farnese collection were modern. Among the classical treasures at the Villa Borghese, Bernini's two 'plainly stupendous' masterpieces, *David* and *Daphne*, more than held their own. While next door, at the Villa Ludovisi, the same artist's *Rape of Proserpine* jostled happily with the assembled antiquities.

Bernini was considered exceptional, but not quite unique. His one rival among contemporary sculptors, according to Evelyn, was François Duquesnoy – or Il Fiamingo, as he was called in Rome, on account of his Flemish origins. He had died the year before Evelyn's arrival, driven mad, so it was said, because his statue of *St Andrew*, made for one of the four column niches supporting the cupola at St Peter's, had been 'plac'd in a disadvantageous light' by Bernini – who was jealous that it outshone his own companion piece of *St Longinus*.†

The very high regard in which sculpture, both ancient and modern, was held by visitors to Rome, had inevitable consequences for other branches of art. In the cultural hierarchy of the early seventeenth-century British tourist, painting held a lesser place. Not that it was ignored absolutely. Michelangelo's exceptional reputation ensured

Bernini's *David*

† Four statues adorn the niches: *St Veronica* by Francesco Mocchi; *St Longinus* by Bernini; *St Helena* by Andrea Bolgi; and Fiamingo's *St Andrew*. A plaster model for the *St Andrew* was displayed in 1629 in the north-west niche now occupied by *St Helena*, but – eleven years later – the finished marble work was set in the opposite south-east niche. Although Duquesnoy certainly did regard this as a slight, his death in July 1643 was probably the result of typhoid.

that his pictures were duly esteemed, even if they were ranked rather lower than the other expressions of his genius. During a visit to the Sistine Chapel, Evelyn expended a certain amount of 'time and wonder' in contemplating Michelangelo's 'incomparable' *Last Judgement* on the end wall. The 'vast design', which Michelangelo had completed in 1541, three decades after his work on the ceiling, had become the main – almost the only – reason why the chapel was 'so much celebrated'. Its pre-eminence had been fixed for later generations by Vasari, who described how, when the fresco was uncovered, Michelangelo 'was seen to have vanquished not only all the painters who had worked there before, but even to have surpassed his own work on the ceiling'.

Indeed the guidebooks of the seventeenth century barely touched on the ceiling decorations. Evelyn spared only a nod towards them: 'the roof is also full of rare work.' He failed even to mention the exquisite quattrocento paintings adorning the side walls, which had drawn Albertini's enthusiastic attention just a century before.

Although Evelyn, following his guidebooks, might occasionally note individual late Renaissance works with approval, the only painter – besides Michelangelo – whom he counted as a recognized genius was Raphael. This was the conventional estimate of the period (again reflecting the judgement of Vasari), though Evelyn was doubtless encouraged in the view by his artist companion Carlo Maratti, who, in the words of his biographer, was 'always reverential toward the name and works of Raphael'. (In 1674 Maratti painted a portrait to adorn the artist's tomb in the Pantheon, and he also restored several of his frescoes.)

Evelyn and Maratti made two trips over the Tiber to the Palazzo Chigi (or the Farnesina, as it now is) to view Raphael's frescoes of Cupid and Psyche – 'esteemed one of the rarest pieces of art in the world'. They climbed up to S. Pietro in Montorio to see his *Transfiguration* (now in the Vatican art gallery – see plate IX), also 'esteemed one of the rarest [pictures] in the world'. And although Evelyn's expressions of enthusiasm sometimes seem rather dutiful, he was certainly impressed at the reputation that Raphael's work enjoyed among painters. The Vatican *Loggie*, he noted, were 'so esteemed that artists come from all parts of Europe to make their studies from these designs'. For his own part he liked the 'the foliage and grotesque[s]' that framed the principal scenes.

At this period the *Loggie* – the long arcaded open corridor, the vaults of which Raphael had decorated with fifty-two scenes from the Bible – were held in higher regard than the so-called *Stanze* – the four reception chambers in the papal apartments that he had also frescoed, and which now draw almost all the touristic attention. Indeed Evelyn was under the impression that the *Stanze* were not by Raphael at all but by his pupil Giulio Romano.

The Vatican *Loggie*, the ceiling panels decorated by Raphael with scenes from the Old Testament, the pillars with grotesques by his pupils

The Catholic priest Richard Lassels declared that Raphael's *Loggie* were 'only inferior to the divine history itself'. He did look over the *Stanze*, admiring the *Sala di Costantino* (which was indeed decorated by Giulio Romano after Raphael's death in 1520), but failing even to mention the *Stanza della Segnatura* – which contains the now pre-eminent *School of Athens*.

Guided by his own taste Evelyn was drawn to a small picture in the Palazzo Barberini: Correggio's sweetly tender *Sposalizio di S. Sebastiano* – 'a table in my judgement Superior to anything I had seene in Rome'. He had Maratti make a copy of it – 'little inferior to the prototype' – to take home with him. Despite this acquisition he always remained rather uncertain of the difference between the various Carracci and Correggio – often combining them under the all-purpose name of 'Caraccio'.

Although both Poussin and Claude Lorrain were working in Rome at the time of Evelyn's visit, and he was aware at least of the latter's work, he singled out the otherwise unknown Antonio della Cornia as the most important contemporary painter in the city, on the grounds that he was the best at copying – or counterfeiting – the works of the old masters.

Correggio's *Sposalizio*, now in the Louvre

When confronted with painting it was ingenuity, or rarity, that was likely to impress him most. The miraculously well preserved portion of a Roman wall-painting – the so-called *Nozze Aldobrandini* – displayed at the Villa Aldobrandini stood 'above all for antiquity and curiosity (as being the only rarity of that nature now knowne to remaine in the World)'. He also took notice whenever he encountered a picture by Lavinia Fontana, because women painters were uncommon.

Trompe l'œil effects, though, excited his greatest admiration. He praised Annibale Carracci's magnificent painted gallery at the Palazzo Farnese largely because 'it would require more judgement than, I confess, I had, to determine whether [the painted figures] were flat or embossed.' While the decorative effects achieved by Cherubino Alberti on the ceiling of the *Sala Clementina* in the Vatican were, in his estimation 'a thing of art incomparable'. He considered the room 'Certainly . . . one of the most Superb and royall Appartments in the world, [and] much too beautifull for a guard of gigantique Swizzers who do nothing but drinke and play cards in it.' (See plate v.)

In the upper chamber of the cloister at SS. Trinità del Monte he was greatly intrigued by an 'excellent Perspective' recently completed by the French friar and mathematics professor, Jean-François Niceron: seen from the front it appeared as a landscape, but when viewed from a oblique angle it revealed the image of St Francis of Paola (see plates VI and VII). Niceron, who had published an influential work on optics, *Perspective Curieuse*, in 1638, was fascinated by such visual tricks. The fresco, one of a pair done in monochrome and stretching along a side wall of the cloister, can still be visited as part of a twice-weekly guided tour of the church and adjoining convent. It is, indeed, a wonderful thing, with a great looming black olive tree framing the bald hills of an imaginary Galilee, dotted with tiny figures from the holy story, which then suddenly resolve themselves into an image of the bearded founder of the Minim Friars. The work, with its bold forms and muted tones, has a ready appeal to modern tastes, but its attraction for Evelyn was unlikely to have been aesthetic.

When Evelyn called on Cassiano dal Pozzo, the sponsor and patron of Poussin, to view his collection of antiquities, pictures, books and treasures, he failed even to register the work of his host's brilliant protégé. Despite the several Poussins on view, the only pictures that Evelyn recalled seeing that evening were some 'very pretty things painted on Crimson Velvet, designed in black & shaded, [and] heightened in white'. (They sound like something one might have discovered on the walls of a 1970s Indian restaurant.)

Indeed in his visits to the great princely and private collections, among the thickly ranged treasures on view, pictures always made the least impression. And this was surely not untypical – of British visitors in particular. After he had admired the antique statues, Evelyn's attention was always drawn next to historical rarities and natural curiosities. Chez Cassiano dal Pozzo, Evelyn was most excited by a rock crystal with some water in it – the fabled *enhydros* described by Pliny. At the *studiolo* of Francesco Angeloni he ignored the collector's numerous Titians to pore over his 'infinity of naturall rarities, dryd animals, Indian habits & Weapons, shells & c . . . a sea-man's skin, as he affirm'd . . . hinges of Corinthian brasse, and one huge nayle of the same metal found in the ruines of Nero's golden house.' And one of the highpoints of Evelyn's tour was a visit to see the various scientific models and ethnographic artefacts assembled by the Jesuit polymath Athanasius Kircher at the Collegio Romano.

To modern eyes there is a certain breadth and generosity – or quaint eccentricity – about the typical seventeenth-century enthusiasms expressed by Evelyn. At the Sistine Chapel he turned away from Michelangelo's ceiling to scrutinize the pope's red velvet slippers, and his favourite part of the whole papal palace was the magnificent library – 'doubtless the most nobly built, furnish'd, and beautified in the world'. Like many English visitors of the period he was anxious to see – among the various bibliographic treats – the book that Henry VIII, before his break with Rome, had written against Luther and presented to Leo X – thus earning for himself the title 'Defender of the Faith'. (After Henry fell out with the papacy, Vatican agents also acquired his lascivious love letters to Anne Boleyn as a means of blackening his reputation, and these too became a popular attraction for British visitors.)

The list of extraordinary objects shown to Evelyn during his time in Rome is a long one. Every princely collection contained its choice curiosities. Highlights included: a crystal altar set at the Palazzo Farnese ('there was nothing which to me seem'd more curious and rare in its kind . . . Truly I looked on this as one of the rarest curiosities I had seene since my being in Rome'); the wonderfully petrified body of a man discovered in the Alps and displayed in a black-velvet-lined coffin at the Villa Ludovisi; an ornate bedstead and a stuffed hydra in the same collection (Evelyn was somewhat disappointed that the hydra measured barely a foot in length, and had clearly been patched up with 'several pieces of Serpents skins'); 'the only Tripod of Apollo extant', a giant's kneebone and a stuffed remora, all in the cabinet of Francesco Gualdo; and – at the Villa Borghese – an ingenious chair 'which Catches at any who but sitts downe in it, so, as not to be able to stir out of it, by certaine springs conceiled in the Armes and back theroff, which at sitting down surprises a man on the suddaine, locking him in armes and thighs after a true tretcherous Italian guize'.

Between peering at a diminutive hydra in some nobleman's *studiolo* and inspecting the massive ruins of the Forum, there emerged a sense that the whole of Rome was itself like one giant cabinet of curiosities. At every step, it seemed, the visitor was assailed by sights of interest, distinction, strangeness or beauty. Evelyn, in his poetic tribute to the city, declared:

> With speaking stone, & breathing statues set,
> Justly art term'd the *World's sole Cabinet*:
> Of all the *Universe* none dares Contend
> With thee o ROME, nor will thy Praises End.

The trouble with any cabinet of curiosities is that it can be broken up. Treasures are moveable. Although Rome itself still retains a strong flavour of the seventeenth century, with its numerous Baroque buildings, its radiating street plan, its obelisks and fountains, even its occasional garden park, many of the individual works and wonders that Evelyn and his contemporaries most admired are no longer to be seen there.

Some – like the petrified man at the Villa Ludovisi – have disappeared. Others have found new homes. Not a few left Rome soon after Evelyn did. The choicest statues from the Villa Medici – the *Wrestlers* and *Venus* – were taken to Florence as early as 1677, and the *Niobe Group* followed a century later; they can all still be seen in the Uffizi. Correggio's painting of the *Sposaliccio*, so admired by Evelyn, was given to the French minister Cardinal Mazarin in 1650. It is now in the Louvre, along with the *Hermaphrodite*, the *Gladiator* and *Seneca* – acquired from Prince Camillo Borghese in 1805 by his brother-in-law, Napoleon. The 'never sufficiently to be admired' *Toro*, with all the other treasures of Palazzo Farnese, was shipped to Naples in 1787 when the last scion of the family married the heir to the Neapolitan throne; they form the nucleus of the National Archeological Museum there.

One of the sights most enjoyed by seventeenth-century visitors has, however, simply passed out of bounds. Familiar concerns with health and safety, to say nothing of accessibility, have closed it to the public. For Evelyn, though, and many other travellers, it was the literal highpoint of a visit to Rome: the ascent of the dome at St Peter's. That may sound like a familiar enterprise to any modern visitor who has ever taken the lift up to the roof and walked up the 320 steps to the narrow observation platform that runs around the lantern at the top of the dome, but in the 1640s they did things rather differently. Having made his way up the narrow spiral stairway that twists between the inner and outer shells of the cupola, Evelyn reached the base of the lantern, where the

The lantern of St Peter's, and a cross-section showing the ascent to the gilded 'Globe or Mundo' on top of it

modern viewing gallery now runs. But then he went on. Following the staircase upwards, inside the lantern, he reached its crown. Within the tapering 'hat' that surmounted the lantern, he discovered a tiny stairway leading upwards, and then – as the space narrowed still further – a ladder. Up he clambered. 'On the very Summit of this is fix'd a brazen Globe or Mundo gilt likewise over, & capable of receiving 35 Persons at once; This I entred, & engrav'd my name in, amongst other Travellors.'

·VII·
ROME AND THE GRAND TOUR

I N 1755, the thirty-eight-year-old Johann Joachim Winckelmann arrived in Rome. He came ostensibly to act as librarian for one of the great cardinals, but his burning desire was to study the numerous antiquities of the city. He took rooms in the Palazzo Zuccari, near SS. Trinità del Monte, in the artists' quarter of the city. The German painter Raphael Mengs lived across the way. And round the corner, in the Via Sistina, resided Giovanni Battista Piranesi, a prodigiously gifted printmaker already renowned for his dramatic images of Rome's monuments, ancient and modern.

Although Winckelmann lived in Rome until 1768, the year of his unfortunate early death, there is no record that he ever met Piranesi. They had friends and patrons in common, but the two men, it seems, studiously avoided each other – or at least avoided mentioning each other. Over the course of a decade and a half they emerged as not just rivals but enemies. Their visions of Rome and its past were almost diametrically opposed. But between them, these very different viewpoints shaped the understanding – and the appreciation – of Rome for almost all visitors during the second half of the eighteenth century. They influenced what was looked at and, perhaps more importantly, how it was seen.

Both men were fascinated by the past of classical antiquity; they viewed the Rome of their own day through its prism, and they regarded it as a sure guide for future endeavour. But whereas, previously, the whole of the classical age had been regarded as a more or less single entity – an entity largely defined by Rome and her conspicuous ruins – for Winckelmann and Piranesi this notion no longer sufficed.

During the eighteenth century Greece, after a gap of many years, began to be visited again. Although the country was under Ottoman rule, a few intrepid antiquarians and architects braved all difficulties to visit the sites of Homeric legend and Greek history. From their observations and drawings a dawning awareness grew of the differences and distinctions between the culture of Ancient Greece and that of Ancient Rome. And where differences and distinctions were observed, hierarchies soon followed.

Winckelmann, the brilliant son of a Prussian cobbler, who had been saved from a life of minor academic drudgery to work in the great library of Count von Bünau near Dresden, felt a deep interest in the subject. Steeped in the works of Homer and the impressive collection of antiquities assembled at Dresden by King Augustus II of Saxony, he began to map out the differences – and the development – of the two cultures. And he asserted the supremacy of the Greeks over the Romans. In 1755, having never visited Rome, let alone Athens or the Hellenic sites of Sicily and southern Italy, he published his treatise, *Reflections on the Imitation of the Painting and Sculpture of the Greeks*. In it he extolled 'the quiet grandeur and noble simplicity' of Greek art as the true and absolute standard of beauty. Ancient Rome, he argued, had merely adopted and debased the ideas of the conquered Greeks. He urged contemporary artists to turn back to the example of the Greeks for their inspiration: 'The one way for us to become great, perhaps inimitable,' he declared, 'is by imitating the ancients.' The book established Winckelmann's reputation, securing him a royal pension, and allowing him to move to Rome – to pursue his studies and advance his thesis.

Winckelmann's ideas had an arresting novelty, and they were eagerly taken up across the European intellectual world. To Piranesi, however, they seemed almost a personal affront. The Venetian-born printmaker had arrived in Rome in 1740, aged just twenty, full of energy and ambition. He had a training in theatrical design, and he brought this sense of drama to bear on his new home town. Through his magnificent series of *vedute* – large-scale prints of the city's monuments and landmarks – he established a reputation as the foremost interpreter of Rome's heritage. He loved the great ruins of the city's past. The architect Robert Adam (to whom he acted as a guide and mentor), recognized his profound knowledge, claiming, 'he alone might be said to breathe the Ancient Air.' As not just an Italian but an adopted Roman, Piranesi felt his racial pride piqued – and his very livelihood challenged – by Winckelmann's Hellenism.

He responded by proclaiming the independent genius of Roman culture. Rome's art and architecture, he argued, far from being based slavishly on Ancient Greek models, had evolved independently from the more ancient – and wholly Italian – Etruscans. (The Etruscans, he suggested, on no very good authority, had learnt their artistic and architectural principles from the Ancient Egyptians.) In a series of lavishly illustrated polemical volumes he praised the practical genius of the Ancient Romans: their great aqueducts, their paved road system, their development and use of concrete vaulting. Carrying the fight into the Greek camp, he contended that the decadence of Roman art and architecture during the late Roman Empire was, in fact, due to the adoption of too much Greek ornament at the expense of sound Roman structure.

'Greek v. Roman', Winckelmann v. Piranesi: these rival visions battled for supremacy during the second half of the eighteenth century. There was much nonsense written on both sides of the debate, by the principals and their supporters, but it was written with passion and power. The contest held, of course, a special practical interest for architects and artists anxious to know which models to follow. But it also brought the whole subject of classical antiquity into a new focus and a new prominence. It coloured, too, the way in which many educated people looked at the remains of the distant past, and particularly the way in which they looked at Rome. And more people were looking at Rome than ever before.

This was the great age of the Grand Tour. During the eighteenth century an extended trip around the Continent became established as an important element in the education of Europe's upper classes. It also became the fashionable thing to do.

The scope was broad. France had to be seen. The Low Countries and Germany held much of interest. Venice, Florence, Bologna, Pisa, Genoa, Milan, Turin and Naples, all boasted splendid treasures – and made the Italian leg of the tour (or *Giro d'Italia*) particularly rich. But it was universally agreed that Rome marked the climax. From across Europe young men (and occasionally young women) of means converged upon the Eternal City: French, Germans, Danes, Swedes, Russians, Poles, Scots, Irish and – above all – English. So many English aristocrats arrived that the Romans came to designate all well-born foreigners as *milordi Inglesi*.

The flow of visitors, already thick in the early years of the century, became a flood immediately after 1763, following the end of the disruptive Seven Years War. That global contest left the victorious British secure in their position as the most powerful and wealthiest nation in Europe. And they brought their wealth to Rome.

The grandest British visitor of the period, King George III's brother, Edward Augustus, Duke of York, stayed for two weeks in April 1764, travelling incognito as the 'Duke of

Ulster'. Lords were legion, and distinguished men many; artists flocked to Rome, and young students were escorted there under the supervision of 'bear leaders'. Among the most notable visitors during the seasons of 1763–4 and 1764–5 were Edward Gibbon, Tobias Smollett, James Boswell, David Garrick and John Wilkes. Many visitors passed whole months in the city, staying through autumn into spring. Not all, however, could spare so much time.

Almost everyone took lodgings close to the Piazza di Spagna in what had become known as the 'English Quarter', or even the 'English Ghetto'. The piazza had been transformed in the 1720s by the construction of the Spanish Steps. Rather than the old path winding up the grassy bank towards the church of SS. Trinità del Monte, there now rose an elegant *scalinetta*. Built to the design of Francesco de Sanctis, it was said that the arrangement of its three broad flights of steps, broken by three broad landings, provided an architectural allusion to the Holy Trinity. Mainly, however, the stairway offered a handsome backdrop to the scene.

There was a sense of community among the visitors – or rather a sense of several communities. With a fine appreciation for the nuances of rank and class, and the

The Piazza di Spagna, with the Spanish Steps by Piranesi

differences of nationality, travellers would seek out their own to enjoy the moments of leisure and the fun of being abroad.

Among the English much time would be spent in playing billiards or drinking in the numerous cafes around the piazza. Foremost among these establishments was the Caffe degli Inglesi, a large vaulted room on the corner of Via delle Carrozze. The walls of the café had been painted with sphinxes, obelisks and pyramids by Piranesi himself. It sounds rather stylish, though the Welsh painter Thomas Jones thought the décor, 'fitter to adorn the inside of an Egyptian sepulchre than a room of social conversation'. (Nothing, alas, now survives of either the café or the decorations.)

The excited visitors would consort with artists and art-dealers, with antiquarians and restorers. They would visit Piranesi's print shop in the Via Sistina. And, if they were well off, they might sit to Pompeo Batoni or Angelica Kauffmann for their portrait, the background enlivened by some fragment of classical ruin.

For those with introductions to the Roman aristocracy there were receptions to attend. And for British visitors there was – at such gatherings – the special interest of perhaps encountering the 'Old Pretender' – or, as he liked to style himself, King James III. The exiled Stuart court had been established at Rome since 1717 but, after the crushing defeat of the Jacobite cause at Culloden in 1746, it had been reduced to little more than a curiosity – and, increasingly, for the papacy a political embarrassment.†

Contemporary Roman life, however, tended to be only a minor element of the Grand Tourist's sojourn. In previous ages Rome had appeared to foreign visitors as a cradle of new philosophies and new modes of living. Cinquecento travellers had been awed not only by the masterpieces of Renaissance art and architecture but also by Renaissance ideas. Evelyn and his contemporaries in the following century had been very ready to appreciate the first flowering of the Baroque spirit in all its forms. The wealth and sophistication of contemporary Roman culture had, for generations, excited the admiration and interest of all travellers from abroad. Rome had been a respected player on the world stage.

Now, however, the balance was shifting. Northern Europeans arrived with a new self-confidence – if not arrogance – born of their nations' increasing wealth, stability, and political power. Rome began to feel provincial. The feeble government and administration of the Papal States frequently provoked contempt.

† The Old Pretender's eldest son, Bonnie Prince Charlie did not return to Rome, following the wreck of his hopes at Culloden, until after his father's death in 1766. He, together with his brother, Henry, Cardinal York, and their father, are buried in St Peter's.

The population of Rome may have risen to around 130,000 but that was only a quarter the size of the London. And the urban plan which had seemed so impressive to visitors only a hundred years before was now felt to be too incomplete and too compromised. Sarah Bentham, one of several English women to make the Grand Tour, confessed to being 'Much disappointed in seeing Rome. The streets are narrow, dirty and filthy. Even the palaces are . . . intermixed with wretched mean houses.' She was shocked that the elegant Piazza Navona, one of the largest open spaces in Rome, should be 'used for the sale of vegetables'.

The Roman aristocrats seemed impoverished, and their palaces in a state of decay, or worse. Smollett complained that the 'corridors, arcades, and even the staircases of [the Romans'] most elegant palaces, are depositories of nastiness, and indeed in Summer the smell is as strong as spirit of hartshorn.'

As children of both the Enlightenment and the Reformation, most Grand Tourists were also apt to be unimpressed by much of Rome's religious heritage. It became a commonplace for the increasingly secular traveller to view contemporary Rome, dominated as it still was by the rites, the rituals and the personnel of the Catholic Church, as a haven of superstition and backwardness.

But, if the present had become less alluring, the past exerted an ever-stronger pull. Italy, no longer a school of politics and learning, was universally recognized as the fount of art and of ancient history. These were the two things that led people to Italy and – above all – to Rome during the eighteenth century. For successive generations of well-to-do young men the Eternal City served as a school of taste and a living library of the classical past. These twin roles, though linked, were subtly different. Certainly they called forth rather different responses. Most visitors, after all, arrived knowing a great deal about the classical world and very little about art.

For classically educated young Englishmen, raised from infancy on a diet of Cicero, Horace, Ovid, Livy and the rest, Ancient Rome was familiar ground. Art, by comparison, was a rather less well charted world. Although the proliferation of prints, and the establishment of a few private collections, had spread some knowledge of Italy's art across the whole of Europe, Britain still lagged behind. The Royal Academy of Arts in London was not formally established until 1768. And many English travellers had scarcely seen a collection of paintings or an antique sculpture before reaching Italy. But, if they were ignorant, they were aware of it, and they were anxious to address their shortcomings. Art, they understood, was not just important, it was in fashion.

At the leading edge of this fashionability stood the Society of Dilettanti, a group of 'young noblemen of wealth and position' that had come together in 1732. Although

Horace Walpole (never one of their number) complained that 'the nominal qualification for membership is having been in Italy and the real one being drunk', the Society – in time – made a deep impression upon the cultural life of the nation. The Dilettanti were among the prime movers in the establishment of the Royal Academy. Through their publications, travel grants and other activities they also did much to raise interest in the art and architecture of classical antiquity. In the great debate between 'Greeks' and 'Romans' the Society offered support to both sides. One of the Dilettanti's rousing toasts was 'Greek Taste and Roman Spirit': both, they believed, were to be found in the Eternal City.

The eighteenth century being an age of reason, the course adopted by visitors during their time in Rome was eminently rational: they sought to see everything, and to understand it according to established rules. That at least was the ideal.

To aid in its achievement, it was considered essential to engage a guide or *cicerone*. These gentlemen were often expatriate artists or antiquarians long domiciled in Rome and adept at turning their knowledge to account. It was indeed possible to engage Winckelmann himself, although he was not particularly fond of the British, after he took the Duke of Gordon on a tour of the city and the noble *milord* not only refused to get out of the carriage once, but spent much of the time yawning. Boswell got on rather better with his guide – a Scottish artist-cum-antiquary called Colin Morison; they added to the pleasure of their tour by conversing in Latin.

Perhaps the most celebrated of the British *cicerone* was James Byres, another rigorous and opinionated Scot. He acted as Gibbon's guide, during the historian's eighteen-week stay, and also – for three weeks in May 1764 – chaperoned one of the first parties of Americans around the city – the young Samuel Powel, a future mayor of Philadelphia, together with three companions. Although he clearly tailored his 'Course of Antiquities' to the needs of his many clients, a 'list of those things which are most worth seeing in and round Rome divided into Days according to Mr Byres' Plan', preserved in the British Library, gives perhaps a standard plan. It maps out an itinerary beginning in the Forum and ending – thirty-eight days later – with the Villa Ludovisi and the Palazzo Albani.

Such thoroughness was, of course, beyond the patience of some visitors. It was reported that one English *milord* had hired a carriage, good horses, and a compliant *cicerone*, so that he might drive through the city, marking the various sights as he passed them. After two days whirling about in this fashion he was able to claim that he had indeed seen everything in Rome – before retiring once more to the pleasures of the billiard table.

As either a supplement or an alternative to a *cicerone*, a guidebook could be useful. They had been proliferating since Evelyn's visit to the city. Totti's two volumes – the *Ritratto di Roma antica* and *Ritratto di Roma moderna* – had proved amazingly durable. They were regularly updated and reissued, before – in 1745 – the bookseller Gregorio Roisecco had the smart idea of combining the ancient and modern elements into a single general work.

As a scholarly guide to the ancient monuments, Byres recommended the 1763 edition of Ridolfino Venuti's *Accurata e succinta descrizione topografica . . . di Roma*, while one of the best informed accounts of the city's treasures was produced – in 1744 – by the noted scholar and art dealer Francesco Ficoroni. (Ficoroni held a special interest for English visitors as the man who had shown Joseph Addison around Rome at the beginning of the century.)

A new work, however, appeared in 1763: Vasi's *Itinerario istruttivo di Roma*. Produced by the popular topographical printmaker Giuseppe Vasi it rapidly established itself as the market leader, being reissued in numerous editions and translations over the following years. The book offered a step-by-step tour of the city divided into just eight days. Nevertheless, as a representative single 'day' might include all the churches on both the Piazza del Popolo and the Corso, the Palazzo Chigi, the column of Marcus Aurelius, the church of S. Ignazio, the treasures of the Palazzo Doria-Pamphili, the vast Palazzo Venezia, the Gesù, the Campidoglio, and the Capitoline Museums, it soon became a familiar witticism that one day of Vasi was equal to a week of anyone else's time. Certainly all the sights on Mr Byres' thirty-eight day tour were included in Vasi's book.

All authorities agreed that there was a great deal to see. Their claims to completeness, however, were illusory. A certain degree of selection was inevitable and, more importantly, several large chunks of Rome's heritage were deemed to be of scant interest. As in previous generations, the vestiges of the Middle Ages were ignored.

Now, though, there was scarcely more concern for Rome's Baroque architecture. Some of Bernini's more conspicuous creations – notably his magnificent curved double colonnade at St Peter's, his angel-lined bridge opposite the Castel S. Angelo and his jolly fountain in Piazza Navona – were still admired, but much else was either disparaged or passed over without comment. Borromini fared even worse. Winckelmann held him personally responsible for exaggerating all the elements of ornamentation and thus bringing about 'a deterioration in architecture which has spread through Italy and other countries'. And this verdict was echoed by the guidebooks. Among the most frequently used epithets for his work (when it was noticed at all) were '*bizzarro*' and 'wretched'.

If the architecture of eighteenth-century Rome received similarly scant coverage it was partly because there had been little construction work in recent times. The exuberant age of Baroque expansion had passed. Cardinal Alexander Albani had used his wealth and contacts to create a delightful villa outside the Porta Salara, and the new Palazzo della Consulta added an imposing grandeur to the Piazza Quirinale. Although Piranesi himself created the elegant the little church of S. Maria del Priorato for the Knights of Malta in 1764, no major new churches had been built. Flamboyant new façades had been added to both S. Maria Maggiore and the Lateran basilica, but neither was highly regarded. Pope Benedict XIV's verdict on the dramatic broken-work frontage created by Ferdinando Fuga for S. Maria Maggiore was, 'He must have thought we were theatrical impresarios. It looks like a dance hall.' The English visitor Edward Martyn found it 'in a very bad taste'.

The only two contemporary structures to attract any sort of general approbation were the Spanish Steps, and the no less theatrical new Trevi Fountain at the terminus of the Acqua Vergine. The grand architectural backdrop rising above a scene of tumbling rocks and water, through which Oceanus drives his shell chariot accompanied by a bevy of Tritons, was hailed as a 'noble prospect'. Begun by Niccolò Salvi in 1732 but not completed until 1762, it was eagerly recorded by Piranesi and the other printmakers, and rapidly assumed a position at the head of Rome's long list of beautiful fountains.†

Of all Rome's post-classical monuments, however, St Peter's remained the unrivalled acme. It was recognized as a modern wonder. Even Winckelmann and Piranesi agreed upon the point. It was the first item in many guidebooks. It continued to astonish all visitors with its scale and splendour. Winckelmann called it 'the epitome of beauty in architecture . . . the most beautiful building in the world.' Piranesi immortalized it in some of his most powerful *vedute*, emphasizing both its hugeness and grandeur.

The vast circular piazza before it, with its double colonnade, its two magnificent fountains, and – between them – the famous obelisk, now created what was deemed a

† The fountain replaced the old one set up by Pope Nicolas V in 1453. According to the contemporary guidebooks it was due to the fact that the old Renaissance fountain had three spouts or *Tre Vii* – that the Trevi Fountain got its name. The etymology, however, is certainly wrong, like several other popular stories: that the fountain owes its name to its position at the junction of three roads – *tre vie*; or that the Roman virgin who first pointed out the source to the Roman soldiers was called 'Trivia'. The truth, it seems, is less colourful: the name derives from the old place-name of the source (near Salone, on the road to Tivoli), which has as its root an Ancient Italic word – *Trebium* – meaning a farmstead or hamlet.

TOP *The Trevi Fountain* by Piranesi   ABOVE *The Piazza in front of St Peter's* by Piranesi

'truly superb' setting for the truly superb building. Even the incorrigibly disobliging Samuel Sharp, who visited Rome in 1765, admitted that the space possessed an 'inimitable éclat'.

All other Roman churches existed in its shadow. A dutiful round was made of the major basilicas: S. Paolo, S. Lorenzo, S. Sebastiano, SS. Apostoli, but there seems to have been little in them to excite the tourist imagination.

Among the smaller churches, the most enjoyed was that of S. Martino ai Monti, close by S. Maria Maggiore. Although a foundation of the fourth century, it had been completely overhauled in 1650, and much embellished. Vasi adjudged it 'one of the finest [churches] in Rome'. (And visitors endorsed his opinion enthusiastically.) The interior had become an harmonious arrangement of soft greys and muted gold; the two rows of fine antique columns had been reset on high square bases; a stucco frieze had been added; and *trompe l'œil* paintings set in the clerestory above. Connoisseurs were particularly taken with the 'bellissimi' landscapes by Poussin's brother-in-law, Gaspard Dughet, adorning the right-hand wall of the nave. (This beautiful church still exists unchanged since the days of the Grand Tour; now unregarded and unvisited by tourists, it is not even mentioned in many modern guidebooks.)

For most eighteenth-century visitors, Rome's ecclesiastical monuments were, however, little more than a sideshow. The main excitements lay elsewhere. They were to be found, first, among the ruins of antiquity. For the legions of classically schooled travellers these were a great draw. If Gibbon's response was extreme it was not untypical: 'My temper', he wrote, a quarter of a century after his visit of 1764, 'is not very susceptible of enthusiasm, and the enthusiasm which I do not feel I have ever scorned to affect. But at the distance of twenty-five years I can neither forget nor express the stong emotions which agitated my mind as I first approached and entered the *eternal city*. After a sleepless night, I trod with a lofty step the ruins of the Forum: each memorable spot where Romulus *stood*, or Tully [Cicero] spoke, or Caesar fell, was at once present to my eye.'

Such was the power of association, that any lump of stone or patch of ground could become charged with meaning, as the spot on which some historic scene had unfolded. Although most visitors arrived with a rich fund of knowledge, one of the reasons for the great success of Vasi's guide was that it provided, as a useful aide-mémoire, the appropriate Latin quotation or reference for every sight.

The Forum, because it had stood at the centre of Ancient Roman life, stood at the heart of the Grand Tourists' experience of Rome. For Gibbon, and many others like him, it mattered little that the place was now a pasture for cows – and on Thursdays and Fridays a cattle market – that the huts of carpenters and artisans stood dotted about, that only a handful of broken ruins rose or protruded from the earth. This was a sacred ground. It helped, too, that the place now possessed a certain picturesque charm: a double avenue of elm trees (planted in 1656 by Alexander VII) ran down the space, offering some pleasant shade. And the bells of the several churches that faced on to the Forum would call out in answer to each other. It had become a fit setting for flights of historical fancy.

The sight must have been a curious one. James Russell, an English painter who studied in Rome during the 1750s, recalled: 'Some I have known stand upon the same spot of ground for a good while, as it were in deep contemplation, where there was no appearance of any thing very remarkable or uncommon. Tho' such a one might be thought non-compos, he might probably, from his knowledge in history, be then calling to mind some brave action, performed upon that very spot; and enjoying a pleasure not to be felt by anyone confined within the walls of a study, or a chamber.'

(The French, Russell noted, were peculiarly deficient in this imaginative faculty. When confronted by the great obelisk before St Peter's, and having heard the full story of is origins and vicissitudes, one typical Gallic visitor, turned smartly on his red-heeled shoe with the remark, 'Eh bien, Monsieur, ce n'est qu' une Pierre.' Such flippancy seems to have been a national characteristic. Certainly Winckelmann counselled a German friend: 'In Rome you must seek out everything with a certain phlegm, otherwise you are taken for a Frenchman.')

The Forum, of course, was not the only field for historical daydreaming. The other hubs of Ancient Roman political life, the Palatine and Capitoline, were equally suggestive spots. While wandering upon the latter, the disagreeable Samuel Sharp took great pleasure in contemplating what the original drop from the Tarpeian Rock must have been. (In his estimation, the steady rise in Rome's ground level meant that there would now be no guarantee of a person breaking their neck if flung from the precipice.)

Archaeological and epigraphic work continued to make advances in the understanding and interpretation of Rome's ruins. But many gaps remained. Gibbon memorably described how the inspiration to write *The Decline and Fall of the Roman Empire* came to him as he sat 'musing amidst the ruins of the Capitol, while the barefoot friars were singing vespers in the Temple of Jupiter'; yet, in fact, the friars in the Aracoeli were singing on what had been the site, not of the Temple of Jupiter, but the Temple of Juno Moneta. The actual remains of the Temple of Jupiter Optimus Maximus lay, still unrecognized, at the other end of the hill, under the Palazzo Caffarelli.

While many monuments and locations owed their importance to the ties that connected them with the great events of Rome's history, some had risen to prominence for slightly different reasons. The mausoleum of Cecilia Metella, a vast drum-like tomb beside the Via Appia, a couple of miles outside the city wall, became a major stop on the Grand Tourist's itinerary, largely on account of its picturesque charm. The monument (known popularly as Capo di Bove because of its conspicuous frieze of ox skulls) was handsome and impressive in itself, but made more special by its setting on the fringes of the desolate Campagna. It was this *mise-en-scène* that made the tomb for many years a favourite subject of the artists who gathered at Rome. And recorded in these numerous *vedute* – paintings, drawings, prints – it became fixed for whole generations of visitors as one of the iconic images, and one of the unmissable sights, of Rome.

This was a special status that it shared with a small group of other easily recognized and oft-recorded monuments: the three great vaults of the so-called 'Temple of Peace'; the half-buried Arch of Septimius Severus; the great basilica of St Peter's. Of all the image-makers who depicted these monuments, the greatest and the most successful was Piranesi. So it is no surprise that most of the classical edifices on the list had the common characteristic of being distinctively Roman structures, owing nothing or little to Greek influence or Greek models. The triumphal arch and the cylindrical mausoleum were both forms unknown in Ancient Greece.

The Pantheon, too, could claim to be uniquely Roman. But then it was unique in many respects: in its form and its state of preservation. Still entire and in use, it was generally accounted 'the most noble and perfect' of 'all the ancient buildings which Ancient Rome has left us'. (Indeed such was the chorus of approbation that the ever-contrary Smollett insisted on claiming that it looked like nothing so much as 'a huge cockpit open at the top'.) As at St Peter's the general setting of the building had been much enhanced. In the prints of the period it appears handsomely framed by an elegant piazza, at the centre of which stands an elaborate fountain – surmounted by an obelisk.

The building was not only much admired and much depicted, it also received the homage of imitation. Ancient Roman models were being eagerly adopted by the rising generation of British architects, and a succession of eighteenth-century visitors chose the Pantheon as a template for their own building projects. Rotundas began springing up all over Britain, to say nothing of the rest of Europe: a garden *bagno* at Chiswick House, a pavilion at Stourhead, James Wyatt's mausoleum at Dartrey in Ireland, the Earl Bishop of Bristol's eccentric mansion at Ickworth; William Blundell's sculpture gallery at Ince Blundell in Lancashire; Belle Isle House on Lake Windermere.

The Colosseum by Piranesi

Copies of the Colosseum are rather scarcer. (McCaig's Tower at Oban in Scotland is a rare example – and it belongs to the late nineteenth, rather than the eighteenth, century.) Nevertheless, of all the ancient monuments in Rome, the great amphitheatre was the most recognized and the most recognizable. Despite some of the outer wall having been brought down by an earthquake in 1703, it remained 'a stupendous and picturesque ruin', and – for most visitors – the defining symbol of Ancient Rome. 'In Antiquities the COLISEUM takes the lead,' declared Edward Martyn at the beginning of his account of the city.

Classically minded visitors, however, tended to rankle at the ever-increasing Christianization of the monument. A hermit was still in residence, but his tiny chapel had been joined by a host of small shrines and altars dotting the perimeter of the arena, while at the centre of the space, a large iron cross had been erected. Such insistent marks of Roman Catholicism seem to have distressed northern travellers more than the animal pens that occupied part of the space, or indeed, the mountain of manure that filled the northern arcades of the amphitheatre (providing vital material for the nearby saltpetre manufactury). William Beckford was not alone in his 'vehement desire ... to break down and pulverise the whole circle of saints' nests and chapels that disgrace [the site]'.

Of all the myriad prints and drawings produced of the Colosseum, those by Piranesi were the finest. The magnificent example of purely Roman architecture was perhaps his favourite subject. Certainly the images he produced – soaring bird's eye views and dramatic low-angled vistas – did much not merely to record the grandeur of the site, but to spread and enhance its fame.

Another of Piranesi's favourite motifs was rather less expected. It was neither a temple nor a theatre, but the great sewer of the Romans – the Cloaca Maxima. The giant stone-dressed mouth of the sewer was (and is) still to be seen in the Tiber wall, close by the small circular building known as the Temple of Vesta, not far from the church of S. Maria in Cosmedin. It was an impressive sight, some 14 foot wide by 10 foot high, with the walls of the drain being made from finely cut blocks of good-quality stone. As Piranesi declared rhetorically, 'Who would not agree that there is beauty in the sewers of the Romans

rather than lack of it?' And, again, it was a distinctively Roman creation, untouched by Greek influence.

He produced two prints of the Cloaca, and it has been suggested that the great vaulted conduit also inspired his famous series of imaginary dungeons, the *Carceri*. Certainly it was Piranesi's enthusiasm that put the Roman sewage system back on the tourist itinerary after a gap of some 1,900 years. Vasi felt it necessary to give a full account of the Cloaca's history, while Mr Byers included it in the '20th Day' of his schedule. Nor were visitors disappointed: Goethe, when he came to peer into the great drain, found it even more impressive than Piranesi had allowed.

A schematic drawing of the Cloaca Maxima by Piranesi

The architectural monuments of Rome's glorious past were not, however, the only things to be looked at. There was also the great world of Art. Gentlemen on the Grand Tour wanted to develop Taste, to understand and appreciate the realms of painting and of statuary, both modern and ancient.

This was a taxing business, and one in which it was believed the English started at rather a disadvantage. Winckelmann certainly considered that 'the lethargic temperament of the English, coupled with the unfortunate climate in which they had to live, was bound to inhibit the development of their aesthetic sense.' All things, however, were susceptible to education and hard work. To develop one's Taste it was necessary to look at Art, and Rome was the place to do that: there were simply more (and, it was believed, better) paintings, more statues and more antiquities there than anywhere else in the world.

Thousands of paintings – and hundreds of sculptures – adorned Rome's legion of churches. There were yet more crowding the long galleries of the princely palaces. And beyond these there were – so Ficoroni calculated in 1744 – some 10,600 pieces of ancient sculpture of one sort or other (reliefs, statues and busts) present in the city. His estimate, of course, was soon out of date. The great collections at the Vatican and the Palazzo dei Conservatori grew with the years, as new finds were made and old works were acquired. In 1734, Pope Clement XII reconfigured the set-up on the Capitoline, establishing the Museo Capitolino in the Palazzo Nuovo, as a pendant to the Conservatori collection on the other side of the piazza. Beautifully laid out – its walls studded with inscriptions and bas-reliefs, its airy galleries lined with some of the choicest works of antiquity – the new museum immediately became one of the great attractions on the Roman scene.†

To traverse the crowded cultural terrain assistance was thought to be essential. Besides their general guidebooks – and their well informed *ciceroni* – British visitors generally felt it necessary to equip themselves with a few specialist volumes. The leading art guides were Italian works, mostly deriving from the later chapters of Vasari and the pioneering late-seventeenth-century volumes of Baglione and Titi. The latter's *Descrizione delle Pitture,[e] sculture . . . in Roma* went through many revisions in the decades after the author's death. A much-expanded edition appeared in 1763, ready to help the great wave of new visitors. Byres recommended it to his charges.

---

† A similar reordering and expansion of the Vatican's collection of antiquities was carried out between 1771 and 1786, during the pontificates of Clement XIV and Pius VI, leading to the inauguration of the so-called Pio-Clementino Museum at the Vatican.

To supplement these authoritative surveys there were also some useful home-grown productions. Aglionby's *Painting Illustrated in Three Dialogues* of 1685, the first English work on Italian art, gave a broad overview of the field. Of more practical use, however, was the 1754 edition of *An Account of the Statues, Bas-reliefs, Drawings and Pictures in Italy* by the two Jonathan Richardsons, father and son. The book had been produced from notes made by Richardson *fils* during a breakneck tour of the country and, despite some glaring omissions and eccentric judgments, it provided a wealth of useful detail. It remained, throughout the period, the principal English-language guide to the art of Italy and Rome.

In Rome itself the ideas and the writings of the Abbé Winckelmann were inescapable. They carried great authority: in 1763 Winckelmann was elected 'Prefect of Antiquities' by Clement XIII. Although his influential magnum opus, *The History of Ancient Art*, only appeared the following year its theories and opinions had already been prefigured in numerous earlier works, and even echoed in the writings of others.

From all this literature a basic hierarchy of Art was established. At its pinnacle stood Greek sculpture, with what Winckelmann called its 'quiet grandeur and noble simplicity'. This was the art that provided the true and absolute standard of beauty. Winckelmann, along with everyone else, believed that many of the classical statues extant in Rome were original Greek works, brought to the city as plunder; and after a decade of studying them he produced – in his *History of Ancient Art* – a systematic analysis of their stylistic development. It ran, he suggested, from the 'Archaic' style of the early Greeks, to the 'High' (or 'Sublime') style of the fifth century BC, to the 'Style of Beauty' ushered in by Lysippus and Apelles, and on to the debased Hellenistic 'Style of Imitation' adopted – and further corrupted – by the Romans.

Relating this to the field of Renaissance painting, Raphael was acclaimed as the greatest of the modern masters because he was the most 'Greek'. He, more than any of his contemporaries, was supposed to have studied the classical statues at Rome. It was even reported by Vasari that he had sent young assistants to Greece to make copies of the antiquities there. He achieved, according to Winckelmann, the equivalent in painting of the 'Sublime' style.

Having established the pre-eminence of Raphael, other artists were then ranked in relation to him: Michelangelo as his immediate and great precursor, Correggio and Daniele da Volterra as his disciples, the Carracci, Guercino, Guido Reni and other members of the Bolognese school as the inheritors of his classically inspired tradition (and the creators of a 'Style of Beauty'). There was almost no interest in Raphael's predecessors. Early Renaissance artists – such as Fra Angelico, Botticelli and Piero della Francesca – failed even to register.

To explain (or justify) this hierarchy, and to discriminate between the various artworks and artists, a whole quasi-scientific theory of art was elaborated, with its own fixed criteria and specialist language. It could range from the crisply specific to the impressively vague. Winckelmann's long study of antique statues gave him the confidence to assert various important rules: 'the so-called [and much admired] Greek profile consists of an almost straight or a slightly depressed line formed by forehead and nose'; 'a wide and deeply arched chest was regarded [by the Ancient Greeks] as the universal mark of beauty'; 'of the testicles the left is always larger.'

Order, clarity, a tendency to the ideal and general rather than the particular and natural, a preference for 'lofty' subject matter and the fit expression of it: these were among the prevailing precepts of the age. Raphael, for instance, was praised by Joshua Reynolds because 'In all the pictures in which he has represented the Apostles, he has drawn them with great nobleness: he has given them as much dignity as the human figure is capable of receiving; yet we are expressly told in Scripture that they had no such respectable appearance.' Bernini's statue of *David*, meanwhile, was condemned because of the 'mean' expression of the subject; he is 'biting his underlip' as he looses his slingshot, an expression that was deemed to be neither 'general' nor 'dignified'. In painting, 'a breadth of uniform and simple colour' was considered infinitely preferable to an excess of varied tints.

Based upon their adherence to these general rules, a set of conventional epithets had, over time, become associated with the various leading Italian artists. The would-be connoisseur soon learnt to deploy such key phrases as 'the Grace of Raffaelle', 'the Purity of Domenichino', 'the Air of Guido', 'the greatness of Taste of the Carraccis', and 'the Sublimity of Michelangelo'. Correggio was invariably praised for his unsurpassed rendering of hair. Caravaggio was always admitted to have had good 'Colour', even if this was vitiated by a total want of discretion.

For more ambitious students, the French scholar Roger de Piles produced in 1708 an influential 'Balance of Painters', in which he awarded marks out of twenty to the various modern masters in respect of what he proposed as the four key elements of painting: 'Composition', 'Design', 'Colouring', and 'Expression'. (Raphael, of course, came out top, dropping points only on the score of 'Colouring'.)

Raphael – 17, 18, 12, 18
Michelangelo – 8, 17, 4, 8
Correggio – 13, 13, 15, 12
The Carracci (Annibale and Ludovico) – 15, 17, 13, 13

Domenichino – 15, 17, 9, 17
Guercino – 18, 10, 10, 4
Caravaggio – 6, 6, 16, 0
Guido Reni – 0, 13, 9, 12
Daniele da Volterra – 12, 15, 5, 8

Armed with theories, epithets and tables such as these, the travellers of the period dutifully set out to investigate Rome's art galleries and museums. The exact route they took might vary, but the principal stopping places remained the same. And so did the verdicts given before the accepted masterpieces.

The great fresco cycles at the Vatican were considered the pinnacles of painting. Although Michelangelo was much preferred as a sculptor than a painter, his *Last Judgement* was still accounted the main draw at the Sistine Chapel, indeed the only thing really worth looking at there. For all its recognized power and importance, however, most eighteenth-century visitors found the great mural of the saved and the damned rather too 'Savage' to be truly admirable. There were some efforts to tone it down. In the 1730s Pope Clement XII had employed the artist Stefano Pozzi to paint draperies over the many nude figures, in an attempt to give a sense of decorum.† The impact, however, was minimal. 'Capricious and Disagreeable' was how the Richardsons described the painting, and this was a judgement echoed by many others. Mr C.J. Elliot, whose carefully annotated copy of Vasi's guidebook is in the British Library, remarked, 'the picture is wonderful, but I dislike it very much, as the subject is so unpleasant.'

The Sistine Chapel ceiling was treated by visitors as pretty much an afterthought. The popular art guide *Saggio Pittorico*, produced by Marc Antonio Prunetti in 1786, failed to mention it at all. The Richardsons were innovatory in not only looking at but also

---

† Concern about the propriety of a religious work in which so many of the figures were naked had surfaced even at the time of its composition. The then papal master of ceremonies, Biagio da Cesena, had denounced the composition as being more suited to a 'public bath-house or tavern' than a 'sacred place' (provoking Michelangelo to introduce a defamatory portrait of him – as the donkey-eared King Minos – among the damned). After Michelangelo's death in 1564, the then pope, Pius IV, commissioned Daniele da Volterra to paint draperies over some of the more conspicuously naked figures. He was also obliged to chisel out and rework the images of St Catherine and St Blaise, as it appeared that the latter was looking at the former's naked behind – if indeed he wasn't actually locked in sexual union with her. This work, however, was interrupted when Pius IV died, and the scaffolding that Daniele was working from had to be dismantled to clear the chapel ready for the ensuing conclave.

Michelangelo's *Last Judgement* on the end wall of the Sistine Chapel

Raphael's *School of Athens*

preferring the ceiling decorations. They thought the sibyls, as subjects, better suited to Michelangelo's particular genius than the souls of the dead. Few others, however, seem to have taken their lead.

Most visitors to the Vatican were, after all, interested principally in looking not at the Sistine Chapel but at the various works of Raphael near by. Almost all contemporary accounts of the papal palace begin with a description of Raphael's *Loggie*, before proceeding to his *Stanze*. The *Loggie*, so highly esteemed by Lassels in the previous century, had suffered rather from exposure to the elements and been substantially overpainted, so it was the *Stanze* that became the main focus of interest and admiration. Martyn was echoing the recognized wisdom when he called them 'the first works in fresco that the world can boast'. All four rooms were dutifully filed through, though the twin highlights were now recognized to be the image in the *Stanza di Eliodoro* of St Peter being delivered from prison – on account of the 'singular' effect created by its having three light sources, the moon, the torch and refulgent angel (see plate VIII) and the 'truly magnificent' *School of Athens* in the *Stanza della Segnatura* – 'for composition, and variety and justness of expression unrivalled'.

Lest the general approval should seem uncritical, minor 'defects' were pointed out. Samuel Powel, the young Philadelphian, was told by Mr Byres to note, in Raphael's *Loggie*, the 'noble but too straddling a fig[ure] of the Almighty' in the scene of the Separation of Chaos. But these were minor quibbles, intended to point up the general level of excellence.

Indeed such was Raphael's exalted position among all eighteenth-century visitors, that even his 'skull' was a major attraction. It was displayed at the Roman art institute, the Accademia di S. Luca (then in a building close to the Forum), beneath what was believed to be the master's painting of St Luke appearing to the Madonna. (Neither item, it seems, was authentic: the painting – still in the academy's collection – is now ascribed to Timoteo Viti, Raphael's sometime teacher; while the skull's true origins – and current whereabouts – are unknown.)

Raphael's *Transfiguration*, then in the church of S. Pietro in Montorio, was esteemed 'the greatest painting in the world'. It headed the conventional list – given by Ficoroni – of 'the four most celebrated pictures' in Rome. The others were: *Deposition* by Daniele da Volterra in the Orsini Chapel in SS. Trinità del Monte; Andrea Sacchi's *Vision of St Romuald* in the church of that saint; and Domenichino's *Last Communion of St Jerome* in the oratory of S. Girolamo della Carità on the Piazza Farnese. (The *Deposition*, as a fresco, remains *in situ* in the church at the top of the Spanish Steps; the other three paintings are now all in the Vatican Pinacoteca.)

This quartet seems to have emerged by slow consensus over the course of the late seventeenth and early eighteenth centuries, reflecting the views of both artists (Poussin especially) and 'professori'†. By the 1760s they were famous for being famous. Certainly by modern standards it is a curious collection, and even by the accepted standards of the eighteenth century it is sometimes hard to work out exactly why they achieved such an exalted status.

Raphael's *Transfiguration* (see plate IX) is a strange image, its upper portion showing the transfigured Christ, aglow in his white robes, floating above the summit of Mount Tabor between the prophets Moses and Elijah, while below the Apostles frantically

---

† The French art writer André Félibien (1619–1695), in his *Entretiens sur les vies et sur les ouvrages des plus excellens peintres* (1666), recorded that Poussin considered the Raphael, the Domenichino and the Daniele da Volterra to be the three finest paintings in Rome. Poussin, moreover, had worked in Sacchi's studio when he first came to Rome.

attempt, without success, to exorcise the evil spirit from a possessed boy. It is still prominently displayed in the Vatican art gallery, but is no longer considered either the world's or even the artist's greatest work.

None of the other pictures currently enjoys any status at all. To the fashionable visitor of the 1760s, however, they were indispensable sights. Daniele da Volterra was a pupil of Michelangelo, and his *Deposition* (see plate x) is a Mannerist riot, swirling with mauve and orange drapery, in which some half-dozen stalwart workmen, perched on ladders, are lowering the body of the dead Christ from the cross while below the three Marys and the Virgin swoon and weep. It is now in rather better condition than it was. All the eighteenth-century accounts complain of its cracked and dirty surface. Nevertheless its supposed excellence remained undimmed by grime. The guidebooks confirmed its position as 'one of the first pictures in Rome'. And it was a verdict to which visitors seem readily to have subscribed: Mr Elliot found it ' a very fine Picture, indeed'.

There were, it is true, some doubts among the cognoscenti about several elements of the composition. The Richardsons, in particular, fretted at the work's 'Absolute want of Harmony', and its many 'grievous improprieties'; not the least of these – in their opinion – was that one of the women approaching the Cross had a Handkerchief 'not at her Eyes, but at her Nose'.

Amazingly, the Richardsons do not seem to have minded the even more striking oddness of Domenichino's *St Jerome* (see plate xi). Painted in 1614 at the height of the Counter Reformation, it shows the aged and emaciated saint, wearing little more than a loincloth, being supported by his disciples as he prepares to receive his last communion. The scene is set in the fancifully imagined church at Bethlehem; Jerome's faithful lion (looking like an overgrown pussy cat) sits in the foreground, while overhead some angelic babes cavort. Domenichino's established reputation, however, was as the great inheritor and continuer of Raphael's classical style, so his work was always accepted as being pure and classical, no matter what it looked like. Constable was particularly charmed by the landscape in the background of the scene, calling it 'a requiem to soothe the departing spirit... its effect like that of solemn music heard from an adjoining apartment'.

Andrea Sacchi's painting was rather more staid. Sacchi, who died in 1661, was ranked as the last great painter of the classical tradition. The fame of his *St Romuald* (see plate xii) rested on its carefully orchestrated arrangement of pale tones: it is an essay in white. The saintly white-bearded founder of the Camaldolese Order sits among his white-habited followers, while in the bright haze of the distance scores more monks ascend a miraculous ladder towards a glowing heaven. In Prunetti's judgement it presented the most delightful image of tranquillity.

Besides this illustrious 'top four', there were a few other pictorial highpoints on every Grand Tourist's itinerary – all of them works of the sixteenth or early seventeenth Centuries. The many Correggios at the Palazzo Barberini could not be missed: 'Their Beauty is Inconceivable,' proclaimed the Richardsons.† Standing before these pictures of shy Madonnas and pert deities it was customary to expatiate upon their peculiar 'Harmony' and 'Grace' and to compare both – not unfavourably – to the same qualities in Raphael's work, while lamenting a certain deficiency in the 'correctness of proportion' of the artist's 'Design'.

The only one of Caravaggio's paintings viewed with any enthusiasm at this period was *The Cardsharps*, also then in the Barberini collection (and now in the Kimbell Art Museum, Fort Worth, Texas). The image of the two dandified cardsharps gulling an earnest youth became a hugely popular print. The artist's bracing – if highly theatrical – realism was thought better suited to low rather than religious subjects. Reflecting this popular view, the poet Thomas Gray suggested that, 'If this master had known his own talent, which was that in painting, which comedy is in writing . . . he would have surpassed the Flemish School.'

At St Peter's *The Burial of St Petronilla* by Guercino was eagerly sought out. This huge altarpiece, over 4 metres (14 feet) high, depicted in its lower portion the interment of the beautiful virgin saint (daughter of St Peter), while in the upper section she is being received in glory. The picture's merit – according to Prunetti – lay in its 'Invention' and its colouring. The latter, a boldly contrasted arrangement of deep blues and dark shadows,

Caravaggio's *The Cardsharps* or *I Bari*

was done in what the Richardsons described as the artist's much-admired 'Black Strong manner'. (The painting is now in the gallery of the Palazzo dei Conservatori.)

A special trip had to be made to see the *Aurora* painted by Guido Reni on the ceiling of the garden pavilion at the Palazzo Parravicini-Rospigliosi: 'one of the finest frescoes in the world', in the conventional estimate of Martyn, Prunetti and many others. The picture of the chariot of the sun, being led towards the dawn by a posse of tripping goddesses was, according to the Richardsons, 'A Gay Subject', and the 'Enchanting

LEFT Guercino's *The Burial of St Petronilla*
RIGHT Guido Reni's *Aurora*

[Guido] the fittest of any to execute it'. The 'Airs' of the goddesses' heads were considered particularly 'Exquisite'. (The palace is no longer open to the public, and the picture can only be seen on the first day of each month.)

And, beyond even the much-admired *Aurora*, there was the 'most excellent Gallery of the Carracci', the sumptuous decorative cycle depicting the love lives of the classical gods, created at the end of the 1590s by Annibale Carracci and his pupils on the first floor of the Palazzo Farnese. While Evelyn had merely admired its *trompe l'oeil* effects, the work was now praised as combining the virtues of all the great masters. It was a veritable Art primer, displaying, as the Richardsons put it, 'a Copious, and Rich, a Solid, and Judicious way of Thinking, Strong, and Just Expressions, a Colouring between the Gravity of *Rafaelle*, and the Gaiety of *Guido*, and inclining to that of *Correggio*, whom [Annibale Carracci] had much study'd; the noble Attitudes, and Contours of the Antique, and the *Roman* Schools somewhat reduced towards Common Nature, but very Great, and Open . . . In a Word all that . . . can be Wish'd for in Painting is here to be found.' (This work has become almost as difficult to see as the Rospigliosi *Aurora*; the French Embassy is now installed in the Palazzo Farnese and tours can only be made by prior arrangement.)

Aside from such accredited masterworks there were, of course, many lesser artistic pleasures littered through Rome's princely collections. The numerous 'landskips' by Claude Lorrain, Salvator Rosa, Poussin, Dughet, and other seventeenth-century practitioners, were much enjoyed. But there was little interest in more modern art – beyond, of course, the fashionable portraiture of Pompeo Batoni, Angelica Kauffmann and their lesser rivals. An exception was also made for the German artist Raphael Mengs. As the protégé of Cardinal Albani, the friend of Winckelmann and the erstwhile tutor of Byres, he was certainly well connected. Byres would lead his charges to the church of S. Eusebius to see Mengs' frescoed cycle there, extolling the 'remarkable . . . strength of ye colouring'. The artist's *Parnassus*, painted on the ceiling of Cardinal Albani's villa, was praised as a masterpiece by Winckelmann. For the most part, however, it was believed that the arts in contemporary Rome had suffered a sad decline.

Michelangelo's *Moses*

The one exception, according to all the sources, was the practice of mosaic. In this the modern Romans were considered to have achieved 'a perfection beyond even that of the ancients'. As Ficoroni explained, by manufacturing the individual *tesserae*, not from natural stone, but from 'paste or composition' contemporary practitioners were able 'not only to represent all the principal colours in a strong and lively manner, but all the different shades and degrees of each, as far as they are wanted'. This skill was directed towards creating highly polished and vastly expanded versions of famous oil paintings. A huge and garish version of Domenichino's *Last Communion of St Jerome* created for St Peter's (and still *in situ*) achieved great fame on account of its size, its subject matter, and its having cost the stupendous sum of 15,000 crowns. (Raphael's *Transfiguration* and Guercino's *St Petronilla* were among the several other works to be rendered in the same way, and at the same cost.)

Away from paintings, 'the four most celebrated works of the modern sculptors in Rome' were accounted to be Michelangelo's *Moses*, Algardi's *Story of Attila*, Duquesnoy's *St Susanna* and Bernini's *St Bibiana*.

Of these only Michelangelo's bearded patriarch at S. Pietro in Vincoli still holds its position on the tourist's itinerary. In the eighteenth century it ranked as a 'treasure' – to borrow Titi's term. It was, however, one of those works perhaps more esteemed than liked. The Richardsons complained that the figure had 'much the Air of a Goat'. And indeed Moses' horns seem to have been a constant distraction to British visitors. Boswell likened the patriarch to a satyr. Such cavils, however, did nothing to dampen the work's high repute. (Meanwhile Michelangelo's *Pietà* at St Peter's was noticed largely because it was the great man's 'first work', done when he was only twenty-four, while his naked figure of *Christ the Redeemer* at S. Maria sopra Minerva – adorned with a bronze loincloth – seems to have been viewed as an 'object of curiosity'.†

The other favourite sculptures of the Grand Tourist now have to be searched out. They are unsignposted, and indeed unmentioned in all but the most exhaustive of guides. Alessandro Algardi's large relief, completed in 1653, can still be seen adorning the altar front in St Leo's chapel in the left transept of St Peter's. Unfortunately, the crowd-control barriers mean that often it cannot be approached. Nevertheless

† Raphael was not a sculptor, but in the church of S. Maria del Popolo, 'the most remarkable thing', according to Edward Martyn, was the 'statue of Jonah standing on the fish, executed by Lorenzetto from a design by Raffaelle, who himself, as they say, attended every stroke of the chisel'. The figure, looking more like Antinous than an Old Testament prophet is still to be seen there, in the Chigi Chapel.

its scale is such that, even from a distance, Pope Leo I can be made out, remonstrating sternly with an alarmed-looking Attila the Hun, while Saints Peter and Paul fly overhead in close formation, their swords unsheathed. For all the conspicuous drama of the scene, there is a sober classicized restraint about the work: Ficoroni compared it to a bas-relief in the Museo Capitolino representing Marcus Aurelius pacifying the barbarians.

The *St Susanna* by Duquesnoy stands in a niche to the right of the altar in the little church of S. Maria di Loreto, close to Trajan's Column. It is easy to see why this serene noble-browed matron in a flowing robe appealed so much to eighteenth-century taste and supplanted the *St Andrew* in St Peter's as Duquesnoy's most highly regarded work: she looks very like a classical goddess. Indeed the head appears to have been copied from the Venus in the Museo Capitolino, and the robes from a statue of *Urania* there. Ficoroni, always ready with the appropriate praise, considered the statue equal to the creations of the Greek masters. It enjoyed, moreover, an international reputation, after the French sculptor Guillaume Coustou made a marble copy of it, which was transported to Paris in 1739 and displayed at the Lourvre. There were also casts taken for the Academies of Madrid and St Petersburg.

ABOVE Duquesnoy's *St Susanna*
OPPOSITE Algardi's *Story of Attila*

199

A rather fainter air of classicism hangs over Bernini's *St Bibiana*. The statue stands, as it has always done, in a grey scalloped alcove above the altar in the tiny church of the same name, which now finds itself squashed awkwardly beneath the railway tracks leading into Stazione Termini, but in the eighteenth century lay in a bosky corner of the *disabitato*. St Bibiana was a Roman virgin, martyred during the persecutions of Julian the Apostate in the fourth century, and Bernini has treated her with rare restraint. The work, done in 1624, was his first religious commission and his first draped figure. If there is a trace of sensuality in the saint's parted lips and dreamy upward glance, it seems largely spiritualized. And that of course was why the statue became so admired. 'The chastest of his works,' remarked one visitor approvingly, 'and without flutter.'

Bernini's *St Bibiana*

The more exuberant manifestations of Bernini's genius (which are now so well regarded) tended to be treated with a mixture of hostility and suspicion during the eighteenth century. Byres liked to tell his charges that Bernini had 'spoilt the taste for Sculpture in Italy (as Borromini [had] the taste for architecture)'. Winckelmann, with his absolute faith in classical models, disapproved of Bernini's irrepressible individualism and eccentricity; he suggested that all the sculptor's figures 'looked as if they were suffering from dropsy'. And certainly those agitated saints and impassioned goddesses, spilling out of their swirling drapery, were very far removed from Winckelmann's Greek ideal of 'quiet grandeur and noble simplicity'.

At the Villa Borghese Bernini's *Apollo and Daphne* was generally disparaged. Samuel Powel (following Byres' lead) found it, 'not pleasing – She is a little like a fury – the fig[ure]s too long and lank'. The 'mean' expression of his *David* has already been noted. Even worse, though, was the *Ecstasy of St Theresa* at the church of S. Maria della Vittoria (see page 252). It lay entirely beyond the pale. Although conceived as a representation of intense spiritual union, the image of the ecstatic, prostrate saint – lips aquiver, eyes shuttered, head thrown back – and the smiling angel armed with his golden dart, seemed to suggest an altogether more profane interpretation. Confronted with it, one scandalized cleric exclaimed, 'I feel within myself, if I may so say, a kind of mental blush.' It was not what visitors expected to encounter in a place of worship. A few bold spirits did, of course, enjoy its very dangerousness. The worldly French scholar Charles de Brosses commented with wry amusement 'If that is divine love, I know all about it.'

The works of Bernini, Michelangelo, Raphael and the rest provided a useful prelude to the Grand Tourist's encounter with the masterpieces of classical antiquity. The faculties of discrimination could, it was supposed, be honed through a course of 'modern' masters, before classical statuary – the highpoint, and also the main point, of any visit to Rome – was reached. (Hofrat Reiffenstein advised Goethe to start his artistic education with the Carracci Gallery at the Palazzo Farnese, and then work up to Raphael, before setting off to see the antiquities in the Vatican collection.)

Antique statues, it was understood, provided the absolute standard against which all art must be judged. As Winckelmann proclaimed, 'Let no man, who has not formed his taste upon antiquity, take it into his head to act as the connoisseur of beauty; his ideas must be a parcel of whimsies.'

Even among classical statues, however, there was a hierarchy. The 'best' works had to be sought out. All the authorities had strong views on which were the finest pieces, and although there might be quibbling about the exact order of a 'Top Ten', a general consensus did exist – and about the very finest works there was even unanimity. Although the list contained many of the sculptures admired by Evelyn and his contemporaries in the seventeenth century, there were also many notable changes and additions.

The polychrome works that had appealed so greatly to the Baroque spirit were now reviled. The *Seneca* emerging from his bath at the Villa Borghese could, according to the German connoisseur Baron von Stosch, 'hardly be considered worthy of the art of antiquity'. Purity was preferred.

The *Farnese Hercules*

The *Callipygian Venus*

The *Meleager* (still, then, in the Palazzo Picchini) remained one of the undisputed stars. Naked and slightly larger than life, even Smollett admitted that the statue of the youthful huntsman was beautiful. At the Palazzo Farnese, however, the *Toro* had been overtaken by the hulking muscle-bound *Hercules* as the most valued work in the collection (a collection which, though still much frequented, was no longer rated supreme).† Samuel Sharp, of course, dissented from the general view, announcing that he could not admire the work, as no man ever looked like that. (The *Callipygian Venus* – or 'Venus of the beautiful buttocks' – was, perhaps unsurprisingly, still considered one of the gems of the collection by the succession of male Grand Tourists. Samuel Powel, the Philadelphian Quaker, noted it as, 'most exquisite – a lovely face & sweet A–').

Another statue that had risen in status during the course of the eighteenth century was the languorous *Sleeping Faun* at the Palazzo Barberini. This sculpture had belonged to the Barberini family for many years, but – left incomplete and lying on the ground – it attracted little notice. Only after it was 'restored' (in 1679), and artfully arranged in a lolling position upon a marble tree stump, did it become a popular draw. Byres pointed it

† As mentioned in Chapter 6, all the sculptures from the Palazzo Farnese were removed to Naples in 1787.

out to his charges as 'one of the first Things in Rome' – while noting that the legs were 'modern and bad'; Edward Martyn endorsed it as 'an admirable Greek work'; while Charles Burney (the music historian, and father of Fanny Burney) rated it 'the fifth or sixth statue in Rome'. (It is now in the Glyptothek at Munich having been bought in 1814 – amidst much controversy – by Crown Prince Ludwig of Bavaria).†

Historical rather than aesthetic distinction accounted for the celebrity of a large nude statue of *Pompey* at the Palazzo Spada. It was believed to be the very piece at the feet of which Caesar had been assassinated. Some even suggested that a faint reddish tinge visible on the legs of the figure might be a trace of the great man's blood. (Gibbon, to his credit, had doubts about the correctness of the attribution. Few other visitors did.)

The story of the statue's discovery also contributed to its popular appeal. According to the established legend it had been unearthed back in the 1550s, during the construction of a cellar beneath a house on the Vicolo dei Lentari (near the site of the Theatre of Pompey – though not really so close as to justify the grand historical claims made for the work). Although the greatest part of the statue lay beneath the house where the cellar was being dug, the head rested in the ground under the neighbouring property. This occasioned a dispute over ownership between the two householders. The case came before a judge who ordered that the statue be decapitated, and the two parts divided between the claimants. Fortunately the then pope, Julius III, heard of the judgement, and to prevent the vandalism bought the work for 500 scudi. He subsequently presented it to Cardinal Capodiferro, owner of the Palazzo Spada at that time.

---

† Among eighteenth-century visitors to Rome the desire to buy antiquities was quite as keen as the desire to look at them. And the English, with their great wealth, were the most enthusiastic purchasers. It was said that, if they could have carried it off, they would have bought the Colosseum. Although a huge quantity of stuff was brought back to Britain, papal export licences prevented foreigners acquiring the more celebrated works from the established princely collections. Instead, if they were not to be content with copies and casts, visitors were obliged to buy up recently discovered and heavily restored pieces from the numerous dealers and middlemen who offered their services. The doyen of the profession was the sculptor Bartolomeo Cavaceppi (friend of Cardinal Albani and restorer-in-chief to the papal collections), but almost every *cicerone* and expatriate artist was involved in the trade. Indeed James Byres was among the leading practitioners. He maintained a team of artists to restore the pieces that his agents dug up or found. Broken statues were supplied with missing noses, limbs or heads, fragmentary vases were made whole – a practice approved by Winckelmann and the taste of the times. Byres' greatest coup, however, was to sell – and get an export licence for – the so-called Portland Vase, now in the British Museum, but formerly in the collection of the Princess of Palestrina.

The statue's dramatic provenance has long since been discredited. It is now thought to have been a statue from the barracks of the Green chariot-racing team, which stood near the Campo dei Fiori. It remains, however, in the Palazzo Spada, in what has become the council chamber of the Consiglio di Stato, and as a result it can only be visited by special arrangement.

At Cardinal Albani's elegant new Villa there was – set above the chimneypiece in the main salon – an equally celebrated and very much more beautiful work: a bas-relief of *Antinous* which had been discovered during excavations at Hadrian's Villa in 1735. (Gibbon found it 'admirably finished, soft, well turned and full of flesh'.)

Hadrian's Villa at Tivoli was proving very rich ground for antiquity hunters. It was from there that many of the newest and brightest stars in the Museo Capitolino had come. They can still be seen, almost exactly as they were arranged for eighteenth-century visitors: a full figure of *Antinous* (now thought to be *Hermes*) bought from Cardinal Albani, the laughing *Satyr* in *rosso antico* marble, 'the well known mosaic of the pigeons', and (from 1765) the two magnificent centaurs in *bigio morato*, standing in the middle of the main gallery.

RIGHT ABOVE The *Sleeping Faun*
RIGHT BELOW *Pompey* in the Palazzo Spada

They joined there other important works, most notably the far-famed *Dying Gladiator*, which had been bought for the museum from the Ludovisi family in 1734. Even Samuel Sharp was impressed by the stricken warrior: 'The expression is so strong, a man may walk round and round the statue till he almost forget it is stone.' Edward Martyn found the man's 'countenance vulgar' but felt that that was exactly how it would have been (see page 220).

Also on view at the museum was the so-called *Capitoline Venus* (see page 98). Discovered in 1670 near the basilica of S. Vitale, the image of the goddess 'issuing from the bath' had gradually grown in status to fill the void left by the removal of the *Medici Venus* from Rome to Florence. By the time the statue was installed in the Capitoline collection (in 1752), it was ranked as the best and most celebrated representation of Venus in Rome. Lady Anne Miller was not completely convinced, remarking, 'She has a great share of grace ... yet I think, was she dressed, she would appear too plump for the present taste.' Most male visitors, however, do not seem to have shared her opinion.

The collection was – so connoisseurs agreed – best seen by torchlight. (Nocturnal tours of the museum became a popular feature of the period.) It was believed that the flickering play of light on the smooth, pale, isolated marble forms revealed the beauty and drama of the works with a rare intensity.

Great though the Museo Capitolino was, for a visitor of the 1760s, it ranked second to the collection at the Vatican, or – more especially – to the Belvedere sculpture court. This marked a return for the courtyard to the unassailable position that it had enjoyed during the years of the High Renaissance. Its shuttered niches were once again acknowledged to contain the very 'finest works of the Greek chisel' in Rome.

Opinion as to exactly which were the 'finest works' had, however, shifted yet again. Some of the pieces most admired by Evelyn and his contemporaries only a century before had fallen rather from favour. The two recumbent river gods – *Tiber* and *Nile* – were passed over by the guidebooks and actually dismissed by Richardson as 'not of a good taste', while the *Dying Cleopatra* (the darling of the Baroque period) no longer enjoyed a special status. The books often relegated her to a footnote, and Lady Anne Miller, though interested to see the notorious heroine, complained that she was not struck by the statue 'as with a perfect piece of sculpture'.

For the men – and women – of the Grand Tour the preferred works were now *Antinous* ('a model for grace'), the *Torso* 'so greatly admired by Michael Angelo' and *Laocoön*, which was still revered both for itself and on account of Pliny's recommendation. Edward Martyn called it 'the noblest group in the world'. Boswell considered it 'supreme', and found his 'nerves so contracted by it' that everything else paled in comparison.

The *Belvedere Torso*

The subject was admitted to be 'horrible', but – as Lady Anne Miller remarked – the 'expression [is] so just'.

Certainly the statue's power does not seem to have been diminished by the fact that the main figure's missing arm was supplied by a terracotta substitute – done, according to some guidebooks, by Bernini. Behind the statue, in the niche, lay the not very well finished marble arm that had been produced by Michelangelo's pupil Montorsoli – though the guidebooks, always ready with an exaggeration, pointed it out as the work of Michelangelo himself, claiming that the artist had left it unfinished because 'he found he could do nothing worthy of being joined to so admirable a piece'. It lay there as a mute witness to the superiority of the best ancient artists to the best 'moderns'. (A further intervention, carried out in the 1720s by the sculptor Agostino Cornacchini had given Laocoön's elder son an upraised arm, to echo the gesture of the central figure.)

Nevertheless, despite the flood of praise and admiration, *Laocoön* was now deemed to rank only second among the masterpieces of the Belvedere. In pole position stood the serene yet forceful image of *Apollo* – 'incomparably the finest single figure in the world'.

The elevation of the *Apollo Belvedere*, after some two centuries of comparative neglect, to the very first place among all the statues in Rome was very largely due to the enthusiasm of Winckelmann. He loved the work, and extolled its virtues unstintingly. It represented – as he explained – Apollo 'in a state of anger over the serpent, Python, slain by his arrows, and at the same time with a feeling of contempt for his victory, which to a god was an easy achievement. As the skilful artist wished to personify the most beautiful of the gods, he expressed only the anger in the nose, and the contempt on the lips. The latter emotion is manifested by the elevation of the lower lip, by which the chin is raised at the same time; the former is visible in the dilated nostrils.' The image of the god seemed the very embodiment of that Greek ideal: 'quiet grandeur and noble simplicity'.

In a celebrated passage from his *History of Ancient Art*, Winckelmann described its effect: 'Before this miracle of art I forget the entire universe and my soul takes on a nobility befitting its dignity. From admiration I pass to ecstasy; I feel my breast dilate and expand as if at the height of prophetic frenzy; I am transported to Delos and to the groves of Lycia, places that Apollo honoured with his presence; the statue takes on life, as did the beautiful creation of Pygmalion.'

This was heady stuff. And although most travellers of the period did not achieve quite such dizzying heights of ecstasy while contemplating the statue, they knew they were supposed to be bowled over. And almost invariably they were. The tones of Winckelman are echoed in dozens of travel accounts: 'His attitude is beautiful,

The *Apollo Belvedere*

natural, unaffected; his countenance composed and elegant, the workmanship of every part exquisite . . . he has an unspeakable sublimity, that inspires admiration, awe and reverence.' With more originality, but equal enthusiasm, the young American artist Benjamin West, when confronted by the work, exclaimed, 'My God, how like it is to a young Mohawk warrior!' (West's Italian companions were initially shocked that he should compare their divine statue to a savage. But after he had explained the nobility and beauty of the Red Indians to them, they were delighted by the allusion.)

In the face of the general tide of enthusiasm there were inevitably some few small voices of dissension. It was suggested by some that the god's ears were too large. And one expert in archery (the British traveller, Philip Francis) claimed that if the god was supposed to be loosing an arrow from his bow, he ought to be resting upon his left leg, rather than his right. Such quibbles, however, did nothing to detract from the work's celebrity or status.

It became an iconic image, and also a merchandizing phenomenon. Indeed it can claim to be the first artwork to achieve this distinctly modern dual status, paving the way for such later examples as Michelangelo's *David*, the *Mona Lisa* and Munch's *Scream*. All the available methods of reproduction were pressed into service to spread its fame. It was reproduced in prints and drawings, and even in micro-mosaic. For a small additional charge Pompeo Batoni might include it in the background of a portrait. Miniature versions were available in bronze, ivory and ceramic. Full-scale casts could also be acquired – and they were.

Dozens of versions of the *Apollo Belvedere* still stand in the draughty hallways and sculpture galleries of Britain's stately homes – serene and erect, their nostrils flaring slightly and their blank eyes fixed upon that distant time when Rome was considered the climax of the Grand Tour – and the *Apollo Belvedere* was considered the very climax of Rome.

·VIII·
ROMANTIC ROME
AND THE VICTORIANS

'I ABSOLUTELY WILL HAVE no antiquary to go prating from fragment to fragment, and tell me that were I to stay five years in Rome, I should not see half it contained.' William Beckford, while visiting Rome in October 1780, dispensed with convention; rather than making the Grand Tourist's dutiful round with a learned *cicerone* and a fat guidebook, he preferred to 'struggle and wander about just as the spirit chuses', relishing the sights and sounds of the city as they came to him. Not cool analysis but emotional engagement and gentle reverie directed his investigations. The measure of the traveller, for him, was not the depth of his erudition but the profundity of his emotional response. Great spirits were likely to be greatly affected by Rome.

Goethe, one of the greatest spirits of the age, was shaken to the very core, during his sojourn at Rome in 1786–8: 'One is, so to speak, reborn, and one's former ideas seem like child's swaddling clothes,' he announced, before generously suggesting that such rebirth was open to all: 'Here the most ordinary person becomes somebody. Everywhere else one starts from the outside and works inward; [in Rome] it seems to be the other way round.'

These passages reverberate with a new and distinctive tone. It is the note of Romanticism – unfettered, intense, reflective and personal. Earlier generations arrived in Rome with a determination to be both thorough and objective. The Grand Tourists wanted to see everything and to judge it according to established rules. By the end of the eighteenth century, however, such certainties were crumbling. A new mood of brooding self-absorption was becoming ever more prevalent.

Increasing numbers were now content to wander as the spirit chose. Before the masterpieces of art and antiquity subjective reaction supplanted objective criticism. Visitors became anxious to proclaim their own feelings, and display their own temperaments in the face of the city and its marvels. A visit to Rome was no longer a social finishing school cum art appreciation course cum classical history tour: it was a transformative experience.

Europe, too, was being transformed. The great age of the aristocratic Grand Tour ended with the cataclysm of the French Revolution and the Napoleonic wars that followed it. The immediate impact was to interrupt all travel. But, as the smoke of war cleared, following Napoleon's final defeat at Waterloo in 1815, it revealed a new landscape. In France the old order and the old certainties had been overturned, and it seemed likely that the same sort of radical change might spread across the whole unsettled continent.

It was in the shadow of these upheavals that many of the great figures of the Romantic Age made their way to Rome. Chateaubriand, who had created the archetypal brooding, pessimistic romantic hero 'René' in his novel *Le Génie du christianisme*, arrived in 1803 to serve in the Napoleonic legation. (His consumptive mistress, Pauline de Beaumont, followed him south, and expired – in suitably romantic fashion – after a visit to the Colosseum.) Madame de Staël toured the city during her 1805 visit to Italy. Lord Byron stayed only twenty-two days at Rome (29 April to 20 May 1817) but drank it all in. Shelley spent a fruitful autumn – in 1818 – as well as the spring of the following year, wandering about the place. Keats arrived in November 1820, and never left; he died of consumption on 23 February 1821 in a small flat beside the Spanish Steps.

Each responded to the city with an intensity that not only changed them but also changed the way that others would come to view the place. Dispensing for the most part with the time-worn itineraries of the previous age, they lighted upon new objects to admire, or else found new ways to see old sights. And they recorded their experiences in enduring form – in poems, plays, novels, letters and other literary works.

Chateaubriand returned often to his memories of Rome in his various autobiographical writings. Mme de Staël's novel *Corinne, ou Italie* achieved an instant, and international, success when it appeared in 1807 – and Rome stood at the heart of the story, as the setting for the doomed love affair between Corinne (a glorious Italian poetess) and the upright Scottish aristocrat Oswald, Lord Nelvil. Byron provided a full poetical tour of the city in Book IV of his best-selling epic *Childe Harold's Pilgrimage*, while Shelley littered his works with specific Roman references.

Ironically, these various Romantic reactions to the city took place against a backdrop of rather unromantic modernization. In the last decades of the eighteenth century and the first of the nineteenth, Rome itself was being transformed. The political turmoil stirred up across Europe by the French Revolution and its bloody aftermath marked Rome in many ways, both deep and direct.

In the immediate wake of the Revolution, the then pope, Pius VI (1775–99), had allied the Papal States with Austria and various other powers against the schismatic Republicans of France. But his justifiable expectation that this alliance would secure a swift and easy victory over the supposedly disorganized revolutionary forces had not been fulfilled. The genius of Napoleon ensured a succession of French military triumphs. Italy was invaded, and Rome was invested twice by French troops – in 1798 and 1808. After the first occupation the pope was exiled and a short-lived republic established. Following the second, Rome became part of Napoleon's European possessions, and the second city of the new French Empire.

Such upheavals made their mark upon the fabric of the city. Although Napoleon's ambitious schemes to remove Trajan's Column and the two *Horse-Tamers* to Paris were abandoned, much else was taken. In accordance with the onerous terms of the Treaty of Tolentino, the hundred most famous artworks from the papal and Capitoline collections – including the *Laocoön, Apollo Belvedere* and Raphael's *Transfiguration* – were shipped to Paris to adorn the Louvre (or the Musée Napoléon as it was then known).

All of these, it is true, with the exception of the *Tiber* river god from the Belvedere sculpture court, were returned to Rome following Napoleon's eventual defeat at Waterloo in 1815, but other losses were permanent. The French authorities used the excuse of any opposition to their occupation to confiscate the collections of several Roman aristocrats. The treasures of the Palazzo Braschi and the Villa Albani were carried off to the Louvre and, for the most part, remain there still.

Napoleon also bought, for a rather over-generous sum, all the antiquities in the great collection of his impoverished brother-in-law Prince Camillo Borghese, thus adding the celebrated *Borghese Gladiator* and the *Hermaphrodite* to his museum – and further reducing the number of acknowledged masterpieces in Rome.

Pius VI's successor, Pius VII (Chiaramonti), did try to make good some of the sore losses to the papal collections. After the papacy's return from exile in 1800, he pursued an active policy of acquisition and excavation, gathering up many newly discovered antiquities. None, perhaps, was of the first quality, but – elegantly displayed in one of the long wings flanking the Vatican Palace courtyard – they added a new feature to Rome's cultural trail.

The arrangement of the various pieces in this so-called Chiaramonti Gallery was undertaken by the brilliant Neoclassical sculptor Antonio Canova. It was one of many services he performed for the papal court. (Following the defeat of Napoleon he would negotiate the return of Rome's plundered art treasures) He also – of course – carried out numerous sculptural commissions. And indeed it must have seemed providential that, at a moment when Rome had been stripped of so many of her great classical sculptures, the city should have been provided with an artistic genius almost capable of replicating the achievements of antiquity.

The twenty-three-year-old Canova had arrived in Rome in 1780 and rapidly confirmed his reputation as the greatest sculptor of the age. Classical restraint, high finish and a

Canova's *Perseus*

graceful purity of vision were the hallmarks of his art. He came to be regarded as the heir to Phidias and Praxiteles. When the Belvedere sculpture court was left almost bare by the depredations of Napoleon, Canova's statue of *Perseus* was installed – as a not-inappropriate substitute – in the niche vacated by the plundered *Apollo Belvedere*. (It can still be seen in the courtyard, together with his sculptures of the two Greek wrestlers, *Kreugas* and *Damoxenos*.)

For all the turmoil of the times, however, Rome's annexation to the French Empire in 1809 was not without its practical benefits. Napoleon and his officials saw themselves as the new Romans and they wanted old Rome to be a fit setting for their rule. As a result, during their seven-year hegemony, they carried forward the many schemes of restoration, construction and excavation that had been initiated by Pius VII and his brilliant Secretary of State Cardinal Ercole Consalvi, during the previous decade, as well as initiating several new ones of their own.

Rome's ancient monuments were treated for the first time since the fifth century to a campaign of systematic care and investigation. Excavations became more concerned with gaining historical information than discovering art treasures. And the whole operation was centralized under the newly created Commission for the Embellishment of Rome, directed by the city prefect. Much was accomplished. The piecemeal accretions of the past began to be stripped away: the full extent of Trajan's Market was gradually revealed; the so-called 'Baker's Tomb' attached to the Porta Maggiore was discovered enclosed within a mediaeval house. Many of the tombs along the Via Appia were restored. The fractured outer wall of the Colosseum was shored up by a massive brick-built buttress, and a huge quantity of ordure was removed from the arena. Exploratory investigations were carried out in the Forum of Trajan, the Domus Aurea, and the Baths of Diocletian.

But the largest project in hand was the excavation of the Forum. The cattle market was banished, and the archaeologists arrived, together with gangs of diggers (often chained convicts). The thousands of tons of earth that had buried the Temple of Vespasian (or Temple of Jupiter Tonans, as it was then called) were cleared away. The lower portions of the Arch of Septimius Severus were dug out; the pavement of the Via Sacra was uncovered. The identity of the Column of Phocas was revealed when the buildings surrounding it were demolished, and the base – with its inscription – was excavated.

At the opposite end of the *campo* the Arch of Titus was freed from its flanking mediaeval walls, and then restored (or pretty much rebuilt) by the favoured architect of the period, Giuseppe Valadier. The convent attached to the church of S. Francesca Romana was demolished, and many of the recent buildings that had grown up around the massive vaults of the *soi-disant* 'Temple of Peace' were also stripped away.

A map of 'Ancient and Modern Rome' from the 1819 edition of Vasi's guidebook

Napoleon also instituted several schemes of urban renewal. There was a dawning recognition that Rome presented a unique challenge to planners. The population had risen to over one hundred thousand, and although the city still retained its distinctive sense of spaciousness – with the demarcation between the *abitato* and *disabitato* as striking as ever to visitors from the crowded cities of the north – the pressure on space was beginning to tell. The constant discoveries of the archaeologists posed additional problems.

Two parallel cities – it was understood – would have to be accommodated: a modern one in which classical monuments and superfluous churches might be demolished to make way for important new developments, and an historical one, in which the great relics of the past were uncovered, restored and preserved in the midst of the contemporary scene. (The tension between these two competing visions still exists, but it first came into focus during the early nineteenth century.)

To enhance the 'modern' city Valadier was commissioned to tidy up the Piazza del Popolo, framing its sides with classically ordered, if rather dull, *palazzi*. He also created the charming Casino Valadier, in the new park on the Pincian hill, just above the square. And on a practical level St Peter's and other important monuments were fitted with lightning conductors.

This was the Rome to which so many of the great Romantics came in the years following Napoleon's defeat: a city of building projects, Neoclassical flourishes, large-scale excavations and practical safety measures. It was not, however, these sights that drew their attention and stimulated their reveries. They wanted something else.

The Mausoleum of Cecilia Metella, from a contemporary print

For the Romantic visitor Rome was pre-eminently a city of death, of disappointed hopes and slow decay, a place of weed-choked ruins and departed spirits. And that was why they liked it so much. 'The impression of [Rome] exceeds anything I have ever experienced in my travels,' enthused Shelley in December 1818; '[It] is a city, as it were, of the dead, or rather of those who cannot die, and who survive the puny generations which inhabit and pass over the spot which they have made sacred to eternity.' Or, in poetic vein, he urged: 'Go thou to Rome, at once the Paradise,/The grave, the city and the Wilderness.'

In their quest for the haunts of melancholy, travellers of a Romantic disposition would be sure to spend a late afternoon wandering – and musing – among the old tombs that flanked the Via Appia Antica. They would invariably pause just before the third milestone, on the fringes of the still desolate Campagna, to contemplate the great stone drum of Cecilia Metella's mausoleum (generally acknowledged, according to the contemporary guides, to be 'the most beautiful sepulchral monument in the world').

Though built to lavish specifications in the first century AD for the wife of the suggestively named nouveau riche consul Marcus Licinius Crassus, the structure – with its rich entanglement of ivy and 'useless flowers' – could inspire flights of poetic fancy.

Madame de Staël's Corinne spent a wistful afternoon there with Lord Nelvil, finding something 'gentle and soothing' in the spot's admixture of natural beauty and remembered grief. Chateaubriand too enjoyed the 'charm' of contemplating the resting place of the long-departed Cecilia in the face of his mistress's recent death. Byron, for his part, devoted seven stanzas of *Childe Harold* to the 'stern round tower of other days' and his reveries upon the age and moral character of its otherwise unknown inmate ('Was she a matron of Cornelia's mien,/ Or the light air of Egypt's graceful queen'?) before concluding:

> But whither would Conjecture stray?
> Thus much alone we know – Metella died,
> The wealthiest Roman's wife: Behold his love or pride!
>
> I know not why – but standing thus by thee
> It seems as if I had thine inmate known,
> Thou Tomb! and other days come back on me
> With recollected music, though the tone
> Is changed and solemn, like the cloudy groan
> Of dying thunder on the distant wind;

Back in the centre of Rome, among the city's more famous monuments, the two that most appealed to the Romantic imagination were the Colosseum and the Baths of Caracalla. Confronted by these broken remnants of the ancient past Shelley and his confrères did not see – as their brisk eighteenth-century forerunners had done – a useful model for some classically inspired building project of their own, or the site where some Latin author had declaimed a famous line. They saw the poignant history of man's pride and fall.

The Colosseum had, of course, long been a source of special wonder to visitors. Its great size, its great age, its supposed associations with Christian martyrdom, had all assured its status with previous generations. But, with the coming of the Romantic era, it began to be looked at in a new light: moonlight.

Goethe was among the first to extol the 'exquisite sight'. He considered that, 'unless a person has walked through Rome in the light of the full moon he cannot imagine the beauty of it. All individual details are swallowed up in the great masses of light and shadow, and only the largest, most general images present themselves to the eye . . .' The Colosseum, he explained was 'particularly beautiful' under such conditions.

It is closed at night, a hermit lives there in his tiny little church, and beggars nest in the dilapidated archways. They had laid a fire on the level floor, and a quiet breeze drove the smoke first toward the arena, so that the lower part of the ruins was covered and the huge walls above jutted out over it darkly. We stood at the grating and watched the phenomenon, while the moon stood high and clear in the sky. Gradually the smoke drifted through the walls, holes and openings, looking like fog in the moonlight.

Byron carried the image into verse. In his poem *Manfred*, the hero is struck by the dramatic contrast between the Colosseum's enduring magnificence and the broken down ivy-clad ruins of the imperial palaces silhouetted on the Palatine.

> . . . the gladiators' bloody Circus stands,
> A noble wreck in ruinous perfection!
> While Caesar's chambers, and the Augustan halls,
> Grovel on earth in indistinct decay. –
> And thou didst shine, thou rolling moon, upon
> All this, and cast a wide and tender light,
> Which softened down the hoar austerity
> Of rugged desolation, and fill'd up,
> As 'twere anew, the gaps of centuries.

A rather different Romantic trope was employed by Shelley in his description of the 'bloody Circus'. Despite the best efforts of the papal and Napoleonic clean-up campaign, the great amphitheatre retained a defiantly rough edge. Weeds and wild flowers grew rife among the stones. (In 1855 an English doctor, Richard Deakin, produced a handbook, *Flora of the Colosseum*, illustrating 420 different species of plant; some of the rarer foreign interlopers were supposed to have germinated from the dung of the wild animals that had once fought in the arena.) Clambering among the floribund tiers of broken masonry, Shelley apostrophized the scene in terms of the triumph of wild Nature over the works of Man:

> It has been changed by time into the image of an amphitheatre of rocky hills overgrown by the wild olive, the myrtle, and the fig-tree, and threaded with little paths, which wind among its ruined stairs and immeasurable galleries: the copsewood overshadows you as you wander though its labyrinths, and the wild weeds of this climate of flowers bloom under your feet. The arena is covered with grass, and pierces, like the skirts of a natural plain, the chasms of the broken arches round.

The same idea animated his enthusiasm for the equally massive, and considerably more overgrown, ruins of the Baths of Caracalla. 'Never,' he declared, 'was any desolation more sublime and lovely.' It was there that he spent his solitary hours, and there that he composed much of his lyric drama *Prometheus Unbound*, perched, as he described it, 'among the flowery grasses, and thickets of odoriferous blossoming trees, which are extended in ever winding labyrinths upon its immense platforms and dizzy arches suspended in the air'. The great imperial monument overwhelmed by luxuriant herbage served, he explained, as an inspirational metaphor for his tale of the triumph of Liberty (represented by Prometheus) over Tyranny (in the guise of divine Jupiter).

The image of the lone Romantic poet lost in contemplation among the odoriferous thickets atop the dizzying arches of an antique ruin was a beguiling one, and it became permanently fixed by the painter Joseph Severn in his posthumous portrait of *Shelley at the Baths of Caracalla* (see plate XIV).

If the Romantics responded most keenly to weed-strangled ruins, they were not immune to the charms of art. It is, however, a striking fact that, daring and innovatory though they were in their literary work, their political opinions and personal lives, they all remained remarkably conventional in their appreciation of sculpture and painting.

Among connoisseurs at the leading edge of taste there was, in the early nineteenth century, a certain downgrading of Rome's far-famed classical statues. The opening up of Greece to travellers, artists and collectors – and, in particular, the acquisition of the Elgin Marbles (the great frieze from the Parthenon in Athens) by the British Museum in 1816 – had served to introduce true Greek art to the connoisseurs of the age. Confronted with the real thing, it began to become clear that most, perhaps all, of the great works of antique sculpture in Rome were – whatever their merits – mere copies of lost Greek originals. Little of this, however, seems to have registered with Romantic visitors to Rome.

If they took only a limited interest in the city's great classical artworks it was not due to any scholarly or aesthetic considerations – but more because the calm sanity of the works left so little scope for their reveries. As Mme de Staël noted, 'scarcely any traces of melancholy can be found in the [Romans'] statues.'

The Romantic visitors to Rome were, for the most part, content to admire those established favourites of the Vatican collection, *Laocoön* and the *Apollo Belvedere*, and then pass on. Shelley, being himself a wavy-haired poet, was said to have felt a special affinity with the *Apollo*. Byron gave both works full – if dutiful – poetic treatment in *Childe Harold*, urging his readers to:

The *Dying Gladiator*

... go see Laocoön's torture dignifying pain –
A father's love and mortal's agony
With an immortal's patience blending ...
Or view the Lord of the unerring bow,
The God of Life, and poesy, and light –
The Sun in human limbs arrayed ...

He also touched briefly on the celebrated *Pompey* in the Palazzo Spada, at the foot of which Julius Caesar was supposed to have been murdered ('Thou who beheldest, mid the assasins' din/At thy bathed base the bloody Caesar lie') and the even more famous bronze of the she-wolf, the *Lupa* ('the thunder-stricken nurse of Rome'). But the one antiquity that really fired his imagination was the so-called *Dying Gladiator* in the Capitoline Museums. And here he achieved a real success. He took the fallen figure as his model when imagining the scene of combat and carnage that was once played out in the Colosseum:

I see before me the Gladiator lie:
He leans upon his hand – his manly brow
Consents to death, but conquers agony,
And his drooped head sinks gradually low –
And through his side the last drops, ebbing slow
From the red gash, fall heavy, one by one,
Like the first of a thunder-shower; and now

The arena swims around him: he is gone,
Ere ceased the inhuman shout which hailed the wretch who won.

He heard it, but he heeded not – his eyes
Were with his heart, and that was far away;
He recked not of the life he lost nor prize,
But where his rude hut by the Danube lay,
THERE were his young barbarians all at play,
THERE was their Dacian mother – he, their sire,
Butchered to make a Roman holiday ...

William Hazlitt, writing only a few years following its publication, pronounced it 'the finest [passage] in Lord Byron'. And many came to share this verdict.

Painting, it seems, had even less impact than sculpture upon the consciousness of the Romantic age. The myriad pictures of Rome's princely galleries and richly endowed churches failed to strike a truly resonating chord – with one great exception: a small portrait in the Palazzo Barberini of a young woman, looking back over her shoulder, her head wrapped in a loose white turban, a strand of hair corkscrewed upon her neck. No artwork in Rome, perhaps, provoked deeper reveries and sadder reflections than this small panel. It was listed as 'Portrait of Beatrice Cenci' by Guido Reni (see plate xv). Here was a potent coming together – as artist and subject – of two of the great names of the High Renaissance.

For almost all educated men of the early nineteenth century Guido Reni remained a great painter – the acknowledged master of the female face. Even Hazlitt, who delighted in pricking established reputations, conceded that 'no other painter has expressed the female character so well'. Guido's women, he thought, were 'the true heroines of romance, the brides of the fancy such as "youthful poets dream of when they love"'. And Beatrice Cenci was an ideal subject for his brush.

She was the daughter of a noble house, who was, in 1599, tortured, tried and executed – along with her brother and stepmother – for plotting the murder of her tyrannical father. It was a tale fraught with tragedy: Beatrice was young and beautiful; she had a reputation for piety; the father had been a monster, violent, malicious and unstable; he had imprisoned Beatrice and raped her; he had abused and dishonoured his wife and quarrelled with his son. Despite such extenuating circumstances the papal court had insisted on exercising the full rigour of the law (perhaps, it was whispered, in order that the Church might acquire the forfeited estates of the disgraced Cenci family). Beatrice went to the executioner's block – calm and beautiful still – a martyr among the Roman people.

According to an earlyish tradition, recorded by the great Italian historian Muratori in his twelve-volume *Annali d'Italia* (1749), Guido Reni had visited Beatrice in her condemned cell on the eve of her execution, and had made a portrait of her then. The result, it came to be thought, was the work hanging in the Palazzo Barberini.

The picture had only recently come to light, entering the Barberini collection in the late eighteenth century. The catalogue of paintings compiled in 1783 listed it cautiously as 'Picture of a head. Portrait believed to be of the Cenci girl. Artist unknown.' But the clouds of doubt and uncertainty were soon dispelled. A few years later the caption beneath a copy of the painting boldly asserted the identity of the sitter and, even more boldly, attributed the original work to Guido Reni. This was done on the strength of little more than wishfulness, a vague stylistic similarity, and the echo of Muratori's anecdote. The attribution, however, stuck. And it was as a definite portrait of 'Beatrice

Cenci' by 'Guido' that the image came to be designated in the numerous prints that spread the painting's fame and raised its reputation.

Shelley, already interested in the sad story of Beatrice's fate, sought out the picture and fell in love with it.

> It is most interesting as a just representation of one of the loveliest specimens of the workmanship of nature. There is a fixed and pale composure upon the features: she seems sad and stricken down in spirit, yet the despair thus expressed is lightened by the patience of gentleness.... The moulding of her face is exquisitely delicate; the eyebrows are distinct and arched: the lips have that permanent meaning of imaginations and sensibility which suffering has not repressed and which it seems as if death scarcely could extinguish. Her forehead is large and clear; her eyes, which we are told were remarkable for their vivacity, are swollen with weeping and lustreless, but beautifully tender and serene. In the whole mien there is a simplicity and dignity which united with her exquisite loveliness and deep sorrow, are inexpressibly pathetic.

The haunting image provided a reference and an inspiration for the five-act verse drama *The Cenci*, which Shelley composed during the spring of 1819. From this hectic tale of incest and parricide, Beatrice herself emerges as a tragic but flawed heroine, fatally provoked to confront evil with evil, and forced to pay the heavy price. The play was never performed but, published in two modest editions in 1820 and 1821, it attracted a generous budget of hostile criticism on account of its atheistic tone and immoral subject matter. Such publicity served, if nothing else, to carry the name and the story of Beatrice Cenci into the English-speaking world.

The *Dying Gladiator*, the condemned Beatrice Cenci, the Mausoleum of Cecilia Metella, the ruins of the Colosseum: death's shadow lay across almost all the sights favoured by the Romantics. So it is no surprise to discover that another of their especial haunts was 'the English Burying-ground', held in the curve of the city wall close by the Pyramid of Cestius. This small Protestant (or, more properly, non-Catholic) Cemetery had been established in the mid-eighteenth century to provide a consecrated burial place for Rome's ever-growing population of non-Catholic visitors and residents. Madame de Staël's Corinne called it 'a gentle haven, tolerant and liberal'. (And Lord Nelvil fantasized about being buried there, as the only way in which he might be able to stay always with his beloved.)

Shelley responded readily to the charm of the 'romantic and lonely' spot, shaded by pines and set beneath the 'massy walls and towers, now moulding and desolate', its open ground 'covered in winter with violets and daisies'; he felt the site 'might make one in love with death, to think that one should be buried in so sweet a place.'

These sentiments were set down in the preface to *Adonais*, the elegy Shelley wrote to commemorate John Keats, who died in Rome, aged just twenty-four, in 1821 – and was buried in the shadow of Cestius' Pyramid. His self-penned, and self-effacing, epitaph ran, 'Here lies one whose name was writ on water.'† Within a year Shelley – who drowned off the Italian coast – had joined his fellow poet in the 'so sweet' burial ground beneath a Shakespearean epitaph of his own (taken from the 'Song of Ariel' in *The Tempest*):

> Nothing of him that doth fade,
> But doth suffer a sea-change
> Into something rich and strange.

Although Keats and Shelley both died feeling unappreciated and misunderstood, their posthumous reputations rose steadily – borne upwards not a little by the romance of their early deaths. Byron, too, died young, in 1824, while on his way to fight for Greek liberty; a circumstance that served further to enhance his never slight fame and popularity. It was little wonder that the doomed and beautiful English Romantics became a fixture in the cultural imagination of the dawning Victorian age. Their colourful lives and idealized features were busily recorded. Their works were known, reprinted, and even read. They cast a long twilit shadow – and it was a shadow that fell full across Rome.

The middle years of the nineteenth century were, in Britain and Germany and the United States especially, the great age of middle-class emancipation and prosperity. A new world of bourgeois leisure opened up, and one of its provinces was travel. Well-to-do merchants, businessmen, professionals, and financiers – together with their families – began to explore the continent. In ever-increasing numbers they visited northern France and Belgium. They cruised down the Rhine. They turned Switzerland – with its

---

† This poetic phrase (derived from a line in Shakespeare's *Henry VIII*) was, on the gravestone, rather bathetically prefaced by Keats' friend Joseph Severn, with the explicatory lines, 'This Grave contains all that was Mortal of a YOUNG ENGLISH POET Who on his Death Bed, in the Bitterness of his Heart, at the malicious Power of his Enemies, Desired these Words to be engraven on his Tomb Stone' - in allusion to the supposed role played by the critics in hastening his end.

vertiginous Alps and tranquil lakes – into 'the playground of Europe'. They discovered Italy. And they went to Rome – in their thousands.†

These tyro travellers were eager for instruction and entertainment. For all their excitement they were also anxious about 'abroad'. And – almost always – they were pushed for time. They required assistance. It arrived dressed in red.

During the 1830s and 1840s a new generation of guidebooks was brought into being to cater for the new generation of travellers – or 'tourists', as they came to be called. At the heart of this enterprise stood two publishing companies, John Murray of London and Karl Baedeker of Koblenz. John Murray II wrote and produced his first *Handbook for Travellers* – to Belgium – in 1836. Karl Baedeker wrote and published his first *Handbuch* – to the Rhine – in 1835. Other titles soon followed from both houses, with each company learning from – and even collaborating with – the other.

The books produced by Murray and Baedeker – small, blockish, closely printed in double columns and bound in distinctive red-cloth covers – offered something novel. While earlier guides tended to comprise little more than an exacting step-by-step cultural itinerary, the new handbooks provided readers with a comprehensive, detailed, practical, easy-to-use and largely objective account of the territory under review. There was information about accommodation, health precautions, transport and banking facilities. Strong opinions might be expressed on the cleanliness of inns or the reliability of shipping lines. In matters of taste and art, however, rather more circumspection was used; Murray was keen, as he put it, to avoid 'inflated language'. A general consensus was aimed at – if not always achieved. The necessities of selection and ordering, as well as the occasional irrepressible enthusiasms or prejudices of the individual author, tended to give both slant and colour to even the simplest gazetteer.

Murray was the first to tackle Rome. The first edition of his *Handbook to Central Italy – Including Rome* appeared in 1843, twenty years before Baedeker's three volumes on the peninsula. The author was Octavian Blewitt, a thirty-something classicist who had abandoned the beginnings of a medical training for a career on the fringes of literature.

---

† The one hiatus in this ever-growing traffic occurred in 1848–9, during the 'Year of Revolutions'. As part of the general upheaval against the old European regimes, Rome declared itself a republic, before being besieged by French troops, who eventually restored papal rule. The siege provides the setting for Arthur Hugh Clough's epistolary narrative poem *Amours de Voyage*, in which the etiolated protagonist, Claude, memorably laments, 'Rome disappoints me much; I hardly as yet understand, but/Rubbishy seems the word that most exactly would suit it.'

(He made his debut with a guide to Torquay, dedicated to Bulwer Lytton.) Having lived for a year in Rome he was well acquainted with the city; and although Murray had to chivvy him to finish the work, he did an excellent job of his commission.

The book proved a great success, achieving an undisputed pre-eminence in what was becoming a crowded field. It was regularly revised, and also provided the model for several rivals. As a result the method that Blewitt adopted in composing the work, and the various choices that he made in describing the city, had a huge impact on way Rome was seen by successive waves of Victorian tourists.

Blewitt recognized that for many of his readers time would be severely limited. So, breaking with the tradition of Vasi's exhaustive *Itinerario* and its various imitations, he arranged his account of the city on what he termed 'a more systematic plan than has hitherto been adopted': 'Instead of describing [Rome] in districts, the objects have been classified under separate heads, in order that the traveller may be enabled at a single glance to ascertain how much or how little it contains of any particular class' – or, indeed, of any particular interest. Forums, Temples, Columns, Arches, Tombs, Obelisks, Fountains, Basilicas, Churches and Palaces were all listed independently, and the reader was invited to choose from among them.

It was a format that allowed him to accommodate the many changes and discoveries that had occurred – and were occurring – across the city. Old buildings received new names: it was finally realized, for example, that the monumental ruins at the north end of the Forum belonged, not to the Temple of Peace erected by Vespasian, but to the great fourth-century basilica begun by Maxentius and completed by Constantine. New treasures were unearthed: among the greatest was a perfectly preserved statue of the Emperor Augustus, discovered in 1863 near the Prima Porta. Artworks were relocated: Raphael's *Transfiguration* (plate IX), together with Domenichino's *Last Communion of St Jerome* (plate XI) and several other celebrated works, had after their return from Paris been transferred to the Vatican art gallery, rather than going back to their various churches. Great monuments endured unexpected alterations: in 1823 a fire had destroyed a large part of the ancient basilica of S. Paolo fuori le Mura, necessitating three decades of reconstruction.

In almost all aesthetic matters Blewitt accepted the verdicts and opinions of the eighteenth century. He had no time for Baroque architecture. The little church of S. Carlo alle Quattro Fontane (now ranked as a jewel) was dismissed as 'one of the extravagant and capricious designs of Borromini'. Other examples of that architect's 'capricious style', if not ignored completely, also received harsh treatment. Of Bernini's architectural works only the colonnade of St Peter's was admired without reserve, but then – as Blewitt pointed out – it was 'generally considered his masterpiece'.

The artworks that he singled out for especial praise were the same ones that had been admired during the era of the Grand Tour. Among 'modern' sculptures Bernini's *St Bibiana* (see page 200) retained its place in the first rank. 'It is graceful and pure in style,' Blewitt reported, 'and forms a remarkable contrast to the fantastic taste which characterizes [the artist's] later work.' Duquesnoy's severely classical *St Susanna* (see page 199) was still heralded as 'one of the greatest productions of modern art in Rome', while Michelangelo's *Moses* (see page 196) was defended from the wags who made fun of the prophet's flaming horns and general likeness to a goat, with the quoted assertion that 'the true sublime resists all ridicule'.

Blewitt's one innovation was entirely conventional – an accident of changing time rather than an expression of changing taste. He directed his readers to admire (along with everyone else) the works of Canova. Among the jostling sculptural monuments in St Peter's (most of them – according to Blewitt – 'in the worst style of the decline of art [ie. the Baroque] and entirely beneath criticism') Canova's several creations stood out particularly in their Neoclassical restraint and purity. One of them had moreover the added interest for British visitors of commemorating the now safely deceased Stuart pretenders 'James the Third, Charles the Third, and Henry the Ninth . . . Names which an Englishman can scarcely read without a smile.'

Blewitt's assessment of Rome's paintings also followed the well established eighteenth-century line. The same masterpieces were ranked in the same order. There was as yet only the faintest hint of the slowly growing Victorian interest in the Italian 'primitives' of the quattrocento. (On the lower walls of the Sistine Chapel, he acknowledged in passing the 'series of remarkable frescoes by eminent artists of the Fifteenth Century'; he even had a word of praise for Fra Angelico's decorations in the papal apartments, but largely as 'studies of costume'.) Michelangelo, Raphael and their followers continued to reign supreme.

Blewitt's description of the Sistine Chapel confirmed a new (and still enduring) hierarchy. In a major shift of taste, Michelangelo's decorations for the chapel ceiling were now ranked above the *Last Judgement* as the prime attraction. Of the ceiling it was claimed, 'no language can exaggerate the grandeur and majesty of it.' The *Last Judgement* was still designated as 'extraordinary', but was now considered to appeal 'more to the reason than the heart'. The distinction was telling: the rational sense of the eighteenth century had yielded to the Romantic sensibility of the nineteenth.

It was not the only sign that the old order was passing. Where the gentlemen of the Grand Tour had been concerned to grasp the underlying rules of Art and Taste through their examination of the pictures in Rome's galleries and churches, the new Victorian tourists wanted hard – and, if possible, entertaining – facts. Particular information rather than general theory was what interested them. And Blewitt provided it. Murray's *Handbook* began the trend, taken up by almost all subsequent nineteenth-century guides, of fixing the supposedly important artworks with telling anecdotes.

Some of these stories – for all their colour – had little basis in fact. Domenichino's *Last Communion of St Jerome* (plate XI), still accounted an 'undoubted masterpiece', was described as a work that Poussin had discovered on an old canvas given to him by the monks of the Aracoeli to reuse. (Domenichino, it was said, had painted the work for the monks but they – having quarrelled with the artist – had refused to exhibit it.) According to the story, Poussin at once recognized the genius of the work and refused to paint over it, instead proclaiming the existence of a masterpiece. Given that the picture had been painted for the oratory of S. Girolamo della Carità, and had been displayed above the altar there from the time of its completion in 1614, it is hard to know where this fanciful tale originated.

Scarcely more likely was an anecdote told of Andrea Sacchi's *St Romuald* (plate XII) – also in the Vatican gallery following its return from Paris, and still accounted one of the four finest pictures in Rome. Blewitt reported that the artist had got the idea for painting the old monk and his white-habited disciples from seeing three flour-covered millers under a tree.

Vasari was responsible for the story – also given in Murray – that the *Transfiguration* (plate IX) had been placed at the head of Raphael's bier after the artist's untimely death, and that the contrast between the living work of art and the dead artist had made 'the hearts of everyone who saw it burst with sorrow'. (Blewitt relayed the incident in the bathetic verses of Samuel Rogers' *Italy* – 'And when all beheld/Him where he lay, how changed from yesterday . . .')

If the prevalence of such artistic anecdotes was something new, an even more striking departure from the traditions of the Grand Tour (and the Grand Tour guidebooks) was in the selection of the things most worth seeing. While allowing the importance, of course, of such enduring landmarks as St Peter's and the other major basilicas, of the Pantheon, the Castel S. Angelo and the Vatican Palace, Blewitt and Murray directed their readers even more enthusiastically in various new directions – towards the sights and artworks that had been so much admired, and so well described, by the great Romantics.

Connections with the Romantic tradition were pointed up at every turn. Where Vasi and other eighteenth-century guidebooks had quoted the Latin classics, Blewitt (for the most part) quoted the Romantics, and particularly Lord Byron. It was, he considered, 'impossible to describe the interest with which [Byron's] genius has invested the monuments of Rome, even to the most indifferent of English travellers'. And, in confirmation of his own opinion, he quoted *Childe Harold* extensively at every opportunity.

Through such touches of poetic colour and approbation the various places that had fired the imaginations of Byron and Shelley, of Chateaubriand and Madame de Staël, became the fixed points of the new tourists' Rome: the Mausoleum of Cecilia Metella, the Baths of Caracalla, the Colosseum by moonlight, the *Dying Gladiator,* Guido's portrait of Beatrice Cenci, the 'English Cemetery'.

It was a colouring that gave a new prominence to some previously overlooked monuments. Among Rome's lesser churches, S. Nicola in Carcere became a major destination because it was supposed to stand upon the ruins of the ancient Decemviral prison, the scene of a famous incident of filial piety (when a daughter saved her incarcerated father from a sentence of starvation by secretly breastfeeding him) and – more importantly – because Byron had related this 'celebrated *Caritas Romana*' in some 'beautiful lines' of *Childe Harold*. The church of S. Onofrio on the Janiculum was visited because outside it stood the oak tree under which the poet Tasso (a great favourite of the Romantics) had died, while inside was his tomb. At the church of S. Luigi dei Francesi (where Blewitt – displaying a rare independence of spirit – praised the 'magnificent' Caravaggios), the monument erected by Chateaubriand in memory of Pauline de Beaumont was guaranteed to draw a tear.

The Palazzo Cenci, near the Ghetto, became charged with new interest for visitors through Shelley's description of it as a 'vast and gloomy pile of feudal architecture… in an obscure corner of Rome'. The Trevi Fountain was commended as being the place where Corinne 'came to meditate by moonlight when she was suddenly surprised seeing the reflection of Oswald in the water'. (The notion that if you drank from the fountain you would return to Rome was also well established by the 1830s.)

These Romantic allusions and connections had such profound resonance because they reflected the taste of the tourists and indeed the temper of the times. The Victorian middle classes, for all their self-proclaimed good sense and sound morality, still read the Romantic poets of the previous generation. And, against the steadily darkening background of a rampant industrial age, the attractions of Romanticism glowed with a special brightness.

It is revealing that most of the destinations favoured by mid-nineteenth-century travellers were 'Romantic' in character. The crags and castles of the Rhine valley or the Swiss Alps – when viewed from the deck of a steamer or the terrace of a clean hotel – offered a convenient dose of the sublime. Both territories also had their own literary resonances – which were duly pointed up in the guidebooks. Herr Baedeker larded his guide to the Rhine with quotations from Schiller, while John Murray made extended reference to Byron's epic – *The Prisoner of Chillon* – in his *Handbook to Switzerland*, as well as quoting the lines from *Childe Harold's Pilgrimage* on 'sweet Clarens, birthplace of deep love'. Rome, though, offered an even richer budget of Romantic associations – and visitors were eager to respond to them.

At the Baths of Caracalla, they wanted to recall the image of Shelley clambering atop the ivy-clad ruins. Having reached the tomb of Cecilia Metella they wanted to read Byron's famous lines upon the monument. And they could readily agree with Blewitt's verdict that the stanzas represented 'one of those eloquent bursts of feeling which appeal irresistibly to the heart'. This was the great attraction of the Romantic framing that Blewitt gave to the Roman sights: it let the reader know not only what to look at but also what – or how – to feel.

There was, of course, something faintly absurd – or at least paradoxical – about the idea of being led, book in hand, to some spot where a poet had once wandered by chance, and there dutifully trying to conjure up the same 'burst of feeling' that had spontaneously erupted in the breast of somebody else quarter of a century before. Yet, out on the Via Appia, or even in the Baths of Caracalla among the overgrown ruins, it was still possible for sensitive spirits to capture something of the Romantic frisson. Herman Melville, the author of *Moby Dick*, unimpressed by so much during his visit to Rome in 1856, was deeply moved by the Baths of Caracalla: 'Wonderful. Massive. Ruins form as it were natural bridges of thousands of arches. There are glades and thickets among the ruins – high up. Thought of Shelley. Truly he got his inspiration here. Corresponded with his drama and mind. Still majesty and desolate grandeur.'

Nearer the centre of Rome it was rather harder to achieve such moments of reverie. Not that the attempt was left unmade. Travellers, Blewitt commanded, 'will want to visit the Colosseum by Moonlight in order to realise the magnificent description in [Byron's] "Manfred", the only description that has ever done justice to the wonders of [the place].' (The relevant passage was helpfully given in full.) And, of course, many did want to do exactly that: too many.

The travel literature of the period is littered with accounts of disappointment. Even in 1826 Mrs Anna Jameson, the fashionable art critic (who – according to Ruskin – knew 'as much about art as the cat'), failed to achieve the expected level of rapture on her moonlit excursion to the amphitheatre. First she was disconcerted to learn that, although it was now possible to enter the Colosseum after nightfall, all visitors had to be accompanied by a guard of two soldiers. Their presence alone would have been an antidote to poetic reverie, but once inside the arena the 'sublime and heart-stopping beauty' of the scene was further undercut by the 'empty and tasteless and misplaced flippancy' of various unromantic members of her party who affected 'a well-bred nonchalance, a fashionable disdain for all romance and enthusiasm'.

As the century advanced, and the night-time outing developed into the great cliché of Roman tourism, the unpoetical distractions grew even more insistent and irksome. To gain entry at all (as the 1865 Baedeker explained) it was necessary to acquire a 'permesso' from 'the office of the commander' in the Piazza Colonna, and then the custodian – with his torch – had to be sought out and tipped. Inside, the moonlit arcades echoed with the raucous sounds of philistine fun. Nathaniel Hawthorne in his great Roman novel *The Marble Faun* (1860) described 'a party of English and Americans paying the inevitable visit [to the Colosseum] by moonlight, and exalting themselves with raptures that were Byron's, not their own', while others raced around shrieking, playing hide-and-seek, or flirting.

Moonlight in time came to be considered too dim and too variable to satisfy touristic expectations. The 1862 Baedeker recommended visitors pay for a display of Bengal Lights; for 'about 150 scudi' the whole monument could be bathed in luminous reds and blues. (After the unification of Italy, and the establishment, in 1870, of Rome as the capital of the new nation, the Colosseum was illuminated with patriotic red, white and green lights every year on 21 April – the Natale di Roma – the day upon which Romulus was said to have founded the city.)

A similar gradual coarsening of response affected the so-called *Dying Gladiator* (see page 220). Although the scholars of the period had become convinced that the figure (with its distinctive woven necklace) represented not a stricken gladiator but a dying Gaulish warrior, few visitors to the Capitoline Museums registered any change of designation. And indeed the work continued to be labelled as the *Dying Gladiator* until well into the twentieth century. Byron's genius for phrase-making had established the title too firmly in the popular imagination. From Ralph Waldo Emerson to Florence Nightingale, no tourist, it seems, could stand before the statue without murmuring, 'Ah, "... butchered to make a Roman Holiday".' Indeed Mark Twain, in his mock travel-book, *The Innocents Abroad* (1869), wanted credit as 'the only free white man of mature age' to have written about Rome without quoting the phrase. 'It sounds well,' he admitted, 'for the first seventeen or eighteen thousand times one sees it in print, but after that it begins to grow tiresome.'

The portrait of Beatrice Cenci prompted rather more considered contemplation. Proclaimed in *Murray's Handbook* as 'one of the most celebrated pictures in Rome', the painting certainly drew the general tourist crowds to the Palazzo Barberini – and, once there, they dutifully read Shelley's 'celebrated' description of the work, and the romantic 'family tradition' of how Guido had come to make it. But the haunting image, having been so vividly fixed by Shelley, also attracted the scrutiny and fired the imagination of a succession of fellow writers. Walter Savage Landor mapped out the sad tale in his *Five Scenes on the Martyrdom of Beatrice Cenci*, both Dumas and Stendhal gave rather more lurid accounts of her history. The portrait itself served as a key device in Melville's novel *Pierre* and Hawthorne's *The Marble Faun*. And Dickens, who seemed to wander largely unmoved through the galleries of Rome, thought it 'almost impossible to be forgotten'; he devoted a page of descriptive enthusiasm to the painting and its subject in his *Pictures from Italy*.

Almost none of this Romantically tinted Rome now survives in the modern visitor's experience. The monuments and the artworks, it is true, are still there – *in situ*, intact, and for the most part in better condition than they were. But they have lost their powers of attraction – and in some cases their charm; for an age that no longer quotes Byron, reads Shelley or has heard of Madame de Staël, they have ceased to resonate with poetic associations.

The Mausoleum of Cecilia Metella has dwindled gradually into an undervisited attraction on the outskirts of Rome. In other instances the change has been more drastic, and earlier in date. Back in the 1870s archaeologists working at the Baths of Caracalla eradicated the centuries of vegetable growth among which Shelley had clambered and composed. A tsunami of weed-killer must have swept over the massive brickwork piles. They were left 'utterly denuded', and so they remain (apart from the occasional tenacious caper bush). Augustus Hare, author of the popular *Walks in Rome,* writing in the aftermath of this intervention, considered the baths 'now little worth visiting'. His verdict might sound harsh. The vast bald ruins (still the largest in Rome), framing a clear blue sky, can yet impress by their very scale. But they are no longer a place of poetic reverie.

A similar scorched-earth policy stripped the Colosseum of its 420 species of fauna in 1871 (before Dr Deakin's book could go into a second edition). Shortly afterwards archaeologists, pursuing knowledge at the expense of the aesthetic, also dug up the central area of the arena. They revealed the extraordinary substructures of the monument but denied future generations the pleasure of wandering over the sacred ground where so many gladiators had been butchered to make all those Roman holidays. The amphitheatre was becoming gradually sanitized. More damaging still, however, to the Romantic tenor of the place was the advent of widespread street-lighting. It has destroyed all sense of nocturnal mystery: the pale moon cannot compete against the ambient sodium glow.

The Colosseum is still illuminated on special occasions with elaborate light and laser displays; the effect can be spectacular, but it has nothing of the spirit of Byron's

Manfred, of Goethe or Chateaubriand. And to all visitors the amphitheatre is closed after sunset.

Few people now pause before the statue labelled *The Dying Gaul* – and this despite its prominent position in the first small room at the top of the stairs in the Palazzo Nuovo. It receives a passing glance and perhaps a quick snap from the digital camera. There is nothing to indicate its former fame as Byron's 'Gladiator'. The only literary allusion that it summoned forth from a passing tourist, during the course of the afternoon that I spent beside it, was a glib reference to Asterix and Obelix.

It has, however, fared better than Guido's portrait of Beatrice Cenci. The eclipse of that work has been almost complete. First art historians, at the end of the nineteenth century, undermined the romantic associations of the picture by pointing out that Guido Reni was not actually in Rome in 1599 when Beatrice was executed, so could not have made a portrait from life. Then they asserted that the girl in the picture was not Beatrice at all but just some generic 'Sybil'. And, as a final blow, they decided that the painting was not even by Guido Reni, but merely the work of a follower. By then, however, artistic taste had shifted. The masters of the early Italian Renaissance were preferred to Raphael and his disciples. And Guido's star had fallen so sharply that few registered this last disappointment. The picture was quietly removed from its prominent position to a store room.

It is now back on show at the Palazzo Barberini (or the Galleria Nazionale d'Arte Antica, to give it its new title). It is still labelled optimistically as 'Beatrice Cenci' and 'attributed' to Guido Reni, but it stands as an all-but unremarked exhibit, lost in the shadow of the gallery's current star, Raphael's portrait of his mistress, *La Fornarina*. Interestingly, the desire to make an artistic connection with the death of Beatrice still lingers. The guide to the Barberini collection suggests that Caravaggio's gruesome picture of the beheading of Holefernes, on show in the same room as 'Guido's' portrait, might owe its anatomical exactitude to the fact that the artist witnessed the execution of Beatrice Cenci.

The one sight favoured by the Romantics that still retains some purchase upon the modern imagination, is the Protestant Cemetery. Murray's *Handbook* had commended the place for its 'air of Romantic beauty' and 'melancholy interest'. Aside from quoting the epitaphs of both Keats and Shelley, Blewitt described how 'the silence and seclusion of the spot, and the inscriptions which tell the British in their native tongue of those who have found their last resting place beneath the bright skies of Rome, appeal irresistibly to the heart.' And that appeal has continued in an unbroken flow down the years. The 'banker poet' Samuel Rogers, in the 1830s, was being surprised by the interest and sympathy he felt among the graves. ('You are yourself in a foreign land, and [the dead] are for the most part your countrymen. They call upon you in your mother tongue – in English – in words unknown to a native, known only to yourself.') Henry James, half a century later, was touched by the natural beauty of the place: 'Here is a mixture of tears and smiles, of stones and flowers, of mourning cypresses and radiant sky, which gives us the impression of our looking back at death from the brighter side of the grave.'

It remains something of an oasis, a place of calm and greenery, of dappled shade and gentle order. Shielded from the roar of the Via Ostiense by the great bluff of the Aurelian wall, and the rising point of Cestius' pyramid, it is even a place of relative quiet. The graves and pathways are well tended and well loved. For the modern tourist,

The Grave of Shelley by the Aurelian Wall near the Pyramid of Cestius, by W. B. Scott, 1873

The Byron boutique,
below the Keats-Shelley
Memorial House

too, it provides something different: a change of pace and of gear. It is a break from the
familiar tourist round of museums, galleries, ruins and churches.

There remains for most visitors an interest, too, in seeing the graves of Keats and
Shelley. If their poetry (outside the classroom) is less read than it was, their personalities
still have the power to attract. The young, doomed Romantics yet retain a certain
romance. Keats and Shelley – together with Byron – still exist on the fringes of the
popular consciousness. Their lives are regularly chronicled in television mini-series and
feature films, as well as in impressive biographies. The Keats-Shelley Memorial House,
located in the very rooms beside the Spanish Steps where Keats died, has existed as
a small museum since 1909, and attracts several thousand visitors a year. While, just
below it, on the Piazza, stands the 'Byron' clothing boutique. Among the display of
folded shirts, draped knitwear and designer belts it is just possible to catch the last faint
echo of that Romantic vision of Rome which shaped the visitor's experience of the city
for so much of the nineteenth century.

·IX·
MODERN ROME

'TWENTY-SIX YEARS of Sardinian rule have done more for the destruction of Rome than all the invasions of the Goths and Vandals. If the Government, the Municipality and, it must be confessed, the Roman aristocracy, had been united together since 1870, with the sole object of annihilating the beauty and interest of Rome, they could not have done it more effectually. The old charm is gone for ever, the whole aspect of the city is changed ... the pagan ruins have been denuded of all that gave them picturesqueness and beauty.'

The Victorian travel writer Augustus Hare penned this lament in 1896. And since then the pace of change – or destruction – has been well maintained. The city has grown once more into a vast metropolis. It has now a population of some 3.5 million, sprawling modern suburbs, traffic-choked streets, and even its own modest metro system.

For Hare the trouble began in 1870 when Rome became the final piece in the jigsaw of the unified Italy. The troops of the new Italian king, Victor Emmanuel II, entered the city on 20 September.† The pope, unwilling to surrender his position as the temporal

---

† Victor Emmanuel, though the first king of Italy, was the second member of the House of Savoy bearing the name Victor Emmanuel to hold the throne of Sardinia. He succeeded to that throne in 1849, twenty-two years before becoming King of Italy, so – rather to the chagrin of most Italians – he insisted on being styled Victor Emmanuel II.

head of the Papal States, may have refused to acknowledge the new order, but everybody else did. Rome became the capital of the fledgling nation state, the centre of its political administration and of its public life. The pope was left sulking and disenfranchised in the Vatican, while the quaint old ways of his former domain were transformed.

Following a devastating flood in 1870, the Tiber was rigorously embanked. Some of the attractive riverine aspect of the city was lost; to Hare's great distress the beautiful gardens of the Farnesina were obliterated. The flow of water, however, proved easier to control than the flow of people.

Whole districts had to be created to accommodate the influx of civil servants, administrators, lawyers, professionals and workers, arriving to operate the machinery of the new state. The old *disabitato* rapidly became built over. Two major boulevards – the Via Nazionale and the Via Cavour – were laid down to allow the city's eastwards expansion. The elegant gardens of the Villa Negroni and the Villa Ludovisi were sold off to developers. The grounds of the latter became a new residential quarter built around the grand sweep of the newly laid Via Veneto. (The gentle arc of the street was specifically designed to allow horse-drawn carriages to make it up the steep incline of the Quirinal hill, from the Piazza Barberini.)

To provide readier access between the historic centre of the town and St Peter's, the broad Corso Vittorio Emanuele was driven through the heart of the crowded Campus Martius district towards one of several smart new bridges over the Tiber.

The go-ahead municipal government wanted to raze the old Aurelian Walls to facilitate the city's growth, but luckily a band of far-sighted conservationists intervened. The protestors camped in and upon the ancient walls, defying the workmen, until the plan was eventually abandoned.

Much was, nevertheless, destroyed during the campaign of modernization; but also many new things were discovered, as a result both of building work and of deliberate archaeological investigation. Overseeing these operations was the indefatigable Rudolfo Lanciani, an engineer turned archaeologist, who became – in 1872 – the Director of Excavations at Rome. In numerous books (many written in English) he recounted the unfolding drama. When the area around Piazza Vittorio Emanuele II, near the Termini station, was being developed, the remains of several temples, together with a basilica, a republican necropolis, and a sumptuous imperial villa were uncovered, but subsequently reburied beneath the new streets and squares. Rome, as Lanciani, briskly remarked, 'has always lived at the expense of her past.'

During the first thirteen years of his tenure, Lanciani estimated that a staggering 270 million cubic feet of Rome's earth had been shifted, turning up more than eight

The *Prima Porta Augustus*

thousand separate items. In a brief overview he listed '77 columns of rare marble . . . 405 works of art in bronze . . . 192 marble statues . . . and 266 busts and heads.' Although many of these works were sold off to private collectors and dispersed, some at least made their way into the Museo Nazionale, which was established in 1889 as a showcase for the city's newly discovered antiquities.†

One of the most conspicuous new developments of the period was the vast Victor Emmanuel Monument, or 'Altar of the Fatherland', erected in 1895 at the very heart of the city, in the lee of the Capitoline hill. An extraordinary white marble monstrosity, inspired in part by the great Altar of Pergamum, it has been nicknamed variously the Typewriter, the False Teeth and the Wedding Cake. Its brilliant and rather jarring whiteness is the result of its having been constructed with Botticino marble from near Brescia, the home town – as it happened – of the then prime minister. The building work, though it uncovered some vestiges from the Republican age, swept away many of the Capitoline's post-classical monuments, including the Renaissance tower of Paul III, and the mediaeval convent of the Aracoeli.

The threefold process of construction, destruction and discovery continued with unfaltering pace into the new century. Among the eager – not to say cavalier – archaeologists, special privilege was always given to Rome's classical remains above those of later epochs. In 1900 the handsome Renaissance church of S. Maria Liberatrice, in the Forum, was blown up after it was discovered to be standing on a first-century Roman guard-house (which had then served in the sixth century as a Byzantine church).

This emphasis only increased under the Fascist regime established by Mussolini in the 1920s. Anxious to revive the great days of Rome's classical past, Mussolini announced plans to renovate the city in order that it might be 'worthy of its glory'. Besides creating whole new quarters on the outskirts to accommodate an ever-expanding population (1.6 million by 1933), he also initiated a series of *sventramenti*

---

† Among the most celebrated new works added to Rome's public collections during the nineteenth century were the *Apoxyomenos* (a marble copy of a bronze by Lysippus, showing an athlete scraping the sweat from his body), which was discovered in Trastevere in 1849 and installed in the Pio-Clementino Museum, and the *Prima Porta Augustus*, the triumphant image of the emperor with his arm raised which was discovered in 1863 and also added to the papal collection.

– 'eviscerations' – designed to clean up and rationalize the city's historic monuments, and give them what he deemed to be a fit dramatic setting.

'Everything', he announced, 'which has grown up in the centuries of decadence must be swept away.' Down came the clutter of post-classical buildings around the Theatre of Marcellus, the Mausoleum of Augustus, the Forum Boarium and a host of lesser sites. The Forum and the Palatine were transformed into an enclosed 'archaeological area'. He completed the excavation of the Ara Pacis and had it reassembled on a site near the Mausoleum of Augustus. He connected many of the major monuments with broad, straight thoroughfares. Among the broadest and straightest was the Via dell'Impero (now the Via dei Fori Imperiali), running from the Piazza Venezia – where Mussolini had his headquarters – to the Colosseum, with the ruins of the Forum on one side, and remnants of the Imperial Fora on the other. The new boulevard swept away the warren of small houses – and chapels – that had grown up amidst the half-buried ruins of the Forum of Nerva, as well as eradicating much valuable archaeological information and the last remnants of the ancient Meta Sudans, a curious weeping fountain that had once stood close to the amphitheatre.

To compensate for these losses, and to enhance the visual impact of what remained, fallen pillars were re-erected and realigned, while at the heart of the Forum a partial – and rather fanciful – reconstruction was made of the circular Temple of Vesta.

Having finally effected a rapprochement between the Italian state and the papacy, with the creation in 1929 of the tiny independent Vatican State, Mussolini also remodelled the approach to St Peter's from the Castel Sant'Angelo, knocking the monumental Via della Conciliazione through the remnants of the crowded old Borgo district in front of the basilica.

Mussolini's various interventions – and indeed the whole physical structure of Rome – came through the Second World War largely unscathed. (The Germans, as they were being driven out of Italy by the Allied Advance, declared Rome an 'Open City', withdrawing from it to ensure that it would not be fought through or bombarded.) And in the postwar years Rome emerged as the capital of the *dolce vita*: a charmed world of Campari cocktails, dark glasses and popping flash-bulbs, around which Audrey Hepburn and Gregory Peck might scoot on their Vespa; where Anita Ekberg could be discovered standing in the Fontana di Trevi bursting out of her evening gown; or Anouk Aimée and Marcello Mastroianni might be glimpsed sitting outside some elegant Via Veneto café, wreathed in cigarette smoke and the scent of espresso coffee.

The glamour of the period was fixed when in 1960 Rome hosted the Olympic Games, the first games to receive full television coverage. An international audience not only

A 1949 map of Rome

Zaha Hadid's prize-winning MAXXI

witnessed Cassius Clay (the future Muhammad Ali) winning light-heavyweight boxing gold, but was also awed by the city's confident sense of style, its ability to balance the glorious past with the exciting present. The gymnastic events were held amidst the ancient ruins of the Baths of Caracalla, while the athletic contests unfolded in the ultra-modern Stadio Olimpico, or in the elegant little Palazzetto dello Sport.

And even now, though the rate of change has slowed, the sense of style and the confidence to mix the old and the new remain. Among the latest additions to the city's architectural heritage are an extraordinary concert-hall complex – 'like three tortoises drinking from a fountain' – created by Renzo Piano, Zaha Hadid's serpentine MAXXI (a museum of twenty-first-century art, and winner of the 2010 Stirling Prize) and, in the centre of the city, Richard Meier's new glass and travertine housing for the Ara Pacis.

As Rome has grown and grown over the last century and a half so have the numbers of people visiting it. Now, on average, eight million visitors arrive at Rome each year – and in Holy Years, when mass tourism is supplemented by mass pilgrimage, this number can more than double. Rome is the third most visited city in Europe after London and Paris. The crowds swarm in by road, by rail, by air and by sea (from the cruise ships that dock at Civitavecchia); some pilgrims still arrive on foot.

The variety of this great incoming crowd is extraordinary. Not since the glory days of the Roman Empire have the city's visitors been so various, have come from so many different countries and backgrounds. Luxury and budget, old and young, well informed and ignorant, Americans and Japanese, Finns and Nigerians, travellers and tourists, trippers and backpackers. Two things, however, link them all – and separate them from visitors of earlier generations. They have not been steeped from childhood in the Latin and Greek classics – and they are pushed for time.

The old established 'classical education', based on intensive study of Latin and Greek authors, ceased to be the preferred schooling for Europe's elite in the years after the First World War, replaced gradually by new syllabuses that focus on modern languages, modern history, and the sciences. Now Latin and Greek, if they are not quite unknown, are certainly minority subjects. The literature and the history of the classical age does, of course, remain accessible – in translation, in films and TV mini-series, in historical novels and popular histories. But no longer is the culture of Ancient Rome a second home for the educated man or woman.

The other change has been no less drastic. With every year the pace of life and the pace of tourism seem to quicken. Although more and more people may come to the city, they spend less and less time there. The sojourn of several months favoured during the leisurely age of the Grand Tour has been replaced by the mini-break, the long weekend, and the 'it's Tuesday so it must be Rome' package tour.

As early as the seventeenth century some visitors felt that there might be too much to see in the city. Now, after decades of new discoveries and fresh construction, with the establishment of numerous new museums and opening up of many old collections, the problem has only grown more acute. To try and see everything would be a complete impossibility.

Rome, as a result, has fragmented. For visitors there are now many different Romes to see and to enjoy. This, however, is not merely a result of the city's physical growth. The vast expansion of Rome in recent times has been matched by an almost equally large expansion in taste. Whole fields of Rome's cultural life and history have, after centuries of neglect, been brought back into play. The monuments of Baroque Rome, of mediaeval Rome, of early Renaissance Rome are now sought out alongside the long-established wonders of the classical past and the great works of the High Renaissance.

The passing years themselves have also produced an effect. Several entirely new areas of interest have emerged over the course of the last century. The best examples of modernist architecture, the monuments of the Fascist era, and the sites fixed in the popular mind by popular culture, have all been added to the list of Rome's treasures. And even that is not all. For although high and low culture, together with ancient and modern history, may be the great motive forces of Roman tourism, they are certainly not the only lures drawing the modern visitor to the city. The charms of shopping, of food, of fashion and sport, and – of course – of religion, also exert a pull.

All these different Romes possess their dedicated followers: the high-minded art lovers making the round of lesser-known Caravaggios; the black-clad architectural students tracking down the works of Pier Luigi Nervi and Gio Ponti in the outer suburbs; schoolchildren dragging their parents off in search of the key sites of Mussolini's rule. There are Japanese coach tours that follow the route taken by Audrey Hepburn in the 1953 film, *Roman Holiday*. And you can join a guided tour of the key sites described in Dan Brown's blockbusting thriller *Angels and Demons*.

More importantly, however, these various particular visions have all contributed to the universal experience of the city. Most modern visitors come to Rome just to have a look around, and, in the very limited time available, to see at least some of the key sights. And the understanding of what those 'key sights' are has inevitably been influenced by the great expansion of tastes and interests that has occurred over the last hundred years.

Gradually a new consensus about what is interesting, beautiful and important has emerged − a consensus that is both reflected in and reinforced by the plethora of modern guidebooks and travel-aids. Some of Rome's most admired monuments and artworks in this new order are the same as for previous generations but others − many of them − are very different.

To steer the busy tourist towards the choicest things in Rome, ever-shorter shortcuts have been devised. From the open-topped bus tour and the museum audio-guide to the virtual-reality 'Roman Time Elevator' and the travel website, the means have become gradually more sophisticated. The guidebook, however, remains a constant. Today's guidebooks are certainly not shy of providing firm pointers, with their definitive lists, their 'top tens', and their starred items. This is an important, but relatively new, phenomenon.

A tourist trinket stall near the Castel Sant'Angelo

Although the practice of marking a city's most noteworthy sights with some sort of typographical device can be traced back to 1802, when Mariana Starke, in her *Tour of Italy*, used exclamation marks to denote the major attractions,† it was really when Baedeker adopted the scheme of using asterisks in 1846 that the idea took off – reaching Rome with the first edition of Baedeker's *Central Italy* in 1867. It became an enduring staple of the guidebook genre, allowing the reader to pick out the key elements from a crowded inventory of wonders.

And the trend has continued, from later editions of Baedeker, to the *Blue Guide* and the *Guida d'Italia* produced by the Touring Club Italiano, the Michelin and AA guides, *Let's Go Italy*, Fodor's *Italy*, and numerous other titles. The British publishers Dorling Kindersley now produce a book solely made up of such lists – *Top 10 Rome*.

A sort of tourist shorthand has developed in which Rome has become represented by a very small collection of iconic monuments. The Colosseum, St Peter's, the Trevi Fountain, the Pantheon, the Roman Forum, the Castel Sant'Angelo and the Spanish Steps pretty much make up the roster. Certainly they are the ubiquitous images: on postcards and posters, T-shirts and headscarves, as plastic models enshrined in domes of swirling snow, fashioned into novelty ashtrays and fancy fridge-magnets. These monuments have, of course, been among the defining images of Rome since the time of Piranesi at least. But the selection has narrowed dramatically over time. The list of Piranesi's favourite images was a long one. It included the great arches of the Basilica Nova, the twin churches of the Piazza del Popolo, Trajan's Column, the Cloaca Maxima and scores of other sites that have now drifted rather to the edges of the popular

---

† Starke visited Rome in the late 1790s, at a time when many of the city's greatest artworks were being held captive in Paris, so her selection was rather circumscribed. Michelangelo's frescoes in the Sistine Chapel (the *Last Judgement* and the ceiling combined) received an unequalled five exclamation marks. Raphael's *School of Athens* and *St Peter in Prison* in the *Stanze* had to make do with four – the same number given to Raphael's fresco of *Isaiah* in the church of S. Agostino. Other, less expected, four-mark attractions included: Domenichino's *Cardinal Virtues* in the angles of the cupola in S. Carlo a Catenari, and his *St John* at S. Andrea della Valle; the 'celebrated ceiling' by Pietro da Cortona at Palazzo Barberini; Poussin's *Madonna and our Saviour with angels* in the Rospigliosi collection, and also several 'beautiful landskips' by Claude Lorrain at Palazzo Colonna. Among the antique statues still present at Rome, the masterworks in the Villa Borghese – the *Hermaphrodite*, *Borghese Gladiator* and '*Curtius leaping into the gulph*' – all received four marks, along with 'a beautiful Group supposed to represent Phaedra and Hippolitus' at the Villa Ludovisi (now designated as *Papirius* with his mother, and displayed in the Museo Nazionale).

consciousness. Moreover, as methods of reproduction have proliferated, so the fame of the small handful of key sights has increased, their impact growing both cruder and more forceful.

The Colosseum and St Peter's rank together at the head of the list. Indeed they belong to that select band of buildings that have become the very symbols of their city. As the Eiffel Tower can stand for Paris, 'Big Ben' for London, the leaning tower for Pisa, the opera house for Sydney, or the Statue of Liberty for New York, the distinctive forms of the great amphitheatre and the huge, domed basilica spell Rome even to those who have never been there. That Rome should have two iconic monuments is apt – one to embody its classical past, the other its Christian tradition.

Although both buildings owe much of their symbolic power to their instantly recognizable silhouettes, many tourists do also take the trouble to visit them. Indeed the Colosseum can claim to be the city's most popular paying attraction, drawing in over three million visitors a year. For those, however, hoping to conjure up the blood-soaked scenes of Ridley Scott's film *Gladiator*, the confused sight of the arena's exposed subterranean workings must be rather a let-down.

A similar sort of disappointment can affect visitors to the Forum. The fame of the Forum as the centre of Ancient Roman political and civil life still lingers, and its physical position at the heart of Rome makes it conspicuous. But these things of themselves do not make a successful modern tourist attraction. Even in the days of Edward Gibbon, when the area's surviving ruins were enhanced by a certain picturesque charm, it required a great deal of classical knowledge and even more imagination for the viewer to enjoy a satisfactory visit. Now few people arrive with an ability to quote Cicero at length, and the whole site has become a rather arid archaeological wasteland of exploratory trenches and exposed foundations. Mussolini's reconstructed Temple of Vesta and the nearby Spring of Juturna (rebuilt in the 1950s) are among some of the few photo opportunities.

More readily enjoyable for the great mass of tourists is the Trevi Fountain. Since the time of its extravagant Baroque remodelling by Nicolo Salvi, it has been one of the acknowledged splendours of Rome. But its fame has been greatly enhanced in the postwar years, in part through its memorable appearance in two notable films: the 1954 Hollywood romance *Three Coins in the Fountain*, and Fellini's 1960 masterpiece *La Dolce Vita*, in which the heroine, Anita Ekberg, spends a scene splashing around the fountain one night in her low-cut evening dress. The real root of the fountain's attraction for modern visitors, however, is that it is a monument with which they can actively engage.

As early as 1869 Baedeker was reporting that, 'on quitting Rome the superstitious partake of the water of this fountain, and throw a coin into the basin in the pious belief that their return is thus ensured.' In subsequent decades (perhaps prompted by fears about foreign drinking water), the coin-throwing element of the ritual has taken precedence. And in recent years it has evolved into the yet more elaborate conceit that two coins thrown into the fountain will secure a marriage, and three will produce a divorce. This steady inflation now means that some 3,500 euros are thrown into the fountain every day. Despite the best efforts of local urchins, most of these are gathered up each evening and used to subsidise a low-cost Catholic supermarket for the city's poor.

If the little piazza around the Trevi Fountain is always crowded with tourists, it is only one of several popular gathering places. The Campo dei Fiori has for much of its history been regarded in rather a negative light, as a place of public executions and punishment. And despite the fact that following the unification of Italy it became the site of a daily flower and vegetable market, the sombre statue of Giordano Bruno erected at its centre soon afterwards scarcely adds to the jollity of the place. Nevertheless, in recent decades, it has joined the Piazza Navona and the Piazza di Spagna as one of the great hubs of tourist life in Rome. The cowled figure of the philosopher, who was burnt as a heretic in the piazza in 1600, today looks down upon a colourful alfresco scene.

A designated tourist trail, marked with special signposts, now runs from the Campo, through the Piazza Navona, past the Pantheon and the Trevi Fountain, before reaching the Spanish Steps. This – along with other trails towards the Castel Sant'Angelo and St Peter's, or off towards the Colosseum – provides many visitors with their basic framework for exploring the city. But the framework is broad, and there are always details to be filled in. Between the main iconic monuments there are other distinct – and new – sources of interest.

Rome's Baroque architecture, for so long a source of ridicule, has come back into vogue. Borromini is no longer a name to be scorned. Bernini's achievements are proclaimed without embarrassment. This change of attitude gathered force gradually in the early years of the twentieth century, as the Baroque style came to be understood as a distinct form, rather than merely as a bizarre corruption of the classical Renaissance ideal. Among the pioneers of this re-evaluation was the German-born art historian Rudolf Wittkower (1901–1971). As a young man he developed a deep knowledge and a keen appreciation of the Baroque while working in Rome on a catalogue of Bernini's drawings. In 1927 he was invited to revise the account of the 'Art of Rome' for the new edition of Baedeker, and although he seems not to have taken up the offer, his ideas certainly percolated into the revised text.

While earlier editions of the guidebook routinely referred to Borromini as 'eccentric', the architect was now saluted as 'gifted', and praised for displaying 'rare skill' in his deployment of 'the most spirited Baroque style'. S Carlo alle Quattro Fontane became a tourist destination. His other major works were all listed and starred, and so they remain. The adjective 'grotesque' no longer adheres to the description of his spiral tower atop the church of S. Ivo. Instead the building is described as 'harmonizing well' with the arcaded courtyard in which it stands.

The church of S. Ivo by Borromini

If Rome's post-Renaissance architecture has returned to favour, so too have the monuments of the pre-Renaissance period. It has become a commonplace – but remains a truth – that in Rome you can see the layers of history piled one upon the other. And this is considered to be one of the city's great attractions. Churches and palaces have been built over or among the ruins of old Roman apartment blocks, pagan temples and other buildings. The cellar of a trattoria off the Campo dei Fiori might turn out to be a vaulted arch from the Theatre of Pompey, the basement of a grand palace might be filled with the massive blocks of some temple podium.

One of the most vivid instances of this phenomenon is the church of S. Clemente. And it is this that probably accounts for the basilica's great popularity with modern tourists. The existing church, with its beautifully decorated apse, its cosmatesque pavement and its fine carved pulpit, dates from the twelfth century, but it stands (literally) upon an equally impressive fourth-century basilica, mentioned by St Jerome in 392 and sacked by the Normans in 1084, which now serves as a crypt. And beneath this early church lie the remains of a substantial first-century AD Roman dwelling, which in turn rests upon the vestiges of a Republican era building that appears to have been burnt in Nero's great fire of AD 64.

This extraordinary archaeological sequence was uncovered in the 1860s through 'the praiseworthy exertions' (as Baedeker described them) of the church's Irish prior, Joseph Mullooly. As a further excitement he also discovered that, at some moment in the second century, a Mithraic temple had been constructed in the basement of the first-century house.

Mithras was an eastern divinity whose mystery cult became popular in Rome and across the empire from the late first century onwards. Although firm evidence about the cult and its workings is scant, this did not prevent some scholars from suggesting that the religion, in its early days, was a serious rival to Christianity, and that when the Christian religion did eventually win out, it – tellingly – adopted some aspects of its rival's ritual and belief. It was suggested, for example, (on no very good authority) that Mithras' 'birthday' was celebrated on 25 December, the date later adopted by Christians to mark the nativity of Jesus. And the notion that the physical arrangement of S. Clemente also reflects the layers of Rome's spiritual history has proved an enduring one, adding to the building's popularity and interest.

Having been rather briskly dealt with in all early nineteenth-century guidebooks, the church received a star in the 1875 edition of Baedeker. Since then its status has risen with the passing decades. It is now considered one of the foremost sights in Rome. In Fodor's *Italy* it stands first on the list of Roman churches worth visiting, while the Dorling Kindersley guide rates it the sixth best thing to see in the whole of the city.

Among the myriad artworks assembled in Rome's churches, galleries, museums and palaces a new hierarchy has also established itself. Many of the old favourites of the nineteenth century have been supplanted. In the popular estimate the foremost post-classical statue in the city is no longer reckoned to be Michelangelo's *Moses*, but the same artist's *Pietà*, in St Peter's. As you approach the Vatican the image of the dead Christ stretched over the knees of his grieving mother becomes ubiquitous on the stalls of the souvenir-sellers – adorning the covers of pictorial guides, reproduced on postcards, and fashioned from painted plastic.†

In previous centuries the *Pietà* had been something of a poor relation among Michelangelo's Roman works: Albertini didn't mention it; Evelyn did, but only in passing; Smollett affected to find it indecent. The early editions of Murray's *Handbook* related that 'the critics of Michel Angelo's own time objected [like Smollett] to the youthful appearance of the Virgin, and to the Son being represented older than the mother.' A further complaint was that the work, set up in 1749 on a high plinth, could not be 'seen to advantage'. The best that Octavian Blewitt, the *Handbook* author, would allow was that 'some portions of it are extremely beautiful'.

And it seems to have continued as a sort of sculptural curate's egg until 1875. The fourth edition of Baedeker, which appeared that year, granted it two stars. By 1890 it was being declared 'a masterpiece', praised because 'the depth and truth of the [work's] conception are mirrored in the exquisite finish of the execution. Neither the grief of the mother nor the effect of death on the Son detracts from the ideal beauty imparted.' Whether this re-evaluation reflected a novel preference for the artist's early work above his later, more mannered style, or a new desire for pathos and sentiment, is hard to know. But the verdict certainly stuck. It retains a multi-stellar status in modern guidebooks, along with the recurring epithets 'moving', 'powerful' and 'masterpiece'.

The work's steady increase in fame over the decades has not been without its drawbacks. In 1972 a deranged Australian geologist – announcing 'I am Jesus Christ, risen from the dead' – attacked the sculpture with a hammer, damaging it severely. The statue now sits behind a screen of bullet-proof glass, an arrangement that serves only to increase its aura of specialness.

---

† Although the *Pietà* is now considered the most important sculpture by Michelangelo in Rome, it still ranks well below the artist's celebrated *David* at Florence in the popular estimate. Indeed such is that sculpture's iconic status that even the Roman souvenir-sellers offer statuettes of it, together with an array of printed aprons and novelty underpants.

Michelangelo's *Pietà*

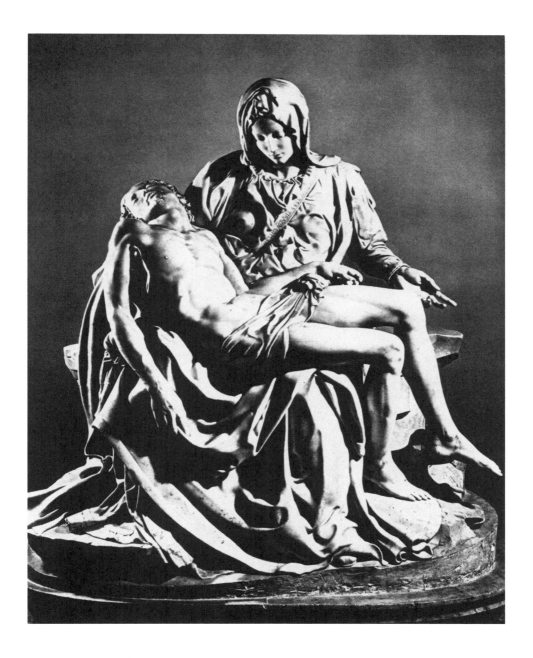

Of Bernini's sculptural works, the flamboyant *Ecstasy of Saint Theresa*, so long disparaged, has risen to the front rank, as the 'chaste' *St Bibiana* has lapsed into obscurity. In the 1890 Baedeker the sculpture of the prostrate saint and attendant angel was passed over in small print as that 'notorious group'; by 1909 this had been modified to 'the notorious group . . . the execution of which is masterly, whatever may be thought of the spirit'. But from 1930, under the influence of Wittkower, the whole tenor had changed. The work received a starred billing, was called 'famous' and described as 'a

LEFT Bernini's *Ecstasy of Saint Theresa*
RIGHT Canova's *Pauline Bonaparte*

fine example of the Baroque style at its zenith; the masterly treatment of the marble and the light effects serve to augment the intensity of expression.' And it is in such terms that it has been treated ever since. (The appearance of the sculpture in one of the key scenes of Dan Brown's *Angels and Demons* will only serve to lead yet more people to the church of S. Maria della Vittoria.)

Bernini's dramatically charged *Apollo and Daphne* has also enjoyed a similar re-evaluation, but even so it probably cedes pole position among the sculptures at the Villa Borghese to Canova's Neoclassical statue of the recumbent, and topless, Pauline Bonaparte as Venus. This has gradually emerged as the artist's most famous work in Rome. Canova's various papal monuments in St Peter's are still accorded a dutiful respect, but it is the suggestive silhouette of Napoleon's sister that has come to command the popular attention. Having been rather ignored in accounts of the Borghese collection, it first received a star in the 1930 edition of Baedeker, at which time it was also described as 'the most famous ideal portrait of the Empire period'.

Michelangelo's *Creation of Man*, on the Sistine Chapel ceiling

The shifts that have taken place in the hierarchies of Rome's architecture and sculpture have been matched in the realm of painting. The most famous piece of pictorial art in Rome is now undoubtedly the ceiling of the Sistine Chapel. Indeed it can sometimes seem as though it is the only painting in Rome. It is represented and reproduced everywhere – in colours that, since the thorough cleaning of 1984–94, have taken on an arresting new brightness and clarity. The detail of God's hand reaching out to touch Adam's finger, to instil Man with life, has become a universal image, borrowed and subverted in a thousand tributes, from the opening credits of *The South Bank Show* to the poster for *E.T.*

Every year over three million visitors traipse through the Vatican museums, and all of them understand that the highpoint of their tour will be the Sistine Chapel and its ceiling. The great expanse of the Cortile della Pigna is now lined with information boards depicting the chapel ceiling, before which the expectant tour parties gather to be instructed about the iconography of the fresco cycle and to prepare themselves for their encounter with the real thing.

Although the audio-guide to the chapel announces that the *Last Judgement* is 'the richest and most important [work] that mankind has ever conceived', it is hard not to feel that the great fresco, for centuries considered the chapel's main attraction, has been relegated to the position of a worthy pendant. It is always upwards, towards the ceiling, that the eyes of the tourists turn.

While Michelangelo's reputation as a painter has risen, Raphael's has sunk rather. His Vatican *Stanze* are still rated as a three-star masterpiece in the guidebooks and are dutifully filed through, but only the *School of Athens* seems to hold the attention of modern visitors for long. And even it tends to be viewed in relation to the Sistine ceiling. The Dorling Kindersley guide remarks that 'after he saw the Sistine ceiling that Michelangelo was painting down the hall, Raphael added the troubled genius, sulking on the steps, as Heraclitus.'

Few visitors to the Vatican museums even stray into the Pinacoteca, or papal picture gallery, and only some of them linger before Raphael's *Transfiguration* – long regarded as the greatest oil painting in the world. The fact that it is accorded its own wall in a specially darkened room makes it clear that this is an 'important' picture. And that sense of importance is still confirmed by most modern guidebooks. (The DK *Top Ten* guide rates the picture the second greatest 'Artistic Masterpiece' in Rome.) But, somehow, the subject is too unfamiliar to allow for any very easy connection with a contemporary audience.

Indeed of all Raphael's Roman works, the portrait of his mistress – *La Fornarina* – is probably now the most famous and the best recognized. The roguish baker's daughter

Raphael's *La Fornarina*

has become the poster girl for the gallery at the Palazzo Barberini. In the eighteenth century she was considered 'coarse looking'. Anne Miller, in her *Letters from Italy*, could not understand what Raphael saw in the girl. Now her hint of less than ideal sensuality is preferred to all those noble-looking Apostles and virgins.

The modern preference for the real and the particular over the ideal and the general has also carried Caravaggio – the great master of early seventeenth-century realism – back into favour. Wherever his pictures appear, they are now both starred and looked at. His *Deposition* is accounted one of the jewels of the Vatican Pinacoteca; the *Crucifixion of St Peter* and *Conversion of St Paul* are thought to be two of the main things that make the church of S. Maria del Popolo such a treasure house of art; and his three pictures chronicling the life of St Matthew are, according to most guidebooks, the sole reason for visiting S. Luigi dei Francesi.

This revival of interest in the artist seems to have begun in the late nineteenth century. Professor Anton Springer, in his survey of 'Roman Art' for the 1890 Baedeker, was less dismissive of Caravaggio than previous writers had been. While acknowledging his limitations in 'drawing' and 'composition', he suggested that his painting was 'presented with such startling reality, and animated with gesture so impassioned that every figure asserts itself, while a corresponding force in colour conveys an impression powerfully suggestive of the turbulent licence then prevailing.' It was, however, only at the end of the end of the 1920s – following a critical reappraisal effected by the Italian art historian Roberto Longhi – that Caravaggio's works began to be widely admired once more. Among other insights, Longhi likened Caravaggio's use of dramatic lighting to the techniques of modern cinema. Soon the artist's pictures were being starred in the guidebooks.

In recent years the attractions of Caravaggio's art have been further enhanced by the drama of his colourful life. Following a Derek Jarman film, and a clutch of more or less sensationalist biographies – in which the principal motifs are gay sex, artistic jealousy and murder – he has entered the popular consciousness as an artistic rebel and a byword for 'turbulent licence'.

With glamour such as this it is little wonder that Caravaggio, alone among the painters from the post-Raphael generations, is now sought out by the tourist crowd. His near-contemporaries, the classicizing Annibale Caracci, Domenichino, Guido Reni and the rest have become, for most visitors, mere names.

Their decline, though, has been matched by a corresponding rise in status and repute of Raphael's artistic predecessors – the great Tuscan and Umbrian masters of the quattrocento: Masaccio, Fra Angelico, Pinturicchio, Botticelli, Filippino Lippi, Ghirlandaio, Melozzo da Forli and the rest. The works of these artists may be relatively scarce in Rome, but where they are found they are admired.

This seismic shift in taste away from the old favourites and towards the 'Italian Primitives' – as they were once called – was effected during the middle years of the nineteenth century by a number of critics and writers, of whom the most prominent and impassioned was John Ruskin. Moved often by their own religious convictions they praised what they saw as the simplicity and the earnest spiritual inspiration of early Italian painting, and – in Ruskin's case – contrasted this with the 'insincere' and flashy works of Raphael's disciples. These bold new ideas, though first voiced in the 1840s, took some time to register with the wider public, and perhaps even longer to register with the average visitor to Rome.

Although Ruskin himself actually revised the section on painting in the 1847 edition of the *Handbook for Travellers in North Italy*, in order that he might promote his ideas and insights to a general readership, that volume of course did not include Rome. It was not until 1875 that Baedeker began giving out stars to the Pinturicchios adorning S. Maria del Popolo and the Borgia Apartments at the Vatican, to Fra Angelico's decorations for the little Chapel of Nicholas V (see plate XVII), and even to one of the paintings on the side walls of the Sistine Chapel (Ghirlandaio's *The Calling of Peter and Andrew*, see plate II). This marked a return, after a hiatus of some five hundred years, to the critical estimates of Francesco Albertini's *Opusculum*.

The works have only grown in repute since then, appreciated increasingly for the strength and simplicity of their aesthetic, rather than the sincerity of their religious vision. In 1890 another of the Sistine Chapel pictures – Perugino's *Christ Handing the Keys to Peter* (see plate III) – got the Baedeker star treatment; and twenty years later two more were added to the list: Botticelli's *Moses Driving the Shepherds from the Well* and Signorelli's *Moses the Lawgiver*. By 1930, the Carafa Chapel at S. Maria sopra Minerva, rather than being praised solely for its 'handsome balustrade', was starred as the site of Filippino Lippi's beautiful fresco cycle. Georgina Masson, the architectural historian and photographer who wrote one of the finest books on the city, the *Companion Guide to Rome* (first published in 1965, but reissued and revised many times since), considered Fra Angelico's frescoes of the lives of the early martyrs in Nicholas V's intimate little chapel 'one of the most exquisite things in the Vatican Palace – indeed in all Rome'.

If the rise of the 'Primitives' has taken time to register with the majority of tourists, so too has the decline of Raphael's disciples. Although Ruskin might have declared back in the 1840s that they belonged to a 'fallen and discredited school', from sheer force of habit the guidebooks continued to mark their works for special attention well into the twentieth century. As late as 1965 the *Blue Guide* was still according Domenichino's frescoes of St Cecilia in S. Luigi dei Francesi a star rating. Now, though, they are not even mentioned.

Among all the figures of the Italian Renaissance Leonardo da Vinci has come to occupy a special place: as both great artist and universal genius, he is seen as the very embodiment of the age. Although he was one of the few artists of the period not to work for any period of time at Rome, his unfinished painting of St Jerome has ended up there, and now ranks as one of the few acknowledged stars of the Vatican Pinacoteca (see plate XVIII). It is a powerful image done in sepia tones on panel: the old, bare-chested saint squatting in the desert with his faithful lion. The fact that it was discovered in the early nineteenth century by Napoleon's uncle Cardinal Fresch in two separate pieces – one supporting a shoemaker's bench, the other for sale in a Roman pawn shop – only adds to its interest.

Early editions of Baedeker merely mentioned the *St Jerome* as 'a coloured sketch' but accorded a rare two stars to a fresco of *The Madonna with Donor* on the upper floor of the cloister next to the little church of S. Onofrio on the Janiculum, which was believed to be by Leonardo. By the turn of the century, however, the picture had been downgraded to the work of a pupil. Now it no longer rates even a mention in the guidebooks.

On Rome's shifting cultural index few things have fallen further than classical statuary. It still retains a certain status, but it has declined from a great, great height. For Renaissance humanists and seventeenth-century curiosity-seekers, for learned dilettanti on the Grand tour and early Victorian sightseers, antique sculpture was the prime draw. *Laocoön, Apollo Belvedere*, the *Dying Gladiator, Meleager, Antinous* and the rest were – over the course of five centuries – a constant focus of interest, of intense study, rapturous contemplation and impassioned debate. Indeed, for many people, they were the very reason for visiting Rome.

Now it seems as though most tourists regard classical statues as something between a chore and a mystery. The major sculptures do have to be seen, of course. And modern visitors file doggedly through the great collections – the Vatican and Capitoline museums, and the Museo Nazionale (at its several sites) – registering, photographing and even filming the ranks of marble deities, the massed busts of the great and good, the nymphs and satyrs, senators and soldiers. But, to a generation with little classical knowledge, the names of these gods and heroes resonate but faintly.†

Responses tend to be limited. In the Pio-Clementino or the Chiaramonti gallery at the Vatican tourists are now likely to point out some statue with a missing penis and remark warmly upon it as an instance of the 'Great Castration'. The reference is to a passage in Dan Brown's thriller *Angels and Demons*: 'It was one of the most horrific tragedies in Renaissance art. In 1857, Pope Pius XI decided that the accurate representation of the male form might incite lust inside the Vatican. So he got a chisel and mallet and hacked off the genitalia of every single male statue inside the Vatican City . . . Langdon often wondered if there was a huge crate of stone penises someplace.' This stupendous piece of nonsense – which also appears in the film of the book – has rapidly become one of the established 'facts' about Rome for an alarming number of modern visitors. Although it is true that over the course of the seventeenth, eighteenth and nineteenth centuries, various statues were fitted with sculptural fig-leaves or scraps

---

† The most striking of the new sculpture displays is at the Centrale Montemartini, on the Via Ostiense, where part of the Capitoline collection is now housed in the old Montemartini power plant, amidst the decommissioned turbines and generators.

of metal drapery, there never was any concerted campaign of emasculation – least of all by Pius XI, who was, in fact, a champion of archaeological research.

The massed sculptures of Rome's museums may be admired in a general way – as being part of any tourist's idea of Rome – but few of them seem to stand out and prompt any real enthusiasm. The *Apollo Belvedere* and *Laocoön* are still starred items, along with many other once-famous works, but one only has to stand beside them for a brief while to see how little impact they have upon the general tourist crowd.

The statue of the she-wolf, the *Lupa*, in the Palazzo dei Conservatori does at least remain an instantly recognized image, one of the great symbols of the city. (This despite a recent scholarly attempt to suggest that it is not a classical work but an early mediaeval production.) More popular, though, with the tourist throng, are the great marble fragments that stand in the museum's courtyard: the pointing hand, the foot, and the giant head.

The colossal marble head
of Constantine

These outsize pieces are now thought to have come from a colossal seated statue of Constantine that presided over the Basilica Nova. (The main body of the statue had been made from some less precious material, with only the protruding foot, hand and head fashioned in marble.) They have stood in and around the Palazzo dei Conservatori since the sixteenth century, and over the years have been variously described as belonging to a gigantic statue of either Apollo or Commodus. The cognoscenti of the eighteenth century paid little attention to them. With their crude workmanship and bombastic scale they were regarded as curiosities rather than as things of beauty.

Now, however, their oddness is accounted a virtue. There is, too, a touch of surreal humour about them. The disembodied foot seems to belong to the animated opening credits of *Monty Python's Flying Circus*. Among the best-selling postcards in Rome are a photograph of a kitten curled up between the toes of the giant foot, and an image of the colossal head, with a hole cut where the nose should be; the recipient is supposed to stick the tip of their own nose through the card, and become part of the work itself.

Indeed, among all the sculptural remains of classical antiquity that survive in Rome the one that exerts the strongest hold over modern visitors to Rome is the great disc-like fountainhead carved with the face of a water god and known as the *Bocca della Verità*.

The 'Mouth of Truth', affixed to the end wall of the porch that runs along the front of S. Maria in Cosmedin, has been a sight of interest since at least the fifteenth century, but not a particularly compelling one. Travellers were aware of the legend that in former times (either classical or mediaeval, depending on the report) people taking oaths were required to put their hand into the mouth of the river god, and risked having it bitten off if they perjured themselves. Nevertheless, for most visitors the story seemed to belong to the vanishing world of the *Mirabilia*. Richard Lassels, in his 1670 *Voyage of Italy*, dismissed the tale with a quip: 'I rather believe it served in some old building for a gutter spout: I know *Truth* may speake lowd, and have a *Wide Mouth*, but he that takes every wide mouth for the mouth of *Truth*, is much mistaken.'

Certainly it was not a feature of the Grand Tour. The English *milordi* did not line up to place their hands in the great stone mouth. According to Augustus Hare, one sceptical nineteenth-century English visitor did, on hearing the legend, immediately plunge his hand in – and was greatly surprised to be bitten by a scorpion. But he seems to have been an oddity, and quite possibly an apocryphal one.

It was the romantic comedy *Roman Holiday* that has made the monument famous. In the film Gregory Peck's character, an expatriate American journalist, takes the truanting and supposedly incognito Princess Ann (played by Audrey Hepburn, in her first starring role) to see the *Bocca della Verità*. He tells her of the effigy's supposed power, and coaxes her to try it. She timidly does so, but then challenges him to the same test. Putting his hand into the stone mouth with a show of bravura, Peck then pretends that he is being bitten. To the shrieking, wide-eyed horror of the princess, he draws his apparently severed arm from the gaping mouth. But – cue relief, laughter, recriminations and hugs all round – he has merely pulled the sleeve of his jacket over his hand. According to legend, the drama of the scene was enhanced by the fact that Hepburn didn't know what was going to happen, and was genuinely alarmed at Peck's sudden cries of panic.

The movie was a great success at its first appearance. It was nominated for the Oscar for Best Film, while Audrey Hepburn received an individual award for her performance. But its popularity has only increased with time, drawn upwards in part by the ready accessibility of old films on video and DVD, and – more significantly – by Hepburn's steady rise to the position of modern style icon. Hepburn's appeal

The *Bocca della Verità*

is international, universal even – but it seems to have particular force among the Japanese. There are, I am sure, learned dissertations on why this should be so. Whatever its causes might be, its effect upon Rome is very apparent. The oriental enthusiasm for Audrey Hepburn has in the last couple of decades transformed the *Bocca della Verità* into a prime tourist attraction.

Japanese sightseers arrive by the coachload at S. Maria in Cosmedin. Few of them ever enter the beautiful early mediaeval church. They are intent solely on having their photograph taken in the appropriate Hepburnesque pose beside the great stone face. They form an orderly queue along the length of the church's porch, as they wait their turn. And, of course, many of the northern races only have to see a queue to want to join it. A fair scattering of British, Americans, Australians, Germans, Belgians and others can now be found standing in line – among the Japanese – waiting for their moment with the Mouth of Truth. An official tourist information board on the piazza next to the church explains the background of the *Roman Holiday* story to anyone unfamiliar with the film.

Although the church has taken to charging each visitor 50 cents for their photo opportunity, this has done nothing to thin the crowds. Along with the Vatican museums, the Colosseum, and the ice-cream counter at Giolitti, the porch of S. Maria in Cosmedin has become one of the few places in Rome where there is almost always a queue.

The last time there were such long lines here was probably in the seventh century, when a building on the site – subsequently incorporated into the church – served as a food distribution centre for hungry pilgrims and the local poor. Back then the 'Mouth of Truth' was no more than a defunct and unregarded water feature. Now it seems the embodiment of the modern visitor's experience of Rome. The truth it utters is as enduring as the Eternal City itself: Rome changes, tastes change – yet everything remains the same.

BIBLIOGRAPHY

The many primary sources – memoirs, travel accounts, diaries, guidebooks, poems and novels – on which this book is based are listed in the text. What follows is a selective bibliography of the most relevant secondary sources consulted.

REFERENCE

In tracking down the primary sources, various reference works have been invaluable.

R. Valentini & G. Zuchetti's four-volume compendium of first-hand topographical accounts of the city in the classical, mediaeval and Renaissance periods, *Codice topographico della città di Rome* (Rome, 1940–1953).

Robert Dudley, *Urbs Roma* (London, 1967) and Naphtali Lewis & Meyer Reinhold, *Roman Civilization* (New York, 1951) for classical texts; N. Maugham, ed., *The Book of Italian Travel* (London, 1903) and John Varriano's delightful *A Literary Companion – Rome* (London, 1991), for more general coverage.

Several works deal with Rome's rich heritage of guidebooks: Amy Marshall, *Mirabilia Urbis Romae – Five Centuries of Guidebooks and Views* (Toronto, 2002); Gaetana Scano, *Guide E Descrizioni di Roma dal XVI al XX Secolo*; and Ludwig Schudt, *Italinreisen im 17. And 18. Jahrhundert* (Vienna, 1959).

Amato Frutaz, *Le Piante di Roma* (Rome, 1962) provides useful facsimiles of old Roman maps.

GENERAL

Christopher Hibbert, *Rome* (London, 1985), gives an entertaining outline of the city's history; Joel Kotkin, *The City* (London, 2005) provides some good background on how cities grow and function.

For the destruction of Ancient Rome and its subsequent rediscovery, there is much of interest in the numerous works of Rudolfo Lanciani, particularly his *The Destruction of Ancient Rome* (London, 1899); also Claude Moatti, *In Search of Ancient Rome* (1989; English translation, London, 1993); and Christopher Woodward, *In Ruins* (London, 2001).

More than a mere guidebook is Georgina Masson's magisterial *Companion Guide to Rome* (first edition London, 1965; revised and updated by Jim Jepson, Woodbridge, 2000).

Several volumes in Profile Books' entertaining Wonders of the World series focus on Roman monuments: Keith Hopkins & Mary Beard, *The Colosseum* (2005); David Watkin, *The Roman Forum*, (2009), Keith Miller, *St Peter's* (2007).

Other, more general, studies include Brian Barefoot, *The English Road to Rome* (Upton-upon-Severn, 1993); Anthony Majanlahti, *The Families who made Rome* (London, 2005); Ernest O. Hauser's *Italy – A Cultural Guide* (New Jersey, 1981).

On many topics *The Macmillan Dictionary of Art* has proved a wonderful resource.

CLASSICAL ROME

For an understanding of the ancient city the several topographical dictionaries are indispensable: Samuel Ball Platner & Thomas Ashby, *A Topographical Dictionary of Ancient Rome* (Oxford, 1968 edition); Lawrence Richardson, *A New Topographical Dictionary of Ancient Rome* (Baltimore, 1992); the five volumes of Eva Margareta Steinby, ed., *Lexicon Topographicum Urbis Romae* (Rome 1993–9); and Amanda Claridge, *Oxford Archaeological Guide to Rome* (Oxford, 1998).

On specific aspects of the city's development and its architecture, of particular use were John E. Stambaugh, *The Ancient Roman City* (Baltimore, 1988); John Stamper, *The Architecture of the Roman Temples; The Republic to the Middle Empire* (Cambridge, 2005); James Packer, *The Forum of Trajan* (Berkeley, 1997); Margaret Scherer, *Marvels of Ancient Rome* (New York, 1955).

Of the various accounts of Ancient Roman social history, I much enjoyed J.P.V.D. Balsdon, *Life and Leisure in Ancient Rome* (London,1969); Florence Dupont, *Daily Life in Ancient Rome* (Oxford, 1992); Ugo Enrico Paoli, *Rome – its people, life and customs* (London, 1963); Jerome Carcopino, *Daily Life in Ancient Rome* (London, 1940).

Also of interest were: Pierre Grimal, *In Search of Ancient Italy* (London, 1964); David Noy, *Foreigners At Rome* (London, 2000); Margaret Miles, *Art as Plunder* (Cambridge, 2008).

The 'Lacus Curtius' website, maintained by Bill Thayer, is a fantastic resource, providing easy access to numerous classical and post-classical texts, together with much sane editorial scholarship.

MEDIAEVAL ROME

Richard Krautheimer, *Rome: Profile of a City, 312–1308* (Princeton, 1980) is essential for an understanding of the mediaeval city.

For general historical background the following are extremely useful: Edward Gibbon, *The Decline and Fall of the Roman Empire*; Bryan Ward-Perkins, *The Fall of Rome and the End of Civilization* (Oxford, 2005); G.P. Bowersock, Peter Brown & Oleg Grabar, eds., *Late Antiquity: Guide to the Postclassical World* (Cambridge, Mass., 1999); J.W. Wallace-Hadrill, *The Barbarian West* (London, 1967) and R.W. Southern, *The Making of the Middle Ages* (London, 1953).

For specific accounts of Rome and its monuments during the period, see Peter Llewellyn, *Rome in the Dark Ages* (London, 1971); Robert Brentano, *Rome Before Avignon* (London, 1991); Herbert L. Kessler & Johanna Zacharias, *Rome 1300* (New Haven, 2000); Tilman Buddensieg, 'Criticism and Praise of the Pantheon in the Middle Ages', in *Classical Influences on European Culture AD 500–1500* (Cambridge, 1971); Matilda Webb, *The Churches and Catacombs of Early Christian Rome* (Brighton, 2001).

On the subject of pilgrims and pilgrimage, see Debra Birch, *Pilgrimage to Rome* (Woodbridge, 1998); Jonathon Sumption, *Pilgrimage* (London, 1975); Linda K. Davidson, *Pilgrimage in the Middle Ages* (New York, 1993); James Bentley, *Restless Bones – The Story of Relics* (London, 1985).

RENAISSANCE ROME

The best overview of Renaissance Rome is Charles L. Stinger, *The Renaissance in Rome* (Bloomington, Indiana, 1985); also useful are: Loren Partridge, *The Art of the Renaissance in Rome* (New Jersey, 1996); E. Rodocanachi, *Rome aux temps de Jules II et de Leon X* (Paris, 1912).

On the relation between the Renaissance artists and Rome's classical heritage see: Robert Weiss, *The Renaissance Discovery of Classical Antiquity* (Oxford, 1969); Phyllis Bray Beber & Ruth Olitsky Rubenstein, *Renaissance Artists & Antique Sculpture* (London, 1986); Alice Payne, Ann Kuttner, Rebekah Smick, eds., *Antiquity and its Interpreters* (Cambridge, 2000).

On the *Laocoön* specifically see: Salvatore Settis, *Laocoonte: Fama e Stile* (Rome, 1999); Margaret Bieber, *Laocoön* (Wayne State University, 1967); Hans Henrik Brummer, *The Statue Court in the Vatican Belvedere* (1970, Stockholm).

Among studies of individual artists, the ones I found most useful were: Roger Jones & Nicholas Penney, *Raphael* (New Haven & London, 1983), and the various volumes of Charles de Tolnay's study of *Michelangelo* (Princeton, 1945–1975).

FROM THE SEVENTEENTH CENTURY TO THE GRAND TOUR

A good overview of the seventeenth century is provided by Cesare d'Onofrio, *Roma nel Seicento* (Florence, 1969); *The Origins of the Grand Tour*, Hakluyt Society, Third Series, No. 14 (London, 2004), offers interesting background on seventeenth-century travel in Italy (though very little specifically about Rome).

For the eighteenth century the material is much more plentiful. Among the many studies of the Grand Tour, I found the most useful were: Ilaria Bignamini & Andrew Wilson, eds., *Grand Tour: The Lure of Italy in the Eighteenth Century* (London, 1996), Jeremy Black, *The British and the Grand Tour* (London, 1985); and Clare Hornsby, ed., *The Impact of Italy: The Grand Tour and Beyond* (London, 2000).

For an understanding of the developing taste for classical sculpture and Old Master painting, two brilliant works stand out: Francis Haskell and Nicholas Penny, *Taste and the Antique, the Lure of Classical Sculpture* (New Haven and London, 1981); and J.R Hale, *England and the Italian Renaissance* (London, 1954).

NINETEENTH-CENTURY ROME

The lure of Rome for the Romantics is illuminated in the many studies of the individual authors. Among the best are Richard Holmes, *Shelley – The Pursuit* (London, 1974) and Fiona Macarthy, *Byron – Life and Legend* (London, 2002). A stimulating general study is provided by Joseph Luzzi, *Romantic Europe and the Ghost of Italy* (London, 2008).

The history of nineteenth-century guidebooks is mapped out in Nicholas T. Parsons, *Worth the Detour: A History of the Guidebook* (London, 2007); Alan Sillitoe, *Leading the Blind – A Century of Guide Book Travel* (London, 1995); and W.B.C. Lister, *A Bibliography of Murray's Handbooks for Travellers* (Dereham, 1993).

INDEX

Page numbers in *italics* refer to illustrations.

PICTURE CREDITS

The publishers have made every effort to contact holders of copyright works. Any copyright holders we have been unable to reach are invited to contact the publishers so that a full acknowledgment may be given in subsequent editions. For permission to reproduce the images on the following pages, and for supplying photographs and artworks, the publishers thank those listed below.

© 2011. **Image copyright The Metropolitan Museum of Art/Art Resource/Scala, Florence:** plate XIII (Metropolitan Museum of Art, New York, Gwynne Andrews Fund, 1952. Accession Number 52.63.1)

Louvre, Paris, France/Giraudon/The Bridgeman Art Library: plate IV

© 2011. **Photo Scala, Florence:** plate II, plate III, plate V, plate VI, plate VII, plate VIII, plate IX, plate X, plate XI, plate XII, plate XIV, plate XVI, plate XVII, plate XVIII

© 2011. **Photo Scala, Florence – courtesy of the Ministero Beni e Att. Culturali:** plate XV

Private Collection/Photo © Christie's Images/The Bridgeman Art Library: plate I

Matthew Sturgis: 14, 30, 55, 72 above, 88, 96 above, 104, 235, 242, 244, 260, 262